D1550639

A SHORT GUIDE
TO BUSINESS WRITING

Harry J. Bruce
   Chairman, President and CEO,
   Illinois Central Railroad (ret.)

Russel K. Hirst
   University of Tennessee, Knoxville

Michael L. Keene
   University of Tennessee, Knoxville

Prentice Hall, Englewood Cliffs, New Jersey 07632

Library of Congress Cataloging-in-Publication Data
Bruce, Harry J. (Harry James)
    A short guide to business writing / Harry J. Bruce, Russel K. Hirst, Michael L. Keene.
      p.   cm.
    Includes index.
    ISBN 0-13-124728-X
    1. Business writing.   I. Hirst, Russel K.   II. Keene, Michael L.   III. Title.
HF5718.3.B78   1995
808'.06665—dc20   94–11834
                                                           CIP

Editorial/Production Supervision: Ruttle, Shaw & Wetherill, Inc.
Acquisitions Editor: Natalie Anderson
Cover Designer: Tom Nery
Buyer: Patrice Fraccio

© 1995 by Prentice-Hall, Inc.
A Simon & Schuster Company
Englewood Cliffs, New Jersey 07632

Printed in the United States of America
10 9 8 7 6 5 4 3

ISBN 0-13-124728-X

Prentice-Hall International (UK) Limited, *London*
Prentice-Hall of Australia Pty. Limited, *Sydney*
Prentice-Hall Canada Inc. *Toronto*
Prentice-Hall Hispanoamericana, S.A., *Mexico*
Prentice-Hall of India Private Limited, *New Delhi*
Prentice-Hall of Japan, Inc., *Tokyo*
Simon & Schuster Asia Pte. Ltd., *Singapore*
Editora Prentice-Hall do Brasil, Ltda., *Rio de Janeiro*

Dedication

This book is dedicated with affection, admiration, and respect to Mark Egan of San Francisco. I, along with everyone who reads and uses this book, owe Mark a tremendous debt of gratitude.

Now in the middle of his ninth decade of life, Mark Egan continues to turn out business writing of the very highest quality for clients on four continents. As an advisor to scores of grateful business executives and government officials, he has brought his analytical and reportorial skills to bear on business problems in Egypt, Grenada, Samoa, Hawaii, Malaysia, Japan, Taiwan, Uganda, Tanzania, Turkey, New Guinea, Ghana, Guatemala, and Belize. More than a generation before the term "multinational business" had become accepted usage, Mark was a truly global business communicator.

But the impressive geographic scope of Mark Egan's work must not be allowed to obscure its practical impact; wherever he has written, his reports have enabled his clients to follow up with appropriate action. Mark's career has been a living demonstration of the relationship between sound business writing and effective business decision making.

Mark Egan's work over a period of more than fifty years serves as this book's model of effective business writing. More important, his generous sharing of the lessons of those years served as its inspiration.

Harry J. Bruce

Contents

Foreword

Throughout history, businesses of any significant size have faced opportunities and challenges so new or complex as not to be immediately recognizable or comprehensible to any single leader or small group of leaders. The continued success of such businesses has always been dependent on communication systems that made it possible for those in the field who were witnessing changes in the competitive environment to pass information about those changes and possible responses on to those in the headquarters who were responsible for mobilizing and deploying the organization's financial, technical, and managerial resources.

In recent years, the emergence of very sophisticated new producers and marketers here and abroad, and increases in the rate of technological change, have radically altered the competitive environment in which businesses operate. The available evidence suggests strongly that rapid and far-reaching changes in this environment are not temporary phenomena. In the years to come, such changes are more likely to accelerate than to abate. Effective communication systems are likely, therefore, to become increasingly critical elements not only in a firm's continued success, but in its very survival.

Advances in technology have made it possible for businesses today to transmit huge quantities of data and text from one corner of the globe to another quickly and relatively inexpensively. Technology, however, has done and can do little to enhance the quality and readability of the information businesses transmit. Harry Bruce, Russel Hirst, and Michael Keene have written *A Short Guide to Business Writing* to address that need.

Businesses today have many thousands of men and women in their manufacturing facilities, laboratories, sales outlets, and administrative offices with facts and suggestions that could and would be of great value to upper management. In their headquarters, those same businesses have many executives who need and want access to the expertise and views of their associates in the field. In an ideal world, those executives and their associates would exchange views over lunch or in a car pool every day. However, ours is not an ideal world, and most business communication today, therefore, is written.

By encouraging their associates to improve their ability to write concisely and clearly, executives can greatly enhance the competitive capabilities of their firms. By responding aggressively to that encouragement, men and women in the field can assist in improving their employer's competitive capabilities and can enhance their individual careers. *A Short Guide to Business Writing* can assist in accomplishing these objectives.

John J. Nevin, Chairman and Chief Executive Officer,
The Firestone Tire and Rubber Company (ret.)

Preface

Since the great American postwar business expansion of the 1950s, a steadily growing cadre of critics has been accusing the nation's business managers of bad writing. People who respect and practice good writing continue to charge that today's corporate documents simply don't measure up to their predecessors of a generation or two earlier. We see those charges in editorials, in letters to the editor, in feature articles, and in corporate and governmental memo "bloopers" published as humorous filler items in *The New Yorker* and other popular publications.

As a retired board chairman and chief executive officer whose career spanned the same three decades during which the collapse of business writing took place, Harry Bruce agrees. As teachers of professional writing who, year after year, find so many students ill-prepared for the writing they must do at the university, Russel Hirst and Michael Keene have seen the root causes of poor writing in business.

We have all witnessed, both in the academy and in the business world, many of the dreary phenomena the critics continue to bemoan and ridicule: the poorly organized and hard-to-follow structure of so many reports and speeches, the lack of sound research, the inappropriate style, the sloppy diction, the wrong choice of words, the failure to cite sources, the failure to assemble coherent arguments, and the disturbing inability to articulate ideas in ways that suggest their real relationships.

This book had its beginning in two of Harry Bruce's defining personal experiences. Those experiences convinced him that business writing simply didn't have to suffer this kind of abuse.

The first experience was Harry's own business education, which at both the academic and practical levels insisted on excellence in the use of the written word. Unlike most of today's MBAs, he had to complete a master's thesis in order to graduate from the School of Business at the University of Tennessee in 1959. Performing a thorough job of research and then marshaling specific pieces of evidence into arguments leading to a convincing conclusion was an exciting challenge for which he developed a real taste. When he landed his first job, he found that his employer, United States Steel Corporation, not only maintained the same high standards in its written communications but supported those standards with a large, well trained staff of professional writers and editors. They were always willing to help a tyro, as was his immediate superior, Dr. Gayton E. Germane.

Both segments of Harry's business-writing education convinced him of a fundamental truth: Business problems get solved faster if they are first described and analyzed accurately in writing. With that truth goes a corollary: Managers who write effectively will advance faster in their careers than those who don't. Those who can describe a business problem in language that focuses attention on solutions have penetrated to the core of the managerial mission.

The second defining experience began less pleasantly but came to a positive conclusion that led almost directly to the inception of this book. It happened in 1975, when Harry was elected Senior Vice President of Marketing at the Illinois Central Gulf (now Illinois Central) Railroad. Taking up his new position at the company's headquarters in Chicago, he asked the senior managers in the department to analyze and report on the marketing potential of each of the major commodity groups the railroad was transporting.

With all due respect to his former colleagues—some of whom remain friends and all of whom remember the episode—the reports they submitted were terrible. All the errors of style and composition cited by the corporate writing critics were there, along with others the critics had overlooked, including the basic elements of presentation: Several reports lacked covers, and one was even presented with a distinct, ring-shaped coffee stain on its wrinkled first page. Most depressing of all, the reports failed the basic test of all corporate writing: They did not furnish sufficient information, organization, or argument to lead to a business decision. Work was being stymied by the staff's inability to communicate the information needed to get the job done.

The solution was radical. For several weeks, an *ad hoc* school of corporate writing convened after business hours in Harry Bruce's office. From 5:00 to 6:00 P.M. each day, the senior executives would gather for a series of impromptu lessons in business-report writing. The school proved highly effective, and within about a month's time much improved reports began to appear, several of which led to marketing decisions that raised the fortunes of the railroad.

The brief but successful life of this informal school of corporate writing convinced Harry that business managers can learn to write, and they can do it in a short time if they have two essential ingredients: proper motivation and effective instruction. Harry began putting together a book for business managers who needed to prepare reports and speeches, but his own managerial duties forced him to shelve the project until 1989, when he retired. He has now joined up with two coauthors. Hirst and Keene bring to the book their theoretical understanding of human communication, their intimate familiarity with the needs of today's business students, and decades of experience in teaching others to write well. This team of authors now brings to bear on the problem of business writing a combined expertise that has expanded the original core of instructional materials into a comprehensive manual for writing effective reports and speeches.

Harry J. Bruce
Russel K. Hirst
Michael L. Keene

Acknowledgments

Harry Bruce thanks those long-suffering Illinois Central managers of nearly two decades ago who worked so hard to master the fundamentals of corporate writing and who went on to build a better company.

Russel Hirst and Michael Keene thank their students and colleagues, who have taught them invaluable lessons about the needs of writers.

All the authors thank those who have contributed to the substance and physical production of the book, most notably Karmen N. T. Crowther, University of Tennessee Business Librarian and Associate Professor; and William I. Greener, Jr., Consulting Partner, Fleishman-Hillard, Inc., who opened up to us his files full of so many wonderful examples of writing in industry and government. We were ably assisted in the production of the manuscript by Kathryn G. Aycock, Dariel Mayer, and Susanne Nilson.

A number of people have read and responded to drafts of this manuscript: Dr. Scott Buechler, manager of the MBA program at the University of Tennessee, who was instrumental in test marketing two drafts of the book with his students; Dr. Ernie Cadotte, Professor of Marketing, Logistics, and Transportation at the University of Tennessee, Knoxville, who also organized focus groups to test the book; Eugene D. Fanning, Professor of Career Communications at Notre Dame University, who also test marketed manuscript drafts with his students; and F. K. Plous, communications consultant.

We thank the students of the University of Tennessee MBA Program, classes of 1992 and 1993, and the students of the Business School at Notre Dame University, classes of 1992 and 1993, for their responses and contributions.

We also gratefully acknowledge careful readings and valuable comments from these reviewers:

Academics

Dr. Carter A. Daniel, Director, Communications Programs, Rutgers Graduate School of Management, Rutgers University

Dr. Sidney Davidson, Ernst and Young Distinguished Service Professor Emeritus and former Dean, Graduate School of Business, The University of Chicago

Dr. Robert Fulkerth, Assistant Professor, English and Communications, School of Arts and Sciences, Golden Gate University

Dr. Kathleen Kelly, Associate Professor, English, Babson College

Dr. Marianne T. Miller, Penn State University

Dr. C. Warren Neel, Dean, University of Tennessee College of Business Administration

Dr. Pedro Nueño, Department of Production, Operations, and Technology Management, International Graduate School of Management, University of Navarra, Barcelona, Spain

Dr. Judith P. Saunders, Marist College

Dr. Shelby J. Pierce, Owens Technical College

Dr. Julian L. Simon, Professor of Business Administration, College of Business and Management, University of Maryland, College Park

Dr. E. Ray Smith, Dean, College of Business, Western Illinois University

Dr. Bill M. Stiffler, Harford Community College

Prof. W. D. Wagstaff, Department of Operations Management, Golden Gate University

Dr. Heidemane Z. Weidemer, Texas Tech University

Dr. Deborah S. Workman, Dyke College

Executives

Richard P. Bessette, President and Chief Executive Officer, Roman Adhesives, Inc.

John W. Bruce III, Data Security Administrator, Southern California Gas Company

James M. Denny, Vice-Chairman, Sears, Roebuck and Co.

Richard U. De Schutter, President and Chief Operating Officer, G. D. Searle & Company

Robert Douglas, Business Editor, *The Palm Beach Post*

David W. Grainger, Chairman, President, and Chief Executive Officer, W. W. Grainger, Inc.

Rolf Gullans, Vice President, Logistics, International Paper Co. (ret.)

Douglas D. Hagestad, President, Hagestad Associates, Inc.

Paul B. Haley, President and Chief Operating Officer, Marketing Force, Inc.

C. R. (Jack) Kopp, President and Chief Executive Officer, Leo Burnett Co., Inc. (ret.)

Robert D. Milne, Chairman of the Board, Duff & Phelps Investment Management Co.

Ronald J. Mueller, President and Chief Executive Officer, The Florsheim Shoe Company

Philip J. Niehoff, J. D., Partner, Mayer, Brown & Platt

John J. Nevin, Chairman and Chief Executive Officer, The Firestone Tire and Rubber Company (ret.)

James B. Peterson, Managing Partner, James B. Peterson and Associates

Richard J. L. Senior, President and Chief Executive Officer, Morgan Services, Inc.

Raymond C. Tower, President and Chief Operating Officer, FMC Corporation (ret.)

Robert F. Wall, J. D., Partner, Winston & Strawn

Donald D. Wallace, First Vice President and Branch Manager, Robert W. Baird & Co., Inc.

About the Authors

HARRY J. BRUCE is former Chairman, President, and Chief Executive Officer of the Illinois Central Railroad. Prior to that, he was Vice President—Marketing of the Western Pacific Railroad, Assistant Vice President—Plant Operations for Jos. Schlitz Brewing Company, Vice President—Marketing for Spector Freight System, Inc., and Assistant to the Director—Transport Research for United States Steel Corporation. Since his retirement from Illinois Central in 1989, Mr. Bruce has been elected Chairman—Roman Adhesives Corp. Additionally, he holds a number of corporate directorship positions. Mr. Bruce received the Bachelor of Science degree in Transportation and Industrial Engineering from Kent State University and the Master of Science from the University of Tennessee. He also attended the Harvard Business School Advanced Management Program. He has held teaching positions at Duquesne University and the University of Pittsburgh and is currently Adjunct Professor of Business Strategy at Florida Atlantic University. His publications include *How to Apply Statistics to Physical Distribution* (Chilton), *Distribution and Transportation Handbook* (Cahners), and Chapter 25, "Physical Distribution," in *Handbook of Modern Marketing,* Second Edition (McGraw-Hill). He has published over fifty articles in international business and academic journals, and in 1993 he was elected Fellow of the International Academy of Management. The guiding philosophies of *A Short Guide*—the idea of encouraging writers in business and business students to use their writing skills to differentiate themselves and to speed their progress toward promotion, and the idea of employing a systems-thinking approach to writing—are ideas Harry Bruce worked out during his long and successful business career.

RUSSEL K. HIRST, Assistant Professor of English at the University of Tennessee, is a graduate of the doctoral program in Communication and Rhetoric at Rensselaer Polytechnic Institute. While at Rensselaer, he taught composition and technical communication and tutored in the writing center. Before that, he was an instructor in the Program in Scientific and Technical Communication at the University of Washington. He has also taught technical communication at special seminars for gifted students, and he has been a writing instructor for the New York State Public Service Training Program. Professor Hirst has interned as a technical writer/editor for Care Computer Company of Belleview, Washington, and for the Environmental Restoration Division Publications Group at Martin Marietta Energy Systems, Inc. in Oak Ridge Tennessee. As a freelance technical writer, he wrote and edited *Highlights of the Municipal Energy Recovery Facilities Handbook* (New York State Department of Environmental Conservation, 1988). Professor Hirst has published in *The Journal of Technical Writing and Communication* and has essays on the history of communication in *Oratorical Culture in America: The Transformation of Nineteenth-Century Rhetoric* (Southern Illinois University Press, 1993), and *Ethos: New Essays in Rhetorical and Critical Theory* (Southern Methodist University Press, 1994). His current projects include entries for the *Encyclopedia of Rhetoric* (Garland Press, tentative publication 1995) and a collaborative book entitled *Teaching Technical Communication: Academic Programs That Work.*

MICHAEL L. KEENE, Professor of English, created and directs the program in technical communication at the University of Tennessee, Knoxville, and teaches in the graduate program in Rhetoric and Composition. He was also director of technical writing at the Tennessee Governor's School for the Sciences, 1985–1989. Previously, Dr. Keene taught Freshman English, Argumentation, and Technical Writing at Texas A&M University, where he helped create the Undergraduate Writing Specialization. His publications include *The Heath Guide to College Writing* (D.C. Heath, 1992, 1995, with Ralph Voss), *Effective Professional and Technical Writing* (D.C. Heath, 1987, 1992), and the revised Eighth Edition of W. Paul Jones's *Writing Scientific Papers and Reports* (Wm. C. Brown, 1980). He has also published numerous chapters and articles on composition and technical communication. In addition to *A Short Guide,* his current projects include *A User Manual for College Writers* (with Kate Adams, for Mayfield Press); *Writing Articles, Theses, and Dissertations in Science and Engineering* (tentative publication 1995); and *Teaching Technical Communication: Academic Programs That Work.* Dr. Keene is regularly retained as a writing consultant by clients in engineering, marketing, manufacturing, and government.

Introduction

It should not be an unreasonable assumption that people who have risen to positions of power and respect can write without difficulty.

—The Chicago Tribune, *January 14, 1985*

"The firms identified writing as the most valued skill, but said 80% of their employees at all levels need to improve." From a 1992 survey by Olsten Corp.

Success in the business world today requires many skills: writing ability, speaking ability, the ability to work with graphics, interpersonal skills, analytical skills, knowledge of the industry (and its major players), persistence, consensus building, networking, and a little luck, just to name a few. The point of this book is to show you how to make your writing and speaking skills strong assets to your career. To a greater extent than you might imagine, the key to improving your writing and speaking skills is to bring the same intelligence and good work habits to bear on them that you use in all other parts of your business activities.

Writing is another way of delivering quality to customers.

Today's world of business lives on written documents—memos, letters, and especially reports. Everyone in business reads reports constantly. The higher you go in management, the more time you will spend reading reports—and writing them. The same imperative that drives all successful business activities should also drive your performance as you use words to influence superiors, peers, subordinates, and customers: the need to deliver the highest quality of product or service to the customer. The only difference is that here, *the "customer" is the reader.*

By viewing readers as customers, you can improve your writing and speaking. You achieve this by using many of the skills and techniques you have already mastered—such as the ability to organize and categorize, to establish priorities and schedules, to identify and eliminate the unnecessary, to break down complex phenomena into smaller units, and to reorganize simple units to function better in larger systems. Thus, our approach focuses on making writing part of the larger system of business. Writing is another way of delivering quality to customers.

THE NEED FOR WRITING

Contrary to some predictions, the rapid emergence of electronic information technology has not eliminated the need for clear writing. In fact, by making it easier to create printed documents, to enhance them with visuals, and to reproduce and distribute them, high technology has accentuated the importance of the printed word. As you probably know, computers do not abolish paperwork; they multiply it.

Consider these situations:

- Your boss is a fanatic about record keeping and reporting. Every week you are expected to turn in a one-page progress report on every project on your desk. (See Chapter 10 for help with letters and memos.)
- As a middle manager, you have been commissioned by the CEO to research and write a long-range planning report examining strategic options and suggesting new directions for the organization.
- You are a member of the task force charged with writing the company's new policy on strategic development. Someone needs to write up the results in the following forms:

  1. A resolution to be approved by the Board of Directors.
  2. An advisory to be distributed to all managerial-level employees.
  3. A speech to stockholders.
  4. A presentation to customers.

  The task force is sitting around a table, right now, with these "things to do" in front of them. Will *you* volunteer to handle them?
- You see a chance for your company to be the first to move into a new and (you believe) highly profitable area. You tell your boss about it, and you are given a green light to research and write up your proposal. Your boss says, "Be brief, be factual, be persuasive, and above all be right." Can you do it?

Any reasonably intelligent person should be able to read your report without help.

"If you can't explain what you are doing in simple English, you are probably doing something wrong." Alfred Kahn, in *A Treasury of Business Quotations,* 1991.

The people you work for expect you to handle these and many other kinds of writing situations. How forthcoming you are, and how clear and well written the resulting documents are, will play a major role in how well your career goes. Late, unclear, incomplete, or hard-to-read documents are unacceptable. *Any reasonably intelligent and informed person should be able to read your work through to the end and understand it without asking you or someone else for clarification.*

Too much of the writing in business today fails to meet that test. Readers are often asked to wade through swamps of confusing verbiage, and too often they just turn the pages uncomprehendingly—hoping to find a heading or a visual that will return them to the main theme or argument. Nonessential details get the same coverage as essential ones, key ideas are buried, and the writing style is deadly. The sentences are five or six lines long, every verb is "is" or "was," every noun ends in *-tion*, and the jargon makes the reader feel like an outsider. Worst of all from the reader's point of view, there is no sense to the structure.

HOW TO BE A BETTER WRITER

Effective writers in business approach their writing tasks using skills remarkably like those they use in the rest of their work. They seek to articulate a clear purpose for the task. They are organized and focused in searching for information. They use numbers and graphics to support their ideas. They are curious and intuitive, listening to their hunches as well as relying on their quantitative methods. Perhaps most important, they are practical. "Practical" here means that their writing has a *problem-solving, audience-specific orientation*. Usually this also means a *bias toward action*: When you finish reading a good piece of business writing, you should want to get up and *do* something. And because the report is well written, you will know exactly what it is you need to do.

Business writing needs to have a problem-solving, audience-specific orientation.

How can you achieve these qualities in your writing? We believe the answer lies in taking a *systems* approach to your writing:

The systems approach to writing

1. Make sure that in your writing you see yourself and your work as part of the business system, rather than seeing the system as an extension of yourself.
2. Make the steps in your writing process flexible and recursive so that they accommodate your larger project, not vice versa.
3. Develop the habit of seeking feedback on interim drafts of your writing, and especially of listening to criticisms and suggestions.
4. Stay interactive with the larger business system throughout the duration of your writing process.
5. Do not let your "product" (your report) die on the shelf; monitor and "sell" its acceptance and use.

Systems thinking reinforces the notion that any piece of business writing (or speaking) succeeds only to the extent that it furnishes its audience with information that leads to practical business decisions. Writing a memo, letter, or report is one activity within a large and complex enterprise made up of thousands of such activities. Only when those parts serve each other's mutual interests do they form a true system.

You and your writing are valuable only insofar as you add value to the larger system.

As a manager, you are part of many systems. The global economy is an increasingly important and interwoven system. The national economy is another. Your particular field or area of business is another. Clearest of all is your own business. If you are an employee of USX Corp., you have to consider the global picture, the national picture, USX's contribution to the world around it, and your own department's contribution to the company. You and your written contributions are valuable insofar as you serve (add value to) those systems, and detrimental as they add static, clutter, or confusion. You must look at your writing and all of its separate activities in terms of the system(s) it fits into. Only by being responsive to the complex and changing realities of the larger system can your writing serve that system effectively.

1. Make sure that in your writing you see yourself and your work as part of the business system, rather than seeing the system as an extension of yourself. Systems thinking as applied to writing requires first and foremost that you develop the ability to view the system from the outside in. Rather than seeing your department, your company, your industry, and so on as fainter and fainter extensions of yourself (Figure I.1), you need to see your own activity as nested within the larger business activities of which it is but a small part (Figure I.2).

It may be natural for writers to see themselves as the center of the universe. But doing so dulls your sense of the report as serving the larger system. Such *egocentric writing* increases the chances that you will tend to define value in the report as whatever you are putting into it—rather than whatever the readers get out of it. Remember, the true definition of value always resides in how the client, the customer, the user—that is, your reader—sees and uses your product (and not intrinsically in what you put into it).

Systems-centered writing will always put the system <u>before</u> the writer. Consider the following sequence:

Monitor your own writing process to make sure you are supplying exactly what the larger system needs.

- Executive management must respond to various business situations:
  Rumors about new competing technologies that may hurt the company.
  Doors newly opened for expanded sales in formerly communist countries.
  Changes in federal regulations.
  Changes in expectations of U.S. workers.
- Executive management needs information, analysis, and recommendations pertaining to one or more of these situations.
- Your immediate supervisor requests a report.
- You find yourself in charge of a writing project.

All of these situations will have an impact on your writing. If you proceed without considering them, your report will add clutter and confusion to the system rather than value.

Beyond considering the relevant business situation before you begin, being a *systems-sensitive writer* means monitoring your writing process to make sure that your research, text, and graphics supply exactly the information the system needs. As feedback from the system continues to reveal fresh concerns or opportunities, you need to be flexible enough to include this new input in your writing process.

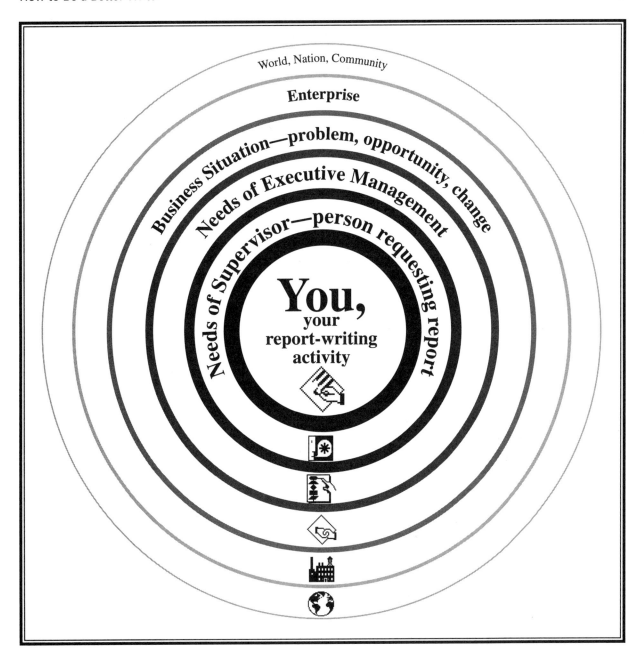

World, Nation, Community

Enterprise

Business Situation—problem, opportunity, change

Needs of Executive Management

Needs of Supervisor—person requesting report

You,
your
report-writing
activity

Figure I.1 Egocentric writing. This erroneous view sees the department, the company, the industry, and so on, as fainter and fainter extensions of the writer's ego.

As the system's needs and goals change, and as your understanding of them sharpens, the writing itself changes accordingly.

2. Make the steps in your writing process flexible and recursive so that they accommodate your larger project, not vice versa. Too many writers get their writing assignments, put their heads down, and plow

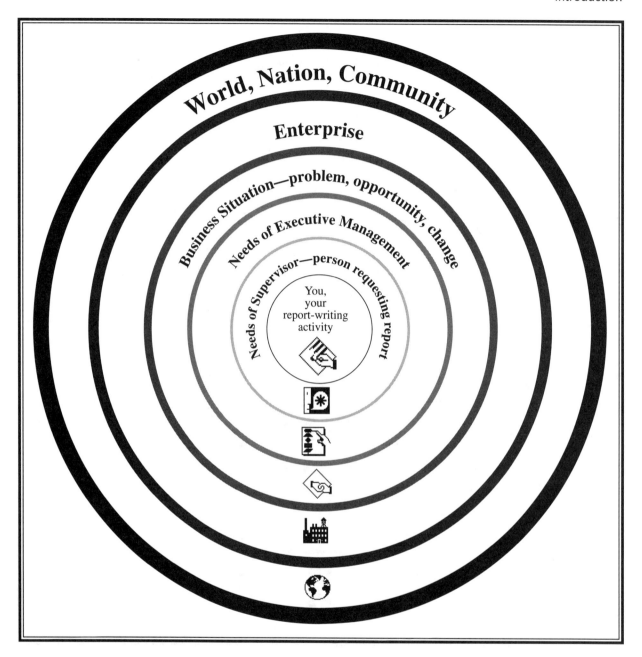

Figure I.2 Systems thinking applied to writing. The writer's activity has meaning only within all the larger systems it must serve.

To serve the system effectively, your writing process must be *intelligently flexible.*

methodically along from page one to page whatever until the report is finished—unaware of impending disaster. If you see your writing as part of the larger system, you can avoid this scenario.

Your writing process must be <u>intelligently flexible</u> in order to serve the system effectively. Most writers go through these stages in their writing: research, writing, revising, and editing (we shall have more to say about these stages in subsequent chapters). One of the most damaging attitudes writers can develop is a reluctance to go back to an earlier stage of the process. Once they have begun researching, most writers do not want to reevaluate their purpose or their audience. Once they have begun writing, they do not want to do any more research. Once they have begun editing, they refuse to see a need to write new material. Even the most accomplished writers must struggle occasionally to resist the tendency to rush the finish.

Successful writers, on the other hand, work *recursively,* ranging freely through the various stages of the process and looping back frequently. As research modifies your understanding, you must reconsider your objectives, audience, and scope. As your writing uncovers holes in your understanding, you *must* go back to your research to fill them in. As your editing shows too much trivia and not enough critical detail, you *must* go back to research and writing to correct the problem. *Remember that the value of your report is not the effort you put into it; the value of your report is what your readers get out of it.*

> The value of your report is not the effort you put into it; value is what your readers get out of it.

3. Develop the habit of seeking feedback on interim drafts of your writing, and especially of listening to criticisms and suggestions. Communicating with the individual who assigned this writing task or who will use the resulting document is a fine art. Fortunately, it is an art that can be learned, practiced, and polished.

Your writing process must be intelligently interactive with the system around you. It is essential to check back with supervisors periodically during your writing project—to define and redefine the report's objectives, to clarify your audience's needs and monitor any changes, to readjust your report's scope, to react to changing circumstances, and to make sure that the approach and organization you are developing are appropriate. You can help yourself in such "check-back" meetings by going in with a brief agenda of your own, even if it consists of only a short list of questions to ask. You can also enlist your supervisor's help by furnishing periodic, concise, written reports of your progress. You can even write those reports in such a way that they can be passed along for tentative approval to those who will receive the final product. In some situations, as you complete parts of the report you may be able to test-market them to friendly readers within your target audience who will give you confidential responses.

4. Stay interactive with the larger business system throughout the duration of your writing process. Interacting with the system is appropriate at nearly every stage of the writing process. Withdrawing into your word-processing cocoon may appear to make the writing easier, but in doing so you risk making all that progress in the wrong direction. Here are two ways to tell you have lost your systems orientation:

> By withdrawing into your word-processing cocoon, you risk making all that progress in the wrong direction.

- You become compulsively inclusive. You do not really know what you should be including, so you include everything. You do not really know what you should be excluding, so you exclude nothing.

- You obsess about things other than the report's content and structure—such as its grammar or its flourishes of style—before you are absolutely certain that your report's content and structure, your understanding of its purpose, and your vision of its audience are on target.

According to Chicago business writer Bob Yovovich, when you find yourself following either of these behavior patterns, you should stop writing and go talk with the person who commissioned the report. Make sure you have the assignment right, probe to discover your reader's real concerns, phrase and rephrase the true goal of the report. When you begin thinking, "Aha—*this* is what the assignment is really about," then it is time to go back to writing.

A substantial benefit of this approach is that you will have gained *incremental acceptance* of your report. The more you interact with the business system as you are doing your writing, the more you minimize the chances that the report will come back to you for a complete revision.

5. Do not let your "product" (your report) die on the shelf; monitor and "sell" its acceptance and use. One of the most frustrating experiences any writer can have is to work hard on an important project, do a good job with it, turn in the report, and never again hear a word about it. Of course it is higher management's responsibility to make better use of both its human and information resources, but saving your report from this kind of living death is your responsibility too, and the best way to do it is to stay system sensitive. You can begin by delivering the report in person, and by making sure that it gets into the hands of *all* the people who need to see it. Then follow up creatively by developing derivatives of the report—slide shows, trade-show talks, shortened versions for customers, employees, or the public—that you can create out of the same basic word-processing file from which you built your report. Once you create these derivatives, you'll find opportunities to use them, and the best time to create them is when all that knowledge is freshest in your mind. If you have built suggestions for future work into your report, you can also beat your peers at coming up with proposals to pursue that future work now.

A REPORT THAT FAILED

Subsystem optimization at the expense of system-wide integration happens to writers, too.

What happens when systems thinking gets left out of the report-writing process? The result is excessive concentration on the parts at the expense of the whole, what systems analysts call *subsystem optimization at the expense of system-wide integration*. Remember the near death of the Detroit automakers? All through the 1970s and 1980s, each function in the car industry appeared to be doing its job adequately, at least when evaluated separately from the rest of the system. Market research turned in reports on consumer preferences; designs changed regularly; management managed; workers worked; cars were built and sold. All the functions went according to the book.

But somewhere along the way, concern for what was going on in the larger

Writers can easily lose sight of the one thing that matters most in business: delivering value to the customer.

business environment was lost. The functions became ends in themselves as subsystem optimization tightened its grip. Cross-functional communications dried up as departments became more introverted. Engineering and design failed to interact with manufacturing; marketing failed to interact with engineering; human resources failed to make clear to workers the essential connections of product quality, corporate success, and job security. Only after a decade and a half of market invasion by foreign competitors, eroding market share, factory closings, product recalls, blue-collar layoffs, white-collar buyouts, billions of dollars in losses, and a Ross Perot tantrum did the industry begin to reform itself—by embracing systems thinking. Automotive management had lost sight of the one thing that matters most in business: delivering value to the customer. That can also happen when people in management write.

When Hawaii's Department of Planning and Economic Development tendered a large contract to a nationally known accounting/management consultant, it requested a development plan for each government entity in the Pacific Islands Tourist Development Council, which included New Guinea, Nauru, Tonga, American/Western Samoa, Cook Islands, Fiji, Tahiti, Hawaii, Micronesia, and Guam. The report's stated objective was to develop a five-year plan formulating recommendations and a course of action for each island area.

The result *looked* like a very professional job: multiple volumes in glossy binders, each addressing a different island and breaking down the problems of that island's tourism into logical categories. The typography was clear and attractive, and the organization was reinforced by outline-style numbering and lettering of the various sections and subsections. Yet the people who had commissioned the report were very disappointed with it. Here is what was wrong:

- Although the report contained a great deal of information that appeared to be useful, there was little relevant interpretation of those data.
- The only mention of the report's objective was in the preface. Large volumes of material were introduced with no indication of how any of it related to the report's original goals. There was no discernible development from one section to the next, and no sequence of specific recommendations flowing from that development.
- There were no graphics.
- The report failed to provide a basis for decision making. For all of its historical background and statistical data, it offered few conclusions and recommendations and failed to show a logical flow from the data collection to the analysis and to the conclusions.
- The few conclusions the report contained were fundamental to any area's development. There was no orderly arrangement of conclusions that could serve as a basis for strategic and tactical planning for each specific island area.

A report that fails to interact with the system during the writing will often fail to deliver value to the customer during the reading.

How did such a failed report happen? The principal contractor had assembled a team from three different firms, each representing a particular skill—organization, regional planning, and marketing. While such subcontracting is common, in this case, the principal contractor failed to articulate a common theme or to manage the project to keep all of the subcontractors in pursuit of that theme. So each firm had written its own section without coordinating its work with the others and without much direction from the principal contractor. There had been very little interim communication between the Department of Planning and the principal contractor, or between the principal contractor and the subcontractors. There had been no check on the competence of the people who actually did the writing, and there was little or no evidence of periodic progress reports or interim review drafts. The final draft was the first substantive piece submitted.

The result was a catchall. Because the report writers did not interact with the system during the writing, the resulting document failed to meet the client's need. No doubt its authors had filled it with many features *they* saw as valuable. The value of business writing, however, is in the eyes of the reader. Measured that way, this report failed.

CONCLUSION

Writing is like many other important tasks in today's business world—often challenging, perhaps perplexing, occasionally discouraging, and ultimately rewarding. When you write well on the job, you receive more than the satisfaction of a job well done. Employees with a reputation for supplying soundly researched and well-written reports will advance faster, acquire more responsibility, and ultimately earn more money than those with weaker writing skills. If you learn to take a systems approach to your writing, as the rest of this book describes it, you too can make the writing you do on the job a less frustrating and more rewarding experience.

PRACTICE

An Inventory for Writers

Answering the following questions can help focus your attention as you read this book. The more you know about your current strengths and weaknesses, the better you can profit from instruction.

1. What were your greatest successes as a writer—
   in the classroom?
   in professional life?
   Choose one successful experience you have had as a writer in the last five years and analyze the source of its success. Pay particular attention to the subjects covered in this chapter.

2. What were your greatest failures as a writer—
   in the classroom?
   in professional life?
   Choose one experience of failure you have had as a writer in the last five years
   and analyze the source of that failure. Pay particular attention to the subjects
   covered in this chapter.

3. What are your skills as a writer—
   in research?
   in brainstorming?
   in getting a good first draft done promptly?
   in revising?
   in proofreading and editing?
   in matching your writing with the situation that required it?
   For each area in which you rated yourself as strong, give one detailed example of that strength.

4. What are your weaknesses as a writer—
   in research?
   in brainstorming?
   in getting a good first draft done promptly?
   in revising?
   in proofreading and editing?
   in making your writing match well with the situation that required it?
   For each area in which you rated yourself as weak, briefly describe one situation that demonstrated your weakness.

Part One

WRITING IN THE BUSINESS WORLD

1

Getting Started: Defining Your Purpose

When does a corporate writing project actually begin? When upper management first discusses a new effort or project? When your boss first mentions it to you? When you get the word that researching and writing up this project is *your* job? When you begin researching? When you first create a document file on your computer for this task? When you write the first word?

In many cases the beginning of a writing project is hard to define exactly. Often a superior will first make some preliminary inquiries about a subject to see if it has possibilities that relate to the organization's goals. You may be asked to check a fact or two, make a few phone calls, or go through some correspondence, reporting what you discover in a brief memo or an oral presentation. Any analysis or conclusions are put off until later.

It is essential to have a good, clear, accurate picture of your project right from the start.

If you do a good job with this preliminary stage of the project, you may then be directed to move from casual exploration to comprehensive study, including an analysis of how this proposed new activity relates to the organization's goals and how the organization can best take practical steps to exploit the information you will develop. At this point, you have a full-scale research and writing project before you.

Defining the task clearly is crucial at this point. All the other phases of the writing process can trade places with each other freely, but having a good, clear, accurate picture of your goal before you begin writing *must* be the first step in the sequence. Figure 1.1 (functional stages of the writing process) presents an overview of an eight-stage writing process:

Getting Started: Defining your purpose

Finding facts and ideas

1 **Getting Started: Defining Your Purpose**
- What objectives does this report have?
- What audiences does this report have?
- What uses will this report be put to?
- What is this report's scope to be?

5 **Choosing and Using Graphics**
- Identifying the functions of graphics
- Identifying the kinds and characteristics of graphics
- Matching graphics to text

2 **Finding Facts and Ideas**
- Getting creativity into report writing
- Connecting creativity and research
- Locating sources of business information

6 **Revising and Editing Your Report**
- Revising and editing for substance
- Revising and editing for structure and function
- Revising and editing for style

3 **Organizing Your Report**
- Using five common structural patterns
- Going from structure to writing
- Beginning to write

7 **Designing Your Pages**
- Seeing each page as a grid
- Coordinating and balancing the elements of pages
- Emphasizing important information
- Using readable typefaces
- Using a helpful heading scheme
- Staying consistent

4 **Writing Your First Full Draft**
- Understanding the composing process
- Avoiding common mistakes
- Practicing good habits
- Keeping your composing process system-sensitive
- Identifying qualities of the first and interim drafts

8 **Checking and Using Your Report**
- Checking your report
- Using your report

Figure 1.1   Functional stages of the writing process.

Organizing your report
Writing your first full draft
Choosing and using graphics
Revising and editing your report
Designing your pages
Checking and using your report

These eight stages correspond to the first eight chapters (Part One) of this book. Remember two points, however:

- No linear, "stages" model can depict the writing process entirely accurately. These stages will always loop back on each other and may even occur in a totally different order from one project to another.
- *You must work through these stages in a system-responsive way.* As Figure 1.2 (system interaction in the report-writing process) indicates, interaction with the larger business system must occur throughout the writing process.

No matter what order your writing process follows, you must begin by getting as clear a picture as you can of the project's purpose. While a complete understanding may not be possible without further study, and while whatever preliminary understanding you may reach can and should change as the project unfolds, this initial conception of your task will have a major and lasting effect on your entire project. You *may* receive explicit instructions, such as these:

- "We need a report recommending a way to significantly reduce our expenses by outsourcing as much of our overhead—physical plant, custodial, cafeteria, health care, and so on—as we can. This is your baby. You've got six weeks."
- "Our walking shoes have been losing market share in the Pacific Northwest for six months now, and our store managers don't seem to know why. Do what you have to do to get to the bottom of this problem, and have a report with recommendations on my desk by the twenty-fourth of next month."

Despite the apparently explicit nature of these instructions, much remains to be determined. Do not assume that your superior will always state in clear and complete terms what you are supposed to do. It is *your* job to ask the necessary questions. If these points are not explicitly stated when the task is presented to you, you need to bring them up:

- What, exactly, are the objectives of this report?
- How much time do you have to complete it?
- How much of your schedule should you clear to do this?
- What should the *scope* and *depth* of the report be?
- What circumstances brought about the need for this project?

Interaction with the larger business system must occur throughout the writing process.

Not understanding your assignment and failing to develop a meaningful goal are major sources of failure in writing on the job.

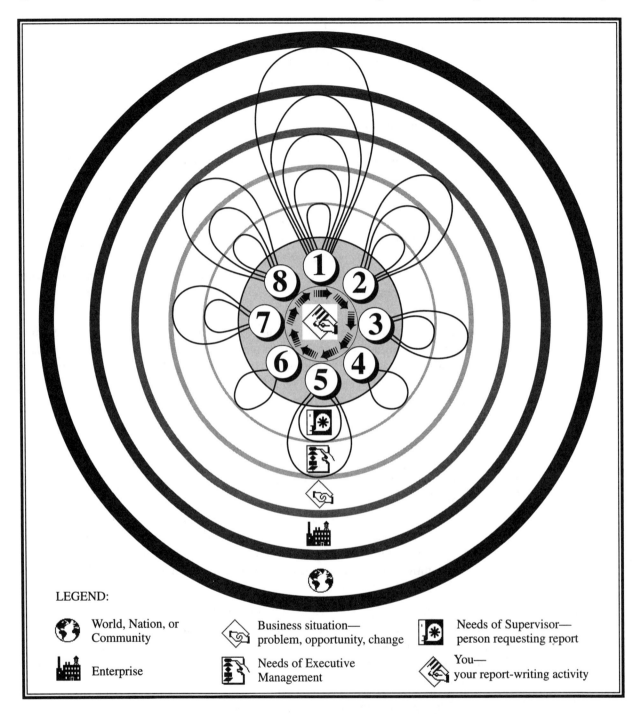

LEGEND:

World, Nation, or Community

Enterprise

Business situation— problem, opportunity, change

Needs of Executive Management

Needs of Supervisor— person requesting report

You— your report-writing activity

Figure 1.2 Recursive interaction in the report-writing process: a systems-thinking approach. Interactivity, recursiveness, and incremental acceptance loops are most numerous in early stages (front-end loaded), may diminish considerably during middle stages, and return to the larger environments to a lesser extent in latter stages.

While your initial sense of the report's goals, direction, scope, depth, and origins will probably come from a meeting with your immediate supervisor, you may also need to consult with higher authorities (with your boss's approval), talk with clients, or look at other documents in order to develop a clear idea of what kind of work is required. Do not skip these steps. *Not understanding your assignment and not developing a meaningful goal are major sources of failure in writing on the job.* You should be concerned not so much with failure to solve the problem but with the possibility of solving the *wrong* problem.

One good way to define your assignment more clearly and develop a meaningful goal is to look for answers to these four questions:

- What *objectives* does this project have?
- What *audiences* does this report have?
- What *uses* will this report be put to?
- What is this report's *scope* to be?

By leaving any of these questions unanswered, you risk writing a report that solves the wrong problem.

WHAT OBJECTIVES DOES THIS REPORT HAVE?

Problem-solving projects can nearly always be broken down into *methods, objectives,* and *goals*. While you may be accustomed to grouping all of these under a more general heading of "objectives," you will find that using the more rigorous terminology explained here will improve both your writing and your thinking. *Methods* are the activities you conduct to accomplish objectives. *Objectives* are results that can be quantified or measured. *Goals* are the highest of the three levels, more abstract than objectives and often somewhat intangible.

When you put down your project's objectives on paper, you gain a clearer focus on its goals.

How methods and objectives shape each other. Consider the walking-shoes assignment (from p. 17). You may already know some of the methods you need to apply on this project, such as visiting major retail outlets for your product in the Pacific Northwest and interviewing sales managers to learn their thoughts on the decline in sales. As you proceed, other methods may come to you, such as conducting focus groups of representative buyers to determine how well or poorly your current advertising is working with them. What *objectives* are you trying to accomplish with these methods? Maybe in your interviews with sales managers you are trying to determine whether the problem is happening in the stores. Perhaps in your focus groups you are trying to determine whether the problem is with the advertising program. When you put down these objectives on paper, you can evaluate the strengths and weaknesses of your current methods and determine what other methods you might need to employ. For example, having covered advertising and the stores, what is left unexamined? You may want to find some way to check on possible distribution problems and on customers' feelings about the product three months after purchase. You may also want to look at what your competitors are doing. Each of these points—distribution, postpurchase satisfaction, and competition—then becomes an objective that must also have a method or methods attached to it.

How objectives help determine goals. Just as there is a reciprocal relationship between objectives and methods (objectives help determine methods, and methods help determine objectives), so there is a reciprocal relationship between objectives and goals. By writing down your project's objectives and clearly defining them, you can get a clearer focus on its goal(s). If you were told "Our walking shoes have been losing market share. . . . Get to the bottom of this . . . have a report with recommendations on my desk by the twenty-fourth of next month," is your only goal that of finding out why the shoes are not selling? No. There is another one—finding out what to *do* about it. Will the same objectives that accomplish the first goal accomplish the second? Maybe, but you may have to come up with other objectives (and other methods) to satisfy that goal.

Once again, just as objectives and methods shape each other, so do goals and objectives. The more you articulate each of these features on paper right from the start, the better you will do at defining them. As Figure 1.3 shows, using a tree diagram to represent goals, objectives, and methods can help you think through their complex, hierarchical relationships. Ultimately, the point of doing this, on paper, right at the beginning of your project, is to define your goals more fully.

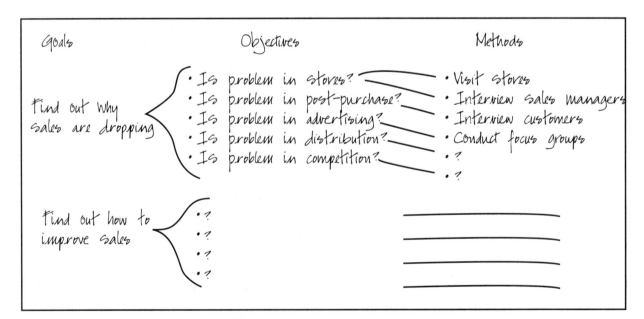

Figure 1.3 Goals, objectives, and methods. The tree diagram, showing the three elements' hierarchical structure, is a good way to work out the relationships (and possible missing pieces) for yourself.

WHAT AUDIENCES DOES THIS REPORT HAVE?

Goals and objectives really have meaning only in relationship to particular audiences. You need to know who your readers will be, what characteristics those readers have, and to what uses they will put your report (uses will be discussed shortly).

Who will your readers be? Reports move through organizational channels in many ways, and they move outside of organizations as well. To define your audiences clearly, you need to envision your report's pathway of acceptance and use:

Never make the mistake of assuming that your report will have only one audience.

- *Upward*—to respond to management requests, to keep management informed, or to seek approval.
- *Downward*—to provide employees with instructions about policy or operations, or to increase their knowledge of the organization.
- *Horizontally*—to elicit cooperation by your peers, or to keep them informed of developments in your area that may affect theirs.
- *Outward*—to clients, other businesses, government agencies, or the public to increase sales, build image, confirm compliance, or provide general information.

Whatever else your writing does or does not do, it must satisfy the primary audience.

Do not assume that your report will have only one audience. Once you put something down on paper, it has a robust life of its own. You cannot generally regard the person who asked you to write the report as its sole audience. Usually, that person's evaluation of the report's quality will be based on his or her opinion of how well the report is likely to accomplish its objectives in connection with audiences beyond (usually above) that person. While the person who commissioned the report is its *primary audience*, he or she may be only a gatekeeper through whom it must pass before it reaches its *secondary audience*, who may be either a higher-ranking person in your own firm or someone outside the firm entirely. Your writing must, whatever else it does, satisfy that primary audience (otherwise, it will never reach the secondary one), but you would be naive to ignore the possibility that a secondary audience exists.

What are your readers' characteristics? Perhaps the most important characteristic of your readers is their expectations concerning your project. For example, if you are writing a recommendation report, what features besides recommendations does your audience expect? How much rationale or background information should you give? How much detail should you include in the recommendations? What kind of physical layout should you use? How much emphasis should you place on graphics? How formal or informal should the writing be? What "red flag" words or subjects should you avoid? What "pet" words or subjects should you include? These kinds of considerations usually become known to you only if you go looking for them. Having lunch with your reader is a good place to start, but it is only a start.

Here are some of the other things you need to know about your readers:

- Level of education.
- Level of hands-on experience with this subject matter.
- Degree of general familiarity with this subject matter.
- Degree of interest (or *personal stake*) in the outcome of the report.
- General attitude toward this subject matter.
- Status in this field of business (Is this person an insider or an outsider, a rookie or an old-timer?).
- Nationality.

Especially in translation situations, the responsibility for avoiding potential problems rests with you, the writer.

This last point, nationality, needs some explanation. If your audience is foreign, and the report is to be translated, you cannot simply write it and send it to the translator. You will need to study the culture and adapt your report to it. Common business practices in the United States (such as setting deadlines) may be seen as meaningless or even offensive in other cultures, and simple language translation will not eliminate such potential cultural differences. Some commonly used business expressions in the United States may become meaningless (or worse) when translated if the translator is not careful.

The magnitude of such cultural differences (and resulting problems in language translation) was dramatized when President Jimmy Carter visited Poland. His interpreter used schoolbook Polish and lacked knowledge of the local idiom. Those listening to President Carter's welcoming remarks were first shocked, then amused, when the hapless interpreter said, "I'm happy to be here to make love to all your women." If your translator is a U.S. native who is fluent in the other language and culture as well, such potential problems may be called to your attention in time to remedy them. If your translator is a native of the country receiving your report, someone who knows only "textbook English," the responsibility for avoiding potential problem areas rests squarely with you.

Graphics can be another problem area for international reports. Each culture has its own graphic conventions—charting methods are different, colors and icons mean different things. Unless your firm has a long-standing and successful relationship with a good translation service, you will need to take the responsibility to be very careful of these matters. Remember, the value of your report is in your reader's (customer's) eyes. If that person is Japanese, or Estonian, or Turkish, it is the norms and customs of that person to which you must appeal.

WHAT USES WILL THIS REPORT BE PUT TO?

It is vital to understand how your report will be used. Is your report just background information? Is it for immediate decision-making purposes? Is it for record keeping? Is it for government regulators? Is it for clients and customers?

Organizing your report based on how you expect it to be used can make your reputation as a writer.

Suppose you have been asked to write a report on three different methods for measuring customer satisfaction with your company's products. The primary audience is executives who must decide which method to use. How can you best serve their decision-making process?

If you know that these executives' typical procedure for decision making is to make holistic comparisons (to look at all of each item, one after another, before making up their minds), you can write a report that gives a full description of Method 1, then Method 2, then Method 3. You would discuss Method 1's cost, effectiveness, and lead time; then Method 2's cost, effectiveness, and lead time; and then Method 3's.

If you know that management's typical procedure is to make analytical comparisons (comparing all three items on one trait, then all three on the next, and so on), you can organize your report around key features instead. Rather than having a section on Method 1, then Method 2, then Method 3, you can have a section on feature A (maybe *cost*) for each method, a section on feature B (maybe *effectiveness*) for each method, and a section on feature C (maybe *lead time*) for each method. This kind of anticipation in terms of organization based on use can make your reputation as a writer.

Suppose you have been asked to write an internal report on the new Local Area Network (LAN) computer system your company is buying. Do not make the mistake of assuming that your report is merely informative. It may well be that you have been asked to write something that will help people begin learning to use the LAN. If so, you must decide what tasks your audience must perform with the new system, and then write your report to enable people to perform those tasks. That could change a heading like "Forum Interlink Feature" into something like "How to Use the Forum Interlink Feature to Write Collaboratively without Leaving Your Office." Once again, different uses dictate different writing.

WHAT IS THIS REPORT'S SCOPE TO BE?

A report's *scope* is the area it covers. Scope is largely determined by three factors:

- Your audience's expectations (for depth and length of coverage),
- Your own time and resources,
- Your own and your associates' capabilities.

Every writer must at one time or another be brave enough to limit the scope of his or her report.

Given the time and resources you have for this project, you must be realistic about what you can produce. Determine what kinds of problems you can realistically hope to investigate within those limits, and learn to recognize uninvestigable topics and unanswerable questions. As necessary, consult with your superiors about what you can rationally hope to accomplish given all of these constraints. Every writer must at one time or another be courageous enough to take the necessary steps to limit his or her report's scope, to defend that limitation against the natural desire to write "the perfect, complete report," and to deal with the criticism of others who may act as though any report not infinite in scope is unacceptable.

In making the project's limitations in scope explicit, you do more than improve its quality. You also move toward making yourself indispensable to any follow-up work. Thus, do not hesitate to indicate the need for further research in the body of your report (perhaps the conclusion or the recommendations). If follow-up studies are indicated, say so. Your readers need to know which questions you did *not* answer just as much as they need to know which ones you did. If management determines that additional research is needed, you will be the one who gets the job.

CONCLUSION

No experienced professional would make the mistake of moving into a new area of business without first carefully surveying the territory. Starting a major writing project without doing a thorough job of defining your purpose is the same kind of mistake.

PRACTICE

A manager who was asked to write a report on safety measures at one of her company's plants in another state sat down with two co-workers to brainstorm ideas for the report before she left to visit the plant. Her notes from that session include these items. Some are questions, some are statements. Help her by arranging these items into a tree diagram on three levels: goals, objectives, and methods. If you come up with additional items, include them in your diagram in square brackets.

Write a report on the South Carolina plant's safety measures.

Is some kind of inspection coming up?

What is the employee safety record?

What kind of safety measures are there?

What kind of safety training is there?

How do employees feel about their safety?

How does the surrounding community feel about the plant's safety?

We need to convince government regulators we are in compliance.

We need to convince local residents our plant poses no threat.

Prove that our procedures are thorough.

Prove our waste management system is "state of the art."

Persuade investors to sink more money into this operation.

2

Finding Facts and Ideas

For business writers, fact finding and creativity are like two strands of a very tightly woven braid.

The demands of business writing make it imperative that you be connected to a much larger system of information—a system that, thanks to modern information technology, now reaches throughout most of the world. But whether you work with files of information from your own company, with librarians, or with computer databases, none of these will write your report for you. All they can supply is facts, statistics, opinions, and arguments.

Only your own sense of this particular report's objectives, audiences, uses, and scope, and above all your own selective and creative powers, can help you shape the facts and ideas you have collected into a successful report. Therefore, at the same time you are doing basic fact-finding, which can sometimes involve considerable plodding, you also need to be creative, which can be exhilarating. For report writers, fact finding and creativity are like two strands of a very tightly woven braid. Lacking either one, the written product simply will not hold together. For that reason, it is useful to think about the process of finding facts and ideas as falling into the two related categories presented in this chapter: creativity and research.

THE NEED FOR CREATIVITY IN REPORT WRITING

Report-writing situations vary infinitely. Sometimes you will find yourself starting from scratch, with very little relevant information available in company files and few (if any) models to work from. At other times there may be vast stores of information to draw on, including information your own research has generated, and plenty of model reports to look at. But both cases—indeed, all report-writing situations—call for creativity if you are going to raise your written product above the ordinary.

You will find a great deal of information just by asking yourself the questions covered in Chapter 1: how to achieve your objectives, accommodate your audiences, fit the report to its uses, and work within its scope. There are also many other *invention techniques* you can use, both alone and collaboratively, to find materials for your report: free associating, questioning, outlining, and capsuling.

If you are going to raise your written product above the ordinary, any report you write will call for creativity.

Free Associating

In free associating, the idea is to unleash your mind's creativity; you *postpone evaluation* of ideas so as not to interfere with their creation. Working from a single starting point—a question, a statement, or even a topic—this invention technique invites you to freely explore associated thoughts. You can try to keep a record of these thoughts with a tape recorder or video camera, but usually the most practical thing is to choose a schematic and diagram your thoughts. You can do this in the form of balloons (Figure 2.1), trees (Figure 2.2), or whatever works best for you.

Some of the best solutions to business problems come to mind outside the office.

Many of the most creative business people find that some of their most inventive solutions come to them outside the office when their linear, logical, verbal faculties are more or less on idle. These successful professionals brainstorm while jogging, swimming, driving the car and listening to a favorite audio tape, or performing some routine task such as chopping wood, mowing the lawn, or pushing a baby carriage.

If you find yourself getting stuck or running out of ideas as you write your report, you may be suffering from an overdose of office environment. A change of scene, pace, and activity can help you switch over to the sort of "right-brain" activity that yields inventive images. Then, when the images have stopped coming—which they usually do after a short burst of activity—you can return to the office to review them logically for an interpretation that makes practical sense.

The more conventional mapping techniques also involve review. After generating a few pages of balloons (or boxes or trees), review them to look for patterns, groupings, anything that particularly strikes you. If you have generated a new idea that seems promising, you can use that as a new starting point and go through the process again—and again. This practice of "review and refocus" becomes one method of *refining* your ideas during a brainstorming session—a technique that can be approached in many ways.

Questioning

An excellent invention technique for finding report material is to create your own list of topics, or questions, and then write out the most substantial comment or reply you can for each one. Some of these, as suggested in Chapter 1, can be direct questions such as how to reach certain objectives or accommodate specific audiences. Often, simply meditating on an objective *in the form of a question* will kick your brain into gear. Instead of writing "Persuade the executive committee to build a new

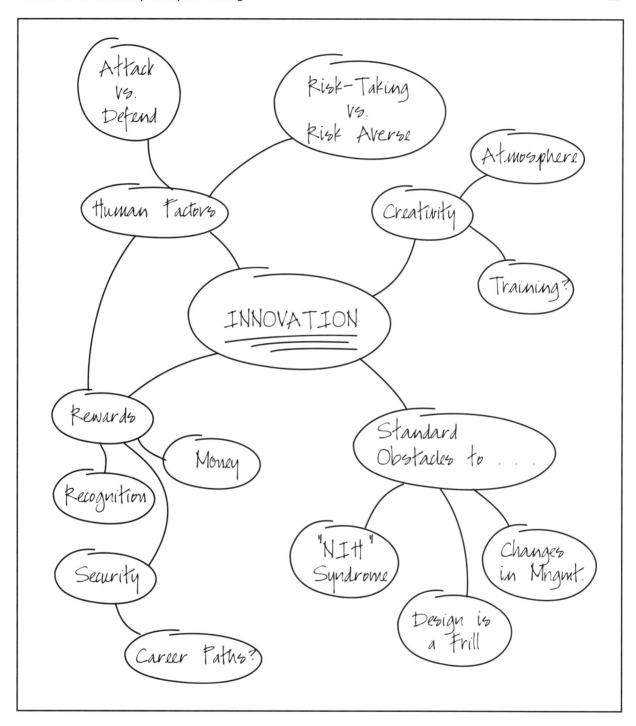

Figure 2.1 Making a balloon diagram is a good way to spark your free association.

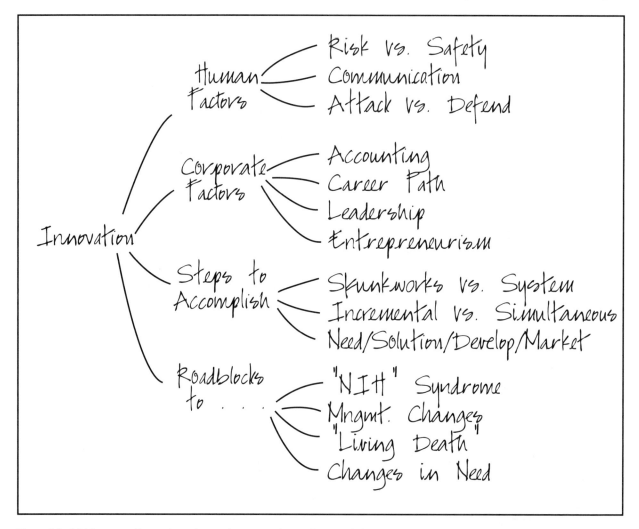

Figure 2.2   Making a tree diagram is another good way to spark your free association.

plant in another location rather than modernize this one," look at the *question* form: "How can we persuade the executive committee that we need to build a new plant in another location rather than trying to modernize and expand the present one?" Other questions can be substantive ones about the subject or problem you are working on:

Often, simply putting objectives into question form will yield ideas.

How advanced has robotics manufacturing become?

Who are the leaders in this technology?

What are the advantages in applying this technology?

What are the drawbacks of this technology?

Has the technology ever been applied to production of X?

In what forms was it applied?

What were the results of this application?

You can even use the old journalistic standby list of "Who, What, When, Where, Why, and How" as questions to begin your flow of ideas.

Outlining

Brainstorming software programs can help you create, group, and rearrange your ideas with a minimum of drudge work.

Often, your brainstorming will produce a number of ideas that you can then begin to group and expand in outline form. There are even brainstorming software programs that will help you do this, such as *Inspiration* and *Idea Fisher*, making it easy to group and rearrange ideas, and even to switch instantaneously between graphical and textual modes. Many word-processing programs, too, have an outlining feature that can be valuable.

The standard sections of various kinds of reports can themselves serve as rough outlines. For example, you can generate materials for a proposal just by making an outline that says, "Problem, Solutions (proposed, rejected, and alternate), Objectives, Method(s), Resources, Schedule, Qualifications, Management, Budget." You may know that the "Problem" involves two principal factors—unreliable technology and public disapproval—and so you are started on an outline. Fill in as much information as you can in each category.

This approach to report writing begins to merge with the next phase, *organizing* your report (discussed in Chapter 3).

Capsuling

This last category of invention involves writing a summary of each section first, and then expanding those summaries into the relevant sections later. For example: An engineer at a major brewery suspected that the company's methods for protecting canned and bottled beer against freezing during shipment were ineffective. He was assigned to write a report that documented the nature of the problem and recommended solutions. To assemble meaningful data, he arranged for some typical trailers to be loaded with cases of beer and subjected to simulated winter temperature and wind conditions in an environmental chamber.

Capsuling allows your writing to move forward on a number of fronts at once.

As the tests proceeded, the engineer read up on heat-transfer systems, insulation, and the effects of low temperatures and temperature fluctuations on fermented beverages. Every time a new piece of data from the lab or a new piece of information from his studies piqued his curiosity, he would jot down his first impression and put it into a large manila envelope. The various envelopes would be labeled Lab Results, Insulating Materials, Heating Devices, Convection, Conduction, or some other useful heading.

Even though he had not yet sat down to start composing a formal document, by the time the testing ended, the researcher already had built up considerable momentum toward writing a report. He had an extensive menu of talking points, all logically filed and easily accessible; after a quick but thorough review of these notes, he was able to write out a two-page Executive Summary, a "capsule" which, for all its brevity, nevertheless was very strong on facts and figures.

The capsule approach is a particularly good technique to apply when you have to wait for others to provide you with experimental data, as the brewery engineer did while the lab technicians were chilling and thawing the trailers. Data trickled in piecemeal; until the experiment was finished there was little the engineer could do but *organize* the data as logically as possible, let them simmer in the back of his mind until all the results were in, and supplement the flow of data with readings on thermodynamics. Careful capsuling of the test results brought about a powerful synergy between empirical studies and book learning, so that when the test period ended, the engineer produced a brief but effective report in a very short period of time.

THE CONNECTION BETWEEN CREATIVITY AND RESEARCH

In our experience, brainstorming works best when you combine it with research. When you start researching the project, do not spend all your time in the office with on-line databases. They are often indispensable, but seldom relaxing. Particularly if the topic of the report is unfamiliar to you, get out of the office and into the nearest library! Introduce yourself to the subject by checking the card catalog (or computer catalog) to identify where most of the materials on the subject are located. Note, for instance, the first three characters of the call numbers for the books on the subject. Most will be common to all the books listed under the topic. Then head for the shelves in the stacks that hold those call numbers and browse. Open books and journals that seem interesting and skim through them. The experienced writer uses this kind of early research to cultivate a state of mind that is open to whatever important information presents itself. The writer browses, follows leads, looks around, sizes things up, and asks questions.

Giving appropriate time and energy to preliminary investigation will feed the "light-bulb effect."

If the project is not primarily a research report (one in which preliminary library work would clearly be helpful), you can often get similar results simply by talking with knowledgeable people, friends, co-workers, and business contacts on your report's general subject. Some of this kind of research may be necessary even for determining your assignment—you may not be able to determine the appropriate scope of your report, for example, until you do this preliminary browsing and talking. More important, this level of research is essential to your creativity: it feeds the "light-bulb effect." Even without *deliberately* using the techniques of invention, you are likely to get light bulbs to blink on in your head if you approach research in this way. Inspiration may come in many forms, including possible solutions to problems, ways to organize the report, mental images of effective visuals, and angles to play in convincing the audience.

All good writing, even a report on shellfish contamination, is creative at some level.

Ultimately, *any* good work is creative. One person may see a topic such as shellfish contamination from sewer outfall as being completely routine, even tedious. But another person may find this subject provocative, likely to lead to creative research and writing. All good writing, even a report on shellfish contamination from sewer outfall, is creative. Not every report requires striking new ideas or approaches, and it is a mistake to try to insert them where there is no need. But a business report writer is paid to take, on some level, a new approach to the subject. Certainly the writer is paid to write a report that addresses a new situation: the business situation facing this company at this time in these circumstances. If there were nothing new to be said, there would be no need to write the report. And when the situation *is* open to radical solutions, you need to be willing to take an innovative approach.

Unfortunately, many people avoid creativity, preferring routine jobs to the uncertainties of unexplored territory. The closer you come to doing genuinely creative work, the more you must strike a balance between the risks of giving offense in the wrong quarters and the potential rewards of creative achievement on the job. We do not advise you to look for toes to step on. But we do encourage you to be creative. There are few things in life as rewarding as developing an independent solution to a problem, one that proves better than existing solutions.

SOURCES FOR BUSINESS INFORMATION

There are various ways to find the background data and facts you need to prepare reports. You may use the telephone to call experts or personal contacts for their insights and information. You may pick up issues of your industry's trade journals or other business magazines and browse, looking for relevant facts. You might stop by a colleague's office to talk about your information problem.

The richest source of background information is generally a library.

The richest source of such information is generally the library. Libraries offer you the broadest range of information—accurate, timely, and easily accessible. Most large cities have a business section in their public library. Colleges and universities with business schools also have extensive business collections in their libraries. You may even be fortunate enough to work for a firm with its own specialized corporate library. Local historical societies often maintain archives containing material with surprising relevance to contemporary business.

Though browsing in a library may turn up a lot of information, there may be more material than you can use efficiently in a limited time, and it may be difficult to pick out key items from the mass of data available. Help is available. Ask a librarian.

Trained in information seeking, librarians are professionals with advanced degrees and experience in assisting researchers like you. A librarian can save you time and effort by identifying definitive texts, suggesting sources you might otherwise overlook, and carrying out electronic information searches for you. As a general rule, librarians assist you in finding the information necessary for your research—they do not do the research for you. However, a growing number of public and academic libraries, as well as freelance information brokers, offer fee-based information services. For a fee, an experienced professional librarian will do your research and obtain relevant documents. This option especially makes sense if you have a tight deadline and an ample research budget.

For a fee, an experienced professional librarian will do your research and obtain relevant documents.

Although librarians are almost always available to help at some level, you have an advantage if you are familiar with the basic reference materials in your own field. You can locate financial data, statistics, names and addresses, and general background information with an ease and facility others will envy. Research is a skill like any other. Learn a few basic techniques and the right tools for specific situations; then practice using them to become an expert. To help you develop your research skills, Appendix A, "Sources for Business Research," pp. 205–220, provides a detailed, annotated, and up-to-date list of the most familiar and valuable business reference materials, divided into these categories:

1. Guides to Business Sources and Research
2. Indexes and Directories of Periodicals and Newspapers
3. Directories of Companies and Organizations
4. Biographical Directories
5. Dictionaries, Encyclopedias, and Handbooks
6. Economic Statistics
7. Corporate Finance and Investment Services
8. Marketing and Advertising Resources
9. Government Information
10. Electronic Information Sources

Although we have placed this material in the Appendix for your convenience, you should spend a few minutes familiarizing yourself with it now before proceeding to Chapter 3. If you are currently preparing a business report, examine Appendix A thoroughly before you begin to write. One or more of the sources listed may be essential to the success of your project. In any case, familiarity with the scope of the sources will almost certainly save you valuable research time on any project you undertake.

PRACTICE

An Inventory for Writers

Here is a short quiz to test your current ability to use a library to find information about your field of business. After you do your best to answer each of these questions, you can use Appendix A to check your work.

1. Name one reference book specifically designed to help you learn about business reference sources.
2. Name one index to information in periodicals and newspapers.
3. Name one directory that gives you basic information about companies.
4. Name one directory that will give you information about top executives with major national firms.
5. Name one dictionary or encyclopedia that is specifically written and published for defining business terms.

6. Name one federal source of information about the nation's industrial and business activity.

7. Name the city nearest you with an SEC regional office.

8. Name one source of information about various advertising markets in the United States.

9. Name one source of information about federal laws and regulations.

10. Name one on-line database specific to your field.

3

Organizing Your
Report

The organization of a report creates the primary lens through which readers see and understand the report's content. A report's organization gathers up the myriad separate bits of information and, by showing how they relate to each other, creates meaning. Reports typically contain a number of standard organizational divisions, covered in detail in Chapter 8. Those standard divisions have evolved because they reinforce and support each other and because they serve particular audiences in the business system in particular ways. That is, reports respond to the larger system by the ways their divisions address the various needs of the people who comprise that system:

Reports respond to the larger system by the way their parts address the system's needs.

- The *letter of transmittal* reminds the primary audience of the authorization for the report and spells out any special conditions concerning its contents.
- The *executive summary* is designed primarily to serve the senior executive who may have time to read only that decision-oriented summary.
- The *body* contains the report's fleshed-out discussion of all its major points, the full narrative of its background, methodology, and findings, for those who need to know "the whole story."
- The *visuals* in the report may be designed to tell the report's story to readers who may just be flipping through the pages.
- The *recommendations section* is designed to be a tool for those who must make detailed decisions within the contexts of a particular business enterprise.
- The technical appendices (if any) serve engineers, accountants, and technicians in various ways that support management's larger concerns.

If you were to look at the typical divisional structure of a report more closely, you would see that within each of those divisions there are certain common structural patterns. This chapter presents a few of the most common structures that operate within divisions of reports. We discuss these structures with two goals in mind: so you may better *recognize* such structures when they are inherent in the report topics you write about, and to help you be more adept at *using* them in your writing. Those structures are shape, process, function, classification, and problem/solution. All five of these patterns can help you write effective divisions of reports, but the last pattern is so important that we devote much of this chapter to demonstrating it.

Remember that your reader will never have a stronger ability to *see* the structure that best fits your topic than you do. If you have to force your material into a certain structure (or try to fake it), you are falling into the trap of building qualities into your product that perhaps you think are valuable, but that your customer—your reader—probably will not. As you try out this or that structure for your report, ask yourself if it will work easily and effortlessly for the reader. If it will not, you probably need to do more digging.

Your reader will never have a stronger ability to see the structure that best fits your topic than you do.

USING FIVE COMMON STRUCTURAL PATTERNS

Shape

One way to organize a report or a division of a report is around the visual shape of the thing being described, such as a computer chip, an airplane, or a robot arm. Suppose, for example, you were describing a manufacturing plant. It may or may not be necessary to describe the simple externals: "The plant is light green, rectangular, two stories high with broad windows on both stories. There is a flagpole in front of the central entryway, and the building is surrounded by parking lots." Often, such extraneous descriptions can be dispensed with. The meat of your description will be more along these lines:

Shape can be the simplest and clearest way to organize a description.

The executive and administrative offices, including the technical-publications department, art department, and print shop, are along the front wall. Behind the executive and administrative offices are the computer data-entry facilities. Behind those facilities lies a 22,000-square-foot product-assembly area housing three assembly lines running from rear to front. A tool room and machine shop occupy a wing running along the west side of the assembly floor. At the rear, an eight-door receiving dock functions as the intake area for raw materials entering the plant. Packaging materials for shipping the plant's output are also received at these docks. Completed products are packaged and dispatched from another five-door shipping dock located along the east wall of the assembly floor. A small area at the rear of the outbound shipping dock is devoted to a waste-disposal facility, including a trash compactor, a dumpster, and a storage area for drums containing hazardous liquid waste.

You may decide to block out the physical characteristics of your subject verbally, schematically, or both. Once the physical shape of the facility has been blocked out, the discussion can focus in more detail on each of the separate categories that have been identified.

When the shape of an object is clearly a part of its nature, this kind of organization is by far the simplest and most effective way of handling the discussion. It would be difficult to imagine describing a railroad line, for example, in a way other than starting at one end and moving to the other, noting important features along the way:

> The Atchison, Topeka & Santa Fe Railway enters Los Angeles from the east over two distinct lines, both of which were built west from San Bernardino: The original line, constructed chiefly to operate passenger trains, runs sixty miles almost due east from San Bernardino to downtown Los Angeles via Pasadena. The second line, built largely to bring freight service to the industrial communities that sprang up south of Los Angeles, proceeds south out of San Bernardino for three miles, then curves southwest for thirty-nine miles into Riverside County and Orange County. At the small town of Atwood the line begins curving back to the northwest, passing through Fullerton before rejoining the original line near downtown Los Angeles. Due to its deep "dip" into the Fullerton area, the seventy-one-mile freight line is eleven miles longer than the passenger line. In recent years it has been the practice to route westbound trains over the southern route through Fullerton and eastbound trains over the older, more northerly route through Pasadena. This circular routing enables the railroad to make the most efficient use of its train crews.

Process

When an object's shape is not so readily apparent, or the subject being discussed is more abstract—a computer's architecture, for example, or employee morale, or a chemical reaction—it may be more effective to organize the discussion around a series of events than a collection of properties.

Often it is helpful to visualize or sketch a flow chart that outlines the process before you actually start to write the description. A list of the steps in an accounting procedure, for example, can help to clarify what is happening and thus make the description easier to understand:

Process as an organizing principle can easily start with a flowchart or a numbered list.

1. Printout generated at close of business every Wednesday and Saturday.
2. Printout kept on shelves in accounting office until month end.
3. Printout sent to bindery and bound each month.
4. Printout sent to files-retention area and kept for two years, then destroyed.

As you proceed from the organization step into composing, you might translate your list into this description:

> Currently, the daily profit-and-loss statement is generated on a line-printer readout and kept on shelves in the accounting department. At the end of each month the accumulated daily outputs for the month are sent to the bindery, where they are bound together. They are then sent to the files-retention area and stored for two years, after which they are destroyed.

Function

Another common organizational pattern is based on what the subject is supposed to do. The following example is from an operations manual for an aircraft test stand:

> The test stand is used to operationally test aircraft components such as valves, actuating cylinders, pressure regulators, accumulators, hand pumps, gasoline engine driven pumps, hydraulic motors, and electric motor driven pumps.
>
> The test stand assembly contains the following flow and pressure circuits:
>
> a. A pump test circuit suitable for testing fixed- and variable-volume hydraulic pumps. The pump drive provides sufficient horsepower to drive a pump of 100 gpm at 3,500 psig at 5,600 rpm and is capable of speeds, at the output shaft, of up to 12,000 rpm. Automatic pump cycling facilities are also provided.
> b. A motor test circuit suitable for testing fixed- and variable-volume hydraulic motors. The motor load system provides sufficient resistance to load a hydraulic motor to 3,000 psi. The motor load system is also designed to assist a small, low-torque motor.

The reader is given no idea of what the test stand looks like, no idea of what steps to follow in testing the components, and no idea of what happens when they are tested. The reader is simply told what the test stand and its subsystems are meant to do.

Function is a good organizing principle for dealing with complex subjects.

Where *process* was helpful in organizing abstraction, *function* can be helpful in organizing complexity. Complicated machinery, complex organizations, and other kinds of large and intricate systems can be broken down according to their functions:

> In the Fire Department, the Bureau of Operations does the actual work of fighting fires. It also performs other functions, such as making certain types of fire prevention inspections and educational and community-relations visits to schools and organizations. The Bureau of Fire Prevention conducts arson investigations, makes mandatory fire-prevention inspections, approves building plans for fire safety, and coordinates education programs for press and broadcast media. The Bureau of Support Services maintains the apparatus and provides supplies. The Bureau of Personnel . . .

Classification

When large numbers of elements are to be discussed—branch offices, products, job classes, and so forth—it may be convenient to group them into larger categories and then base your discussion mainly on the groups rather than detailing each individual case. Branch offices, for example, can be grouped into categories such as those in cities, suburbs, regional centers, and isolated locations. Or they can be grouped by relative size or relative volume of business.

The classification you choose should reflect the purpose of the discussion; do not classify arbitrarily, or simply on the basis of what people are used to seeing. For example, if a company's urban branch offices are considerably less profitable than those in the suburbs, and if this discrepancy in profitability is to be the subject of a report, then branch-office *location* as the basis of the report's structure makes sense. The writer should make clear, however, that for the purposes of this report, location is being used as a proxy for profitability and that differential profitability, not location, is the real subject of the report.

In selecting classifications, it is a good idea to try out several approaches during the first phases of writing to determine which produces the most consistent or useful results. For some topics, statistical procedures such as cluster analysis or regression analysis can be used to good effect, provided the data are suitable and provided the people within the organization are equipped to handle such statistical analysis. Other topics may lend themselves to other kinds of classification schemes.

Problem/Solution

Problem solving may be what humans do best.

Other than doing reverse layups on the third leg of a fast break or playing blues piano, problem solving may be what humans do best. For people who want to succeed in business and professional life, the ability to *conceptualize* a problem, *explain* the problem, and *persuasively present* the solution is indispensable.

The problem may be the declining profitability of one of your firm's manufacturing divisions, the unresponsiveness of a plant's middle management to a renewed corporate concern for quality, the way materials shipped in winter tend to freeze, or just a product that cannot seem to find a market niche. And you may be able to see that pieces of the problem can be described using one or another of the four patterns described above. But the fundamental need for problem-solving reports comes from deep inside our nature as human beings, and the basic structure of those reports must be based more on the reader's needs than on the writer's experiences.

Consider these two structures. Which do you believe is better?

Structure A	**Structure B**
Define the problem.	Recommend a course of action.
Explain why solving it is important.	Give the problem's background, including why solving it is important.
Describe the causes of the problem.	
Explain alternative solutions.	Present the solution persuasively and in detail, explaining the steps required to implement it.
Test solutions.	
Recommend the top-ranked solution.	
	Appendix: Present and interpret test data, present other (less desirable) solutions, provide other similar kinds of background information.

Place the solution first, especially when it is in the form of a recommendation.

Structure B is the better choice in most cases. The reasons lie right at the core of systems thinking. Remember, just as the test of quality is in the perceptions of the customer, the test of the report's success is in the eyes of the reader. Suppose a report written with structure A is twenty pages long; where does your boss have to go to find the solution to the problem? (Remember, the point of the report is to solve the problem!) Do you honestly expect that your boss will be pleased at having to wade through fifteen or more pages of your crunching numbers, spinning your wheels, and racing up various blind alleys before you get to the solution? Or that, having finally found the solution, your boss will be pleased that only a small portion of the report is devoted to it?

Structure B *front-end loads* the solution in the form of a recommendation. The solution, including a course of action that will bring it about, is what most interests your boss, so position it first. Only when the recommendation has been presented do you introduce the problem's background—the circumstances that led to the problem and, unless they are eliminated, presumably will cause recurrence. Finally, you return to the recommendation, but this time in the form of a solution, that is, a detailed explanation of how the recommendation is to be implemented and how it will solve the problem. The solution is persuasive because it gives details, including sequential steps that must be followed if the solution is to be implemented. Where the recommendation is largely informative and suggestive, the solution is practical.

Thus, structure B has these advantages:

Your first job is to help your boss drain the swamp, even when you are both up to your necks in alligators. Leave explanations of the geological origins of the swamp and the evolutionary status of alligators for later.

- It puts first the information the reader most wants to see.
- It uses the other early pages of the report to argue for that solution (rather than to deal with extraneous material).
- It presents a plan of action, which the other structure often lacks.
- It places any material in which the reader may be less interested into the appendix.

If you were to do one report both ways, the two versions would have about the same number of pages. The important difference would be that the structure A report devotes only its *last* five pages to the solution of the problem, while structure B devotes the *first* five pages. Structure B also adds a few pages containing a detailed plan of action that A lacks. Room is created for those additional pages in B by putting the test data and competing solutions into the appendix, which allows that material to be somewhat compressed. Report A, then, may be a twenty-page report, while B is a seven-page report with a thirteen-page appendix. That is another reason your boss probably wants to see B rather than A. Remember: As the report writer, your first job is to help your boss drain the swamp, even when you are both up to your necks in alligators. Leave the explanations of the geological origins of the swamp and the evolution of alligators for later.

Here is a brief extract of the relevant sections of a problem-solving report that uses structure B. We give you just enough of each section of the report for you to see how it implements this structure. Note, too, the elements of other structural patterns within the report. The subject of this report is the problem experienced by a large steel maker (United States Steel) with coal and iron ore freezing in railroad hopper cars.

THE FREEZING OF RAW MATERIALS DURING RAIL TRANSPORTATION

ABSTRACT

Every winter, USS plants have considerable difficulty in the removal of frozen raw materials from railroad cars. Methods currently available include . . .

To eliminate the costly and time-consuming thawing operations by possibly preventing freezing in transit, the Research Group embarked on a joint study program to investigate . . .

The results of the experimental study show that a layer of polyurethane foam sprayed on the walls and bottom of a railroad hopper car greatly reduces the frost penetration into the cargo. The test results also indicate that . . .

RECOMMENDATIONS

Based on the results of the experimental work conducted for this study, the following recommendations are made:

- Urethane foam insulation properly applied to railroad cars will significantly retard the freezing of granular material cargoes. Planning, therefore, should begin for the eventual insulation of all USS hopper cars used in hauling materials subject to freezing.
- This preliminary study shows there is obviously an optimum thickness for the foam insulation based on the effectiveness of the insulation and on the cost of application. Further study should be undertaken, as detailed in this report, to discover that optimum thickness.
- Thoroughness of insulation is also a critical factor. Each square inch of bare steel in contact with the car's cargo will conduct away as much heat as will 3,000 square inches of insulated surface. Therefore, further study should also be undertaken to determine optimum methods for applying insulation in order to ensure that . . .

BACKGROUND

The problem of moist raw materials freezing in railroad cars during winter shipment has been a continuing source of both economic and operational trouble to the United States Steel Corporation and to railroad companies. The difficulties center around the discharging of frozen railroad cargoes into the system that handles plant materials. The usual approach to the problem is to thaw the cargoes before dumping, or shaking the hopper cars. Thawing, dumping, and shaking are costly operations and (in the latter case, especially) are often damaging to the cars. Methods currently available to USS plants for this process include . . .

Also, the company has recently been emphasizing just-in-time operations. The new demands this policy places on the materials-shipping function make the amount of time required for thawing or shaking cargoes an additional factor that legislates in favor of finding an alternate solution that expends less time and money . . . .

IMPLEMENTATION OF SOLUTION

[There is a section for each of the three recommendations proposed above. Here is a sample of the section that concerns the second part of the solution: optimum thickness of insulation.]

Recommendations for Optimum Thickness

The importance of insulating railroad cars with an optimum thickness of insulation cannot be overemphasized. Because the thermal conductivity of steel is about 3,000 times that of urethane foam insulation, with the same temperature gradient across the wall, each square inch of insulated metal in contact with the cargo will allow . . .

Although a layer of about two inches of foam insulation was applied to the test cars, an optimum thickness should be determined from physical and economic considerations. As insulation thickness increases, longer allowable transit times can be achieved. But each additional inch of thickness provides a smaller improvement in these transit times, and costs increase . . .

The effectiveness of insulation can be determined from further theoretical analysis and will be discussed more thoroughly in a future report. The advantages of retarding freezing are lost, however, if improved shipping and dumping schedules are not included in the overall program . . . .

APPENDIX

Arrangements were made with the Budd Company of Philadelphia to lease their environmental test chamber. This chamber is sufficiently large to accommodate two hopper cars at one time . . . .

A survey of the test program is shown in Table I. Figures 3 and 4 show the frost lines in the G39 ore cars carrying Venezuelan ore. These are plots of the 32F isothermal line . . . .

The complete report from which the above sample was taken was fourteen double-spaced pages long. Notice how the sample above focused the reader's attention squarely on how the problem was to be solved. That reflects the report's goal: to sell management on this solution. If this had been a preliminary or interim report on the subject, it might well have had a structure more like the outline in Structure

A, to reflect its purpose of showing the writer's supervisors that the right kind of work is going on in the right way in order to study and eventually solve the problem.

GOING FROM STRUCTURE TO WRITING

Your report's first-level headings must clearly identify the main parts of the report.

Before you start writing, it is important to put some kind of structural plan on paper. Think of the structure of your report as a series of separate sections rather than as a single uninterrupted stream of prose. The *hardest* way to write a report is to ignore its organizational chunks and think only of the whole project. For a problem-solving report, you might start with these five chunks:

RECOMMENDATION
BACKGROUND
SOLUTION
IMPLEMENTATION
APPENDIX

Each of the items above is a *generic first-level heading*. In a book, these headings would be chapter titles. In a report, the first-level headings identify main parts of the report, such as those listed above, or "Introduction," "Summary," and "Discussion." No matter where the previous section's text ended, each first-level heading should be at the top of a new page.

Suppose you were tackling the problem of the unresponsiveness of a plant's middle management to a renewed corporate concern for quality, and you knew what some of the subheadings for the report would be, based on your fact-finding work. Figure 3.1 shows how the skeleton might look.

Notice that in this structural outline the generic, first-level headings have been fleshed out with *second-level headings* that name the topics in each section. By the time you put in those second-level headings, you are well on your way to having a structure that can lead to a good piece of writing.

Even at this early stage of planning, you may be able to take the headings one or two levels deeper in some sections. That would take you into third-level and fourth-level headings. How you represent these levels of headings to yourself at this stage of the writing process is not really important so long as you can see at a glance which headings are at which levels. If you are using pen and paper, you may want to use a scheme something like the one shown below, where level one is centered, two and three begin at the left margin, and four is indented like a paragraph.

[Level one]	IMPLEMENTATION
[Level two]	QUALITY POLICY REPORT
[Level three]	Need for High Visibility "Document of Record"
	Tentative Outline of Quality Policy Report

[Level four]   1. <u>Background of Company's Quality Efforts</u>. [Text begins on same line as heading.]

2. <u>Need for Corporate-Wide Commitment to Quality</u>.[Text begins on same line as heading.]

If you are doing your outlining at the computer, however, you will save time by using the same styles of headings that you intend to use in the final form of your report (see Chapter 7, "Designing Your Pages"). However, whether you are working on screen or on a yellow pad, you should plan your way into this heading skeleton as deeply as you can before beginning to write in earnest. The deeper your planning goes, the easier your writing is likely to be.

BEGINNING TO WRITE

Do not wait for *inspiration* to begin your writing, but do not deny that feeling when it comes, either.

As you are developing your report's structural skeleton, you may begin to feel that it is time to start writing the text that goes under one or more of your headings. If you get that feeling, by all means, begin writing! You can begin in three different ways: using "talking" headings, "capsuling" sections, or diving right into the writing itself.

Use "Talking" Headings

You may want to go back over your basic skeleton and replace the more-or-less generic items with headings made up of phrases, statements, or questions. This step is called *going from topic headings to talking headings*. Think how much more useful the headings in the second (background) section of this quality report would be—both for you and for your readers—if they read like this:

<u>WHY QUALITY IS ESSENTIAL AT THE EL CENTRO PLANT</u>

INCOME FROM NEW PRODUCT SALES STAGNATED IN THE 1980s

BY 2000, SALES FROM NEW PRODUCTS MUST BE 30% OF OUR TOTAL

THE GLOBAL MARKETPLACE OFFERS NEW THREATS AND NEW OPPORTUNITIES

As this example shows, you can enter your writing process by developing each generic heading into a short phrase, statement, or question that more nearly reflects what you envision actually going on in that section.

Write Capsules for Each Section

Remember the brewery engineer (from Chapter 2) who collected his ideas and insights in labeled envelopes? The labels on the envelopes helped him organize the

QUALITY AT EL CENTRO PLASTICS

RECOMMENDATION

CORPORATE COMMUNICATION AND STRUCTURAL CHANGE

BACKGROUND

STAGNATION OF THE 80'S
CHALLENGE OF THE 90'S
GLOBAL MARKETPLACE

SOLUTION

CORPORATE COMMUNICATION PLAN
CONTINUING INFRASTRUCTURE CHANGES

IMPLEMENTATION

QUALITY POLICY REPORT
QUALITY WORKSHOPS
DESIGNATION OF "OWNERS" OF PROCESS IN EACH AREA
INCENTIVES FOR QUALITY

APPENDIX

HOW COMPANY "A" TRIED TO MANDATE QUALITY AND FAILED
HOW COMPANY "B" TRIED TO BUY QUALITY AND FAILED
HOW COMPANY "C" RELIED ON COMMUNICATION AND
        INFRASTRUCTURAL CHANGES TO IMPLEMENT QUALITY
        AND SUCCEEDED

Figure 3.1   First-level generic headings, combined with second-level topic headings.

materials inside into a powerful Executive Summary that needed only two pages to drive home its point.

Developing the skeleton of a report is the ideal time to use this capsuling system. Here's how one section of the Quality report would look when prepared with talking headings and a with little chunk of capsuled text that takes over where the headings leave off. The square brackets around the capsuled text are the report writer's way of remembering that this is just a capsule and will still need expansion.

WHY QUALITY IS ESSENTIAL AT THE EL CENTRO PLANT

INCOME FROM NEW PRODUCT SALES STAGNATED IN THE 1980s

"Capsules" of text take over where the headings leave off.

[From 1955 to 1980, new products typically accounted for 20%-30% of our sales each year. Beginning in 1980, those numbers slid down and stayed down. In 1990, new products were less than 5% of our sales, a new low. Although this reflects a minor trend industry wide, it cannot be allowed to continue if we are to prosper in the future.]

If you hit a section you cannot capsule, you either need to go back to the "generating your materials" stage, or you need to ask yourself whether that section really belongs in the report. After you have done all the capsules possible, you may go back and expand each one appropriately.

Go Ahead and Write the Section

When the words start flowing, let them flow.

Sometimes you will start out to write a capsule and find yourself diving right into writing the section itself. There is absolutely nothing wrong with this. Just let the momentum take you along: Don't stop to worry about grammar, spelling, or style. You can review those elements later. When the words start flowing, let them flow.

Another Style: Decimal Headings

Some report styles and most technical manuals use a decimal method of organizing and outlining material. In this method, the first-level heading is indicated by an Arabic number followed by a decimal point. Here is one section of the quality report with the headings done in decimal style. Notice that all the headings now begin at the left margin.

Decimal headings are especially useful when a long report involves a lot of cross-referencing.

1. IMPLEMENTATION

1.1 QUALITY POLICY REPORT

1.1.1 Need for High Visibility "Document of Record"

1.1.2 Tentative Outline of Quality Policy Report

<u>1.1.2.1 Background of Company's Quality Efforts</u>. [Text begins on same line as heading for this level.]

<u>1.1.2.2 Need for Corporate-Wide Commitment to Quality</u>. [Text begins on same line.]

Decimal headings are especially useful when a long report involves lots of cross-referencing, or when a team of writers is working on very lengthy, complex material. In fields where readers are not familiar with such headings, however, they may actually hurt your clarity rather than help it. And headings that involve more than four numbers give just about everybody (except lawyers) headaches.

CONCLUSION

Clearly, an early concern for structure at even a very basic level can be productive in your report writing. Remember that you should choose a structure your reader will see as clearly as you do. If *you* have to struggle to see how your report will fit into that structure, you cannot expect your reader to see it at all.

PRACTICE

Structuring a Sample Report

Here are the titles of the sections and subsections (in scrambled order) from a problem-solving report on the subject of mechanical controllers. Your task is to decide on a structure for the report in the form of its major and minor headings.

> Appendix C: Sales per Region
>   Methodology
>   Cutting Costs
> Declining Sales and Vanishing Profits, 1983-1993
>   Sales Drop of 38% Since 1983
>   Purpose
> Current Market Demand for Mechanical Controllers
>   Dying Demand in the United States
> Executive Summary
> Letter of Transmittal
>   Growing Demand in Eastern Europe
>   Growing Demand in Pacific Rim
> Introduction
> Forecast of Market Demand, 1993-2003
>   Scope
>   Profits Drop of 25% Since 1983
>   Impact of Technological Obsolescence

4

Writing Your First Full Draft

More than anything else, learning to be a good writer requires that you know your own mind—that you know your own thought processes well enough to discipline and shape them. The other requirements are also qualities we all struggle with in many parts of our lives: persistence, patience, emotional maturity, and the ability to focus concentration, break bad habits, accept criticism, and act on constructive criticism in positive ways.

Learning to write is a hands-on experience.

The ability to write well cannot be acquired in a three-hour seminar (although you can pick up some simple tricks), nor can it be gained from a few days of lectures by a visiting professor. Learning to write is a very practical and hands-on kind of experience: *You learn to write by writing.* Learning to do business writing cannot be done in a vacuum either; it is a cooperative venture that requires at least two people: a writer who is willing to learn—to take chances, make mistakes, be criticized, and change—and at least one reader who is not afraid to give honest opinions. That reader/critic may be a co-worker, a supervisor, or even a close friend or spouse.

UNDERSTANDING THE COMPOSING PROCESS

When you actually begin putting words together into sentences and paragraphs on paper (or, more likely, on the computer screen), the activity you are engaging in is properly called *composing*. On any given project, by the time you begin composing, you will usually have spent a considerable amount of time and energy determining the nature of your assignment (Chapter 1), generating materials (Chapter 2), and making some kind of structural plan (Chapter 3). The more of these activities you have done on paper or on screen, the easier the composing will be. In an ideal situation (such as the Quality report discussed in Chapter 3), your information gathering and structural planning will flow seamlessly into your composing (for example, as you go from a list of generic headings to talking headings, to sub-headings, to capsules). Thus you will find you have begun writing a full first draft of your report without really thinking about whether you are in any particular stage of the process. So if your boss assigns you a project that involves writing a report and you think to yourself, "No problem—I can knock out a first draft this afternoon," then by all means, do so. Some projects go like that. When you feel that momentum pulling you along, go with the flow!

Ideal situations, however, seldom happen, in writing or in life. You need to monitor this process called "composing" just as you would any management or production process. Work at continuously improving your process, and always value and listen to the customers (your readers). Be sure to keep your composing process flexible; if one approach is not working, be willing to try another. The goal of this writing system is to provide quality to your readers, and the point of each functional step within the larger process is to serve the system. If the way you are performing a functional step is detrimental to the system, change that step.

What do you do when you have dutifully followed the steps described in Chapters 2, 3, and 4, and the composing does *not* seem to work very well? You have stacks of material all around you, you are staring at a skeleton outline made up of your report's tentative headings and subheadings on the screen in front of you (some with capsuled text beneath them), and you are still finding it difficult to get past that point. Listed below are seven things people do that make composing *harder*; if you are having trouble on a project, check to see if you are doing any of them, and eliminate any you find. Next are twelve ways to make composing *easier*; the more of these you build into your normal composing process, the better it will go.

> When you feel the momentum of writing pulling you along, go with the flow!

AVOIDING COMMON MISTAKES

By becoming aware of the conditions that seem to make composing harder, you can control them. Some of these conditions are easy to change; others are factors that can only be moderated. But we believe *anything* you do to control these seven conditions will help your composing go better.

Mistakes that make writing harder

- Trying to do a perfect draft the first time.
- Trying to compose when you are too tired.
- Trying to compose when you do not know enough about your assignment, your subject, or your audience.
- Trying to do the whole composition at once.
- Expending your composing energies on noncomposition activities.
- Waiting too late to start.
- Ignoring the ethical implications of your assignment.

Mistake: Trying to Do a Perfect Draft
the First Time

Trying to write a perfect draft the first time inevitably adds so much pressure to the situation that you freeze up.

More writers probably wreck their ships on this rock than any other. There is so much pressure on you in graduate school and in professional life to *get it right*, and especially to get it right *the first time*, that the most natural thing in the world is to impose those same pressures on your composing. Worse, there is never enough time, and you are usually starting too late anyway. Together, these factors nearly always translate into trying too hard to get your writing too right too soon. In doing so, you put too much pressure on yourself. Like a tennis star who has a huge advertising contract riding on getting into the quarterfinals at Wimbledon, you add so much extra and unnecessary pressure to an already tense situation that you freeze up.

Mistake: Trying to Compose When You
Are Too Tired

If you think trying to write perfectly is hard, try writing perfectly when you are exhausted. It will not work. By the end of the business day, to say nothing of the calendar day, you may not have the energy and clarity of mind to produce good prose. Don't be a hero. Even the most accomplished professional writers, the people who make it look easy, always pace themselves, providing themselves not only with ample time for writing but also with frequent breaks. It's the only way to make this intellectually and physically demanding activity tolerable.

Mistake: Trying to Compose When You Don't
Know Enough about Your Assignment, Your
Subject, or Your Audience

Like anything else in business, composing based on ignorance does not work.

You would not expect any other part of your professional life to operate well based on ignorance; why expect your composing to be any different? Investments based on ignorance do not work, nor do sales campaigns, nor does the development of a new product. Psychologist Carl Rogers has shown convincingly that ignorance is one of the two biggest reasons humans have trouble communicating (fear is the other), so why leave yourself open to it? If you do not at least know *about* (and preferably *know*) your audience, you should expect to find composing for that person (or those people) difficult. If you do not know enough about your subject, of course writing about it is going to be hard. And if you do not know enough about your assignment, of course you are going to be plagued by doubts that maybe you are doing the wrong thing.

Mistake: Trying to Do the Whole Composition
at Once

Any serious piece of writing needs to be allowed at least a little time to mature.

Too many writers compound the mistake of trying to make a piece of writing perfect the first time by trying to make the first time the *only* time. Just as the development of writing ability is a *maturational* process, the development of any individual writing project is also maturational. Any serious piece of writing needs to be allowed at least a little time to mature if it is to be done really well. Any piece of writing important enough to worry about, to make a difference in your career, needs time—time to be researched and thought about; time to be planned; time to be composed, rewritten, and revised; time to be looked at in draft form by someone else; time to be edited and polished. Work out a reasonable schedule for these activities and hold to it. If you think you can do all those things in just one pass through your report—and still turn out a really good piece of work—you're kidding yourself.

Mistake: Expending Your Composing Energies on Non-Composition Activities

Composing is more like walking a tightrope than operating a switchboard.

Some struggling writers tend to go off in all sorts of directions right at the moment composing is supposed to occur. This problem is sometimes called the "cleaning off the desk" syndrome. We all have a list of things that have to be done and have not been—from organizing our briefcase, to returning phone calls, to reading last week's sales reports. But if you use the moment you need to be composing as the moment to start taking care of all that other busywork, your composing will never get done. To improve as a writer, you need to be able to summon enough discipline to push those other activities off to the side and keep them there. This need for focus applies not only to getting started composing, but also to keeping your word flow going. Most people cannot do anything like a good job of composing if they are working in 5-, 10-, and 15-minute increments in between answering phone calls, signing purchase authorizations, and talking with passerby co-workers about how the Chicago Cubs lost last night. Composing is more like walking a tightrope than operating a switchboard—you can have only one focus.

Mistake: Waiting Too Late to Start

Waiting too late to start writing is very human. It is also a typical rookie mistake.

Another sure-fire method for making your composing hard or impossible is to magnify the usual deadline pressure of business. Waiting too late to start things is only human, especially for things that we fear we may not be able to do very well even under the best of circumstances. If you are thinking about starting a diet, why make it harder by waiting until the doctor says you absolutely *must* lose weight? If you are worried that the pain in your tooth is a cavity starting, why make the problem worse by putting off going to the dentist as long as you can? If you are worried about that squeak in the left front wheel, why wait until the bearing seizes up entirely before having a mechanic attend to it? Composing falls into the same category: If you wait too long before starting, you can expect to have all these other problems in the bargain—having to do it all at once, having to get it perfect the first time, having to work when you're too tired. Thus, you learn again that you really do have it in your power to make your composing impossible to do, fulfilling your prophecy of disaster.

Mistake: Ignoring the Ethical Implications of Your Assignment

One of the problems that can surprise a writer during the composing stage is facing ethical issues. Any piece of writing, and especially a report of any length, inevitably begins to act as a barometer registering some of the writer's (and the company's) ethical qualities. If you run into an ethical problem during your composing and put off dealing with it, the problem will nag at you and distract you, often without your realizing it.

When management is wrong, you do not help by uncritically reinforcing its views.

For example, many times a report is intended to support an original hypothesis or proposition that is actually the hotly held view of someone in higher management. What should you do if in your research, your interviews, and your sound thinking and writing, you find that the original hypothesis in fact will not work as a foundation on which to build this report? At the very least, you would have to compromise the facts pretty seriously to make that hypothesis even *seem* to stand up. Where does this leave you, ethically?

The professional with integrity may well have to choose to face a superior's displeasure by bringing other viewpoints to light, even if they are contrary to the management view that dictated the original assignment. If management's view really is wrong, you are not helping by reinforcing it uncritically. If management's view is right, you are going to need help in seeing why your research and creativity do not bear that view out. And if, finally, you have to write a report that reflects some serious compromising between the way you think things need to be and the way management instructs you to make them, you can do so with full understanding (and with having gone—gently—on record with pointing out) that unpleasant consequences could follow.

PRACTICING GOOD HABITS

Considering the hazards of composing, why not take a strongly proactive stance toward it? Why not get on top of the problem before it buries you? Here are twelve ways to make your composing go more smoothly. (The first six are the positive sides of the negatives described in the previous section; the last six are valuable additional techniques.)

Good habits that make writing easier

In composing, as in life, the space you do not fill up with good habits will tend to fill itself up with bad ones.

- Learn to "satisfice."
- Compose at the best time of the day.
- Compose from knowledge, not from ignorance.
- Compose incrementally.
- Keep your attention focused.
- Extend your deadline in both directions.
- See what other people have done.
- Try talking it out.

- Try drawing a picture of your report.
- Get some exercise.
- Try composing faster.
- Minimize your reliance on the composing process.

Learn to "Satisfice"

Satisficing, a balance between "satisfying" and "sufficing," means knowing when less than perfect is good enough. If all you are trying to do in this composing session is come up with part of a first draft, your ability to satisfice can keep you from struggling to find exactly the right word, or phrase, or spelling, or punctuation. Try this trick: When you find your composing is getting so difficult that almost nothing is coming out, try *letting go.* Just let any old kind of stuff come out that wants to. If you have to tell yourself, "All I'm doing now is writing the trash out of my system so I can have a clear channel for the good stuff later on," that is absolutely fine.

> Nobody's first draft is ever well written, tight, simple, concise, and soundly developed. Do not kid yourself that yours is.

For many graduate students and professionals having serious trouble with their writing, this inability to satisfice is the single biggest flaw in their approach to composing. All you should want your first draft to do is go from the beginning, through the middle, to the end. *Any* level of quality allowing that movement and coverage is by definition good enough for a first draft. There is a myth in our culture about the writer whose first draft is well written, tight, simple, concise, and soundly developed. Like most myths, this one reflects dreams and wishes more than it reflects reality. Nobody's first draft is ever that good, so don't expect yours to be.

Compose at the Best Time of the Day

Composing is more sensitive to personal energy rhythms than many other activities. For example, many people are at their best early in the day. Too many such writers put off their composing until the end of the day, from 4:00 P.M. to 5:30 P.M. or from 10:00 P.M. to midnight. Composing is too complex a task to withstand such fatigue. If you are a "morning person" and can work at home, try composing first thing in the morning before anyone else is awake. Or try staying at home until 10 A.M. so you can have an hour or so to compose after the family has gone for the day and before you go into your office. Or go into your office an hour early. It's amazing how much good composing you can get done, say, between 7:00 A.M. and 9:30 A.M., before your business day starts to heat up. More than a lack of interruptions is involved; this time shifting lets you do something difficult when you are most alert, energetic, and fresh. If you are a "night person," shift your composing to the evening hours.

Compose from Knowledge, Not from Ignorance

> The more you know about all the "determining your assignment" factors, the easier your composing will be.

The more you know about the subject you are supposed to be writing about, the more you know about all the "determining your assignment" factors, and the better you understanding who you are supposed to be in this document (your *role* in the system), the easier your composing will be. Picture seven scales, one for each aspect of the communication situation. On each scale, 0 represents having absolutely no information on that aspect, and 10 represents having complete information (Figure 4.1).

As you begin to think about starting your composing, rate where you are on each scale. If you want your composing process to go better, do whatever you need to do in order to move yourself farther to the right on more of the scales. If one scale is markedly lower than the others, you need to work on it the most. You will probably never attain a 10 on *all* of them at once—in fact, some writers feel they never attain a 10 on any of them—but you should never try to compose when *any* of them is at 0, either.

Compose Incrementally

Trying to finish any writing assignment in one sitting is a fool's errand.

Just as it is futile to try to compose *perfectly* on the first pass, so it is futile to try to compose *totally*. Trying to finish the assignment in one sitting is a fool's errand. Although individual tolerance for the rigors of composing varies, nobody can stay at it very long. Many professional writers set aside the morning for composing and the afternoon for revising, interviewing, or researching in the library. Unless you are talking about a two-page memo, you can forget about writing the entire report,

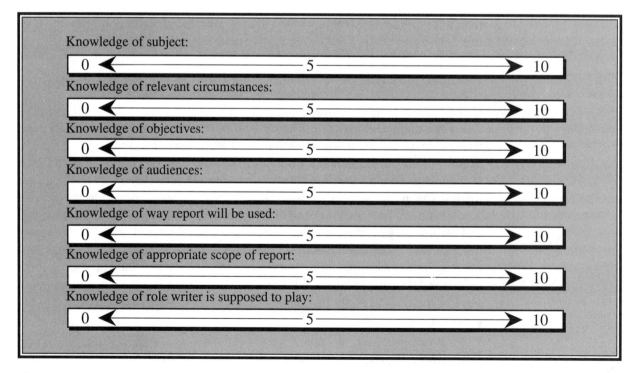

Figure 4.1   Aspects of the communication situation. You should never try to compose when any of these is 0.

even in rough-draft form, the first time around. Use your business skills here. Organize your writing work according to degree of difficulty. Set aside discrete periods for composing, and break them with periods in which you either relax or do work that does not involve composition. You will return to your next composition period refreshed and ready to use your allotted time efficiently.

Keep Your Attention Focused

Writing can be almost impossible to accomplish without *flow*.

People can get into a groove when they are composing. In fact, all productive, motivated, successful people get into a groove when they perform the activities they enjoy most and do best. University of Chicago psychologist Mihaly Csikszentmihalyi wrote an entire book about that special feeling you get when you are really connecting with what you are doing, almost like surfing on the crest of a perpetually breaking wave. He called the book, and the experience, *Flow*. Writing can be almost impossible to accomplish without flow; the words seem to come only when you are at full throttle. If your concentration is broken and the flow interrupted, it is very hard to restore the pace and the exhilaration that seem to be essential to good composition. But what makes for flow in one writer may be different from what makes for flow in another. One of the writers of this book can write only in total seclusion and absolute silence. Another must have classical music in the background and a window to look out of occasionally. If you expect to write, make sure you know what conditions *you* need to establish and maintain flow.

Extend Your Deadline in Both Directions

No writing project is ever really finished; all that happens is you run out of time.

No writing project is ever really finished; it is simply abandoned as the writer runs out of time and has to turn it in. We all fight deadlines and usually extend them as long as we can: As soon as someone says "I need this no later than Monday," we say, "Well, what *time* Monday?" Professional writers and editors are no different from workaday writers in that regard. They *are* different, however, in what they do at the *other* end of the timeline, at the beginning of the project. If a given project has a six-week time span, many people may not even start on it until week two or three, but a professional writer may well start on day one of week one. In that way, the professional extends the deadline in *both* directions. The rest of us would in fact have only three weeks to complete the project, but the professional thus has six. Even if the way you begin is just to put the proper label on a manila file folder (or a computer file) and start stuffing ideas into it (copies of relevant articles, notes from meetings or from reading, quotes from the newspaper, ideas picked up at lunch or on the commuter train, and so on), starting early pays big dividends right on through the rest of the process.

See What Other People Have Done

No tournament golfer would fail to pay attention to how a competitor's putt travels across the green if his or her own ball lies along the same line. Similarly, you probably are not the first person who has been asked to write a report for your company. Whether or not you choose to take the same approach as your predecessors, you cannot help but profit by at least reviewing and assessing what they did. Consult your predecessors' reports. Look at the overall organization, the length, the tone, the use of visuals; look especially for anything that strikes you as unusual or novel—such items may reflect an understanding the other writer had that you may lack, one that may be important. However, you must have a critical eye. If someone else has done a mediocre job, think about how you are going to improve on what he or she did, not about how you are going to copy it.

Try Talking It Out

To get your writing project unstuck, try talking it out with a co-worker or friend.

Sometimes when you cannot get your words to flow out onto the screen, you can go around the composing blockage by working in another language medium: Try talking your project out with a friend or co-worker. Start this way: "All I'm trying to do is to write about the way that . . . ." Use phrases like "The problem I keep running into in my writing is . . ." and "The most important thing I need to get people who read this report to understand is . . ." and "What I want people to be able to do after they read this report is . . . ." Often during a conversation like this you will find not only that you are a little more fluent at producing *speech* than you are at producing *writing*, but also that once you have produced the words as speech you can recapture them quite easily in writing. (Some people can even tape record these conversations, have them keyboarded, and start with the transcript as the core of their first draft.) Be sure to ask your listener to play an active role—to ask questions and point out inconsistencies. That "live audience feedback" can really help get your word flow going.

Try Drawing a Picture of Your Report

Another way to put the subject you are writing about into a slightly different medium than writing, one in which you may be more prolific, is to draw a picture of the report you're trying to write. Try assigning your report different shapes:

- A *line* goes like a story, straight from one point to the next and the next and the next, or from the top of something to the bottom, or from one side to the other.
- A *circle* comes back at the end to where it started, in space, time, or logic, and along the way sets off (and thus defines) the area it encloses.
- A *triangle, square, pentagon,* or *hexagon* has a fixed number of equally important sides, and it takes the whole group of sides to complete a structure.
- A *pyramid* or *funnel* starts narrow and grows broader (or vice versa).
- A *braid* has two or more interlocking strands that weave in and out of each other, alternately surfacing.

Try drawing your report each of these ways, and you may find one that really helps the composing "take off." Does this suggestion to put your report into a visible shape sound anything like some of the brainstorming techniques for invention recommended in Chapter 2? It should. And you should be seeing more and more clearly not only the recursive nature of the writing process, but some of the specific ways in which various techniques are applicable to more than one dimension of writing.

Get Some Exercise

If your composing process is stuck, or going excruciatingly slowly, try getting some exercise—take a walk for about an hour, ride a stationary bicycle, swim, or do some other physical activity. Do not try to think about your writing project at all during this time. You may be amazed at the result. One of the most prolific and successful writers we know often cites as a chief source of her success her long-standing habit of taking a thirty-minute swim at the YWCA every Tuesday and Thursday at lunch. Her best composing, she says, often happens in the time right after that swim. And at age 70+, she is still going strong at her writing and everything else. Another executive found running on a treadmill during lunch break often cleared his head and helped his writing when he returned to work.

Many people do their best composing right after they get some physical exercise.

Try Composing Faster

Just as there is an *upper* limit on most people's reading speed, beyond which comprehension and retention drop markedly, so there is also a *lower* limit. That is, if you read too slowly, you can have serious problems with understanding. Composing has those same qualities. Each person has a range of optimum speeds for composing, *below* which the process is not going to work very well. We have already discussed letting go of worry about grammar and usage while you are composing. Encourage yourself to compose more quickly, to try to find the speed that is most productive for you.

Minimize Your Reliance on the Composing Process

Composing is one of those activities for which trying harder may only result in making it harder. Sometimes you need to try smarter.

Our aim in many of the suggestions presented in this section is to take some of the burden of writing your report off of the composing process. Our system relies *more* on prewriting, revising, and finishing, and less on composing itself. This is because, compared to composing, both prewriting and revising are well understood, can be approached methodically, and can be done better if you simply work harder at them. Composing, on the other hand, is rather mysterious and often seems to defy methodical approaches. In fact, if you work harder at composing, it can get harder to do, not easier. The trick, as in so many areas of business, is to work *smarter*.

Just as a researcher who tries and fails at understanding problem X will then start looking for *parts* of X to try to understand, hoping thereby to minimize the effects of the unknown even if parts remain unsolvable, so we advise writers who have problems with the composing stage to minimize the role it plays in their writing. Lean more heavily on your prewriting, on the information-gathering and planning activities that you are better at, and thus try to approach the composing phase with as much on paper in one form or another as possible. Lean more heavily on the revising stage: Rely more on your processes of revising and finishing to enhance your report's *quality*, such as the orderliness of its development and the smoothness of its language. If you worry about quality in terms of anything other than content during your composing, you may find it hard to get any composing done at all.

KEEPING YOUR COMPOSING PROCESS SYSTEM-SENSITIVE

The point of all the advice offered in this chapter is for you to monitor how you approach this process called *composing*, just as you would do with any management or production process:

The goal of this writing system is to provide quality and value to your reader.

- Keep your approach to composing flexible so that if what you are trying is not working you can abandon that approach and try another.
- Work at continuously improving your composing process. Even if you think it is going along adequately, there may be a much better way to approach composing if you tinker a little with it. How do you know exactly what it is about your process that works, or why it works, until you tinker with it?
- Above all, always value and listen to the customer (your reader). The goal of this writing system is to provide quality to your reader, and the point of the functions—the various steps and approaches presented here—is to serve the larger system(s) of business. If your writing is not truly connecting with your readers, or if you're getting only lukewarm responses from them, you must be willing to change.

IDENTIFYING QUALITIES OF THE FIRST AND INTERIM DRAFTS

What should you expect to have achieved at the end of each of the various phases of your writing task? Although we talk in terms of at least three drafts for any project—a first draft, a good middle-level draft, and a final draft—in the era of word processing it is misleading to imply a crisp demarcation between one draft and the next. Nonetheless, Figure 4.2 outlines a progression of goals through the various draft stages.

Figure 4.2 is meant to be indicative, not exhaustive. Its point is that writing, like any other business activity, can be thought of as the orderly accomplishment of a finite set of previously determined goals. When two goals are right next to each other on this list, or only one or two places away from each other, there is not much point in worrying over which should really come first. Nor is there much point in worrying about whether a particular goal is reached at the end of this draft phase or at the beginning of the next. Even so, it makes sense to talk about a *first draft* (the initial effort we make to flesh out the skeleton of the report with text), a good *middle-level draft* (something that has "all the right parts in all the right places";

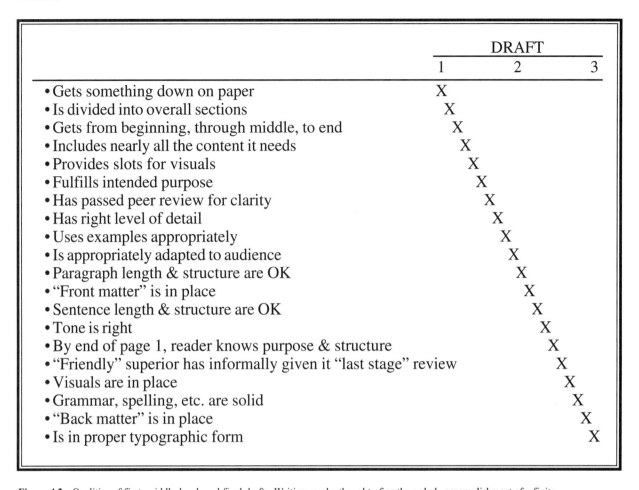

	DRAFT		
	1	2	3
• Gets something down on paper	X		
• Is divided into overall sections	X		
• Gets from beginning, through middle, to end	X		
• Includes nearly all the content it needs	X		
• Provides slots for visuals	X		
• Fulfills intended purpose	X		
• Has passed peer review for clarity	X		
• Has right level of detail		X	
• Uses examples appropriately		X	
• Is appropriately adapted to audience		X	
• Paragraph length & structure are OK		X	
• "Front matter" is in place		X	
• Sentence length & structure are OK		X	
• Tone is right		X	
• By end of page 1, reader knows purpose & structure		X	
• "Friendly" superior has informally given it "last stage" review			X
• Visuals are in place			X
• Grammar, spelling, etc. are solid			X
• "Back matter" is in place			X
• Is in proper typographic form			X

Figure 4.2   Qualities of first, middle-level, and final drafts. Writing can be thought of as the orderly accomplishment of a finite set of previously determined goals.

something good enough to show others for preliminary review), and a *final draft* (the last one before the final printing), at the very least. This chapter has given you some good advice about how to make writing that first draft easier. The next four chapters take you deeper into the territory of the other characteristics listed in Figure 4.2, showing you how to move from a first draft to a final one. A good beginning is important, but to really differentiate your product (your report), you must now raise its quality on every level, from its substance to its structure and its style.

PRACTICE

An Inventory for Writers

Write a three- or four-line description of the last three pieces of writing you did that were of greater than memo length. Label those items "Project 1," "Project 2," and "Project 3." Then, for each project, answer the following questions with a "yes" or a "no."

Bad habits

	Project 1	Project 2	Project 3
Tried to make what you composed perfect the first time.			
Tried to compose when you were too tired.			
Tried to compose without knowing enough about assignment, subject, or audience.			
Tried to do the whole composition at once.			
Expended composing energies on non-composition activities.			
Started too late.			
Ignored ethical implications of assignment.			

There are twenty-one answers to this "bad habits" inventory. If more than seven of your answers are "yes," you need to overhaul your process.

Good habits

	Project 1	Project 2	Project 3
Did you learn to "satisfice"?			
Did you compose at the beginning of the day?			
Did you compose from knowledge, not from ignorance?			
Did you compose incrementally?			
Did you keep your attention focused?			
Did you extend your deadline in both directions?			
Did you see what other people have done?			
Did you try talking it out?			
Did you try drawing a picture of your report?			
Did you get some exercise?			
Did you try composing faster?			
Did you minimize your reliance on the composing process?			

There are thirty-six answers to this "good habits" inventory. If more than twelve of your answers are "no," you are not helping yourself with your process nearly as much as you should be. Start working on building more good composing habits!

5

Choosing and Using Graphics

Get into the habit of thinking both verbally and visually from the beginning of the report-writing process.

Unless you develop a good "theory of graphics," you may have to relinquish control of the important visual dimension of your report.

Well before your first draft is finished, you should be thinking about the visual dimension of your report: A significant part of invention (gathering or generating materials for the report—see p. 28) is coming up with ideas for, or actual examples of, visual information that will help the report achieve its objectives and satisfy its goals. Develop the habit of thinking verbally *and visually* when you are inventing, organizing, and drafting your report. The same information that you discovered while determining your assignment—your sense of the report's objectives, audiences, uses, and scope—will guide your graphical choices for the report.

Many business writers make the mistake of depending almost entirely on graphic-arts departments for the visual dimension of their reports, thereby diminishing their visual thinking and relinquishing too much control over the report to others. But writers who are also effective visual thinkers develop a "theory of graphics"; that is, they know what graphics can do, what varieties are available, when to use them, how to manipulate them, where to place them, how to adapt them to specific audiences, and how to integrate them with the textual and mathematical substance of the report. These writers know they do not have to be graphic artists to work effectively with visuals. This is especially true in the present age of sophisticated computer software; there are dozens of programs that will allow you easily to create and manipulate many of the graphics you will need both for reports and for oral presentations.[1] In addition, optical scanners and "clip art"[2] make it possible to insert all kinds of graphics into your document. When you really need the graphic arts department, use it—but even then, *you* should know what your report

---

[1]Among the most popular computer software packages for producing presentation graphics are *Harvard Graphics, PowerPoint, DeltaGraph Professional, Aldus Persuasion, Aldus Freehand,* and *Adobe Illustrator.*

[2]"Clip art" is artwork, both on physical pages and on computer disk, that you can purchase in finished form. You can insert it into your own document and modify it according to your needs.

needs and be able to describe it to the graphics people accurately. You are the one who is intimately familiar with the report's objectives. You are the one who understands how audiences are likely to react to a graphic and how they will want to use it. You are ultimately responsible for the product.

As part of your own theory of graphics, consider three basic factors:

1. the *functions* of graphics in general—that is, what effects they can have on reports,
2. the *kinds and characteristics* of graphics that are available to you, and
3. the *rules* for using graphics—how to manipulate, place, and label them; integrate them with words; and adapt them to objectives and audiences.

THE FUNCTIONS OF GRAPHICS

There are eight basic functions of graphics: to support, clarify/simplify, emphasize, dramatize, generate interest in, compare/contrast, translate, and correlate/organize information contained in the report

Support

Perhaps the most common function of graphics is to support a discussion or give evidence for claims being made. A map representing reported encounters with African killer bees may be used to supplement a discussion of the spread of the bees into North America or to reinforce a claim about the imminent danger the bees represent to U.S. citizens.

Clarification/Simplification

A graphic can save you a lot of textual explanation, but don't leave it unsupported by text.

In many communication situations, a graphic can enormously shorten the job of writing (and reading) by explaining complex relationships, summarizing facts, or representing physical data that would take pages of written text to approximate. For example, a chart showing relative expenditures in a complex budget over many years can tell a reader far more at a glance than several pages of text explaining the same points. Such a chart should not stand alone, without textual introduction and discussion (nor should virtually any graphic), but it would certainly take a healthy chunk out of the text needed in the report's budget section.

Emphasis

Graphics command attention. They can be used to highlight concepts, to make them stand out. Have you ever seen that old drawing of the winged dollar bill flying away from its distraught former owner, or the shrugging man pulling his pants pockets inside out? How often are we shown a line graph with a single line showing earnings descending at a depressing angle? None of these graphics may be intellectually necessary, but they *emphasize* the concept of real or possible loss of funds.

Drama

Consider using graphics for emphasis and dramatic effect even when you know the text makes a point intellectually clear.

Closely related to the emphatic power of visuals is their dramatic power. Sometimes, even though a point may be quite clear in its textual formulation, you will choose to reinforce it graphically for the dramatic power the graphic lends to the concept. A report on the need to improve the braking system of trains may not need a photograph of a train wreck in any intellectual sense, but the photograph might have a valuable dramatic effect. The introduction of such a graphic certainly makes clear to the reader that the writer takes the subject very seriously.

Interest/Impression

Use artists to *supplement*, rather than *supplant*, your work on the visual dimension of your report.

Graphics can generate interest and promote positive feelings in the reader. A proposal to build an office complex for a client might be more effective if accompanied by aesthetically pleasing drawings of the proposed complex (here is a case where you will need those graphic artists).

Comparison/Contrast

Often, graphics can make the reader's job of comparing and contrasting things much easier; a simple example is a line graph that shows the relationship of two factors over time. This function is just the most obvious expression of the reference function of graphics: Graphic displays of information can make it much easier for the reader to find information and see its relationship to other information—in particular, to compare and contrast pieces of information, such as a drop in traffic fatalities in inverse proportion to the number of law enforcement officers, or a rise in a company's stock price in proportion to sales growth.

Translation/Conversion

Graphics are often the most economical and helpful way to translate or convert information from one language or unit of expression or symbol system to another. We are all familiar with charts that convert miles to kilometers, but graphics can convert *many* kinds of information, numerical, linguistic, or symbolic.

Correlation/Organization

Using graphic techniques to signal organization is a particularly good idea for long reports.

Graphics can function to correlate or organize information. For example, you may decide to use an illustration of some kind to signal the start of each major section of your report, or to tag particular kinds of information with certain colors or icons.

THE KINDS AND CHARACTERISTICS OF GRAPHICS

Many types of graphics are appropriate for business reports. Among the most important are tables, bar charts, pictographs, pie charts, line graphs, flow charts, organizational charts, maps, photographs, and illustrations.

Tables

Tables come in two varieties: informal and formal. Use an informal table to make small bundles of information within a paragraph more readable:

Gross income from our Portland plant has nearly equaled that of our Seattle plant over the last two years:

	1993	1994	2-YEAR TOTAL
Portland	$8.0 million	$8.4 million	$16.4 million
Seattle	$8.3 million	$8.6 million	$16.9 million

This is particularly interesting in view of the . . .

Brief, informal tables need not be boxed or labeled.

Informal tables need no titles because they are so brief and because the paragraphs in which they are imbedded interpret them fully for the reader. Indenting the informal table at both margins is helpful to the reader.

Formal tables contain more information and should be set off from the text by spacing and (when it enhances page design, as it usually does) boxing. Place titles *above* tables and number them with capital Roman numerals; captions (brief descriptions/explanations/comments) usually go below (see Figure 5.1).

Tables help readers find and compare precise pieces of information. They are also useful for showing categories, relationships between categories, and position of information within categories. Tables may also show trends, but not as efficiently as some other types of graphics.

Organize tables in ways that will serve the reader. Don't simply use a chronological or alphabetical organization if that is not the most helpful form for the material.

As with all graphics, you should design tables to serve the needs of your readers and support the objectives of your report. For example, a table that will serve primarily as a reference tool, helping readers to find the names of products and their characteristics, might list those products alphabetically in a row and their characteristics horizontally. But *do not* use an alphabetical listing, or a chronological order, or some other simple organizational form, simply because it is the most convenient thing for *you* to do. If your objective is to persuade the company to discontinue the use of product X and start using product Y, and you know that your audience will want to compare the products principally on the basis of characteristic Z, set up your table to make that comparison easy and to highlight the conclusion you want readers to reach (see Figure 5.2).

Design your tables for easy access and readability.

High-tech computer developments in the past ten years have dramatically affected the writer's product. With a word processor, you have lots of freedom in designing tables. You can manipulate cells, make borders thick or thin, change typefaces, and align material within cells in various ways. Use that freedom to design tables that are attractive, readable, and helpful. For example, if a table turns out to be more easily read when text is centered within each cell (as it often does), use that format. But never center columns of numbers if that throws off the vertical alignment of the unit values and decimal points. Also, if a table fills up with so

Table X. Average Daily Temperature and Total Precipitation during March 1994
in Major Cities of the Southeastern United States

| CITY | AVERAGE TEMPERATURE | | TOTAL PRECIPITATION | |
	DAILY HIGH	DAILY LOW	PRECIP. (INCHES*)	NO. OF WET DAYS
Asheville, N.C.	58	34	5.00	11
Atlanta, Ga.	63	42	6.00	11
Baltimore, Md.	53	33	3.50	11
Birmingham, Ala.	65	42	6.50	11
Charleston, S.C.	69	45	4.50	10
Charlotte, N.C.	61	39	4.75	11
Greenville, S.C.	63	39	6.25	11
Jackson, Miss.	68	44	5.75	10
Jacksonville, Fla.	73	49	3.75	8
Knoxville, Tenn.	58	31	5.50	12
Louisville/Lexington, Ky.	56	34	4.75	13
Memphis, Tenn.	61	42	5.50	11
Miami, Fla.	79	64	2.00	6
Mobile, Ala.	70	50	6.50	10
Nashville, Tenn.	60	33	4.50	9
Norfolk, Va.	58	39	3.75	11
Orlando, Fla.	78	55	3.25	7
Savannah, Ga.	70	47	3.75	9
Tampa, Fla.	76	56	3.75	9
Washington, D.C.	55	35	3.50	11
REGIONAL AVERAGE	65	43	4.75	10

Included are 11 states: Alabama, District of Columbia, Georgia, Florida, Kentucky, Maryland, Mississippi, North Carolina, South Carolina, Tennessee, Virginia.

*Figures are rounded off to the nearest quarter of an inch.

Figure 5.1 A formal, simple table.

Table III. Comparative Interest Rates at Local Lending Institutions

| INSTITUTION | CERTIFICATE OF DEPOSIT RATES % | | | | INTEREST RATES ON LOANS % | | |
| | $10,000 | | $100,000 | | PRIME | AUTO | HOME |
	6 MOS.	12 MOS.	6 MOS.	12 MOS.	RATE	48 MOS.	EQUITY
National Commerce	8.30	8.45	8.40	8.50	11.50	13.25	14.25
Sovreign National	8.35	8.50	8.40	8.50	11.50	13.00	14.00
Security National	8.50	8.60	8.60	8.65	11.50	12.75	13.75
Citizens Bank USA	8.50	8.60	8.65	8.70	11.50	12.75	13.75
American Tenn.	8.50	8.55	8.60	8.90	11.50	12.00	13.00
The Credit Union	8.50	8.75	8.60	9.00	11.50	11.50	12.75
Home Town Bank	8.65	8.90	8.75	9.25	11.50	11.25	12.75

Figure 5.2   Formal table arranged in hierarchical order to drive home a point.

Table IV. Rating of Foundation Bedrock

Rock Class	I	II	III	IV	V
Description	very good rock	good rock	fair rock	poor rock	very poor rock
Velocity	>2,150	2,150–1,850	1,850–1,500	1,500–1,200	1,200–450
Rating	25	20	15	10	5
Hardness	extremely hard rock	very hard rock	hard rock	soft rock	very soft rock
Rating	20	15	10	5	0
Weathering	unweathered	slightly weathered	weathered	highly weathered	completely weathered
Rating	20	15	10	5	0
Joint Spacing	>3,000	3,000–1,000	1,000–300	300–50	<50
Rating	30	25	20	15	10
Joint Separation	no separation	slightly separated	separation 1 mm	separation 2 to 5 mm	separation <5 mm
Rating	30	25	20	15	10
Orientation (strike & dip)	very favorable	favorable	slightly favorable	unfavorable	slightly unfavorable
Rating	25	20	15	10	5
Total Rating	150	120	90	60	30

Figure 5.3   Hard to read table. Adapted from *Manual on Subsurface Investigations*, The American Association of State Highway and Transportation Officials, 1988.

much data that you suspect the reader will have trouble using it, or may even want to skip it, consider breaking up the data into smaller, more manageable tables. If that is not practical, work with the design of the table, using groupings, different typefaces, shading—whatever will make the table more readable. See Figures 5.3 and 5.4. Which of these tables would you rather read?

Bar Graphs

Bar graphs, also known as histograms, represent numerical quantities in the form of rectangular bars whose length is proportional to accompanying tick marks and/or to other bars in the same visual field. They are particularly good at permitting readers to gain a quick sense of comparison between quantities (see Figure 5.5). Bar graphs are also excellent for comparing *groups* of quantities (see Figure

Table IV. Rating of Foundation Bedrock					
ROCK CLASS	**I**	**II**	**III**	**IV**	**V**
Description	very good rock	good rock	fair rock	poor rock	very poor rock
Velocity	>2,150	2,150–1,850	1,850–1,500	1,500–1,200	1,200–450
Rating	25	20	15	10	5
Hardness	extremely hard rock	very hard rock	hard rock	soft rock	very soft rock
Rating	20	15	10	5	0
Weathering	unweathered	slightly weathered	weathered	highly weathered	completely weathered
Rating	20	15	10	5	0
Joint Spacing	>3,000	3,000–1,000	1,000–300	300–50	<50
Rating	30	25	20	15	10
Joint Separation	no separation	slightly separated	separation 1 mm	separation 2 to 5 mm	separation <5 mm
Rating	30	25	20	15	10
Orientation (strike & dip)	very favorable	favorable	slightly favorable	unfavorable	slightly unfavorable
Rating	25	20	15	10	5
TOTAL RATING	150	120	90	60	30

Figure 5.4   Easier to read table. Adapted from *Manual on Subsurface Investigations*, The American Association of State Highway and Transportation Officials, 1988.

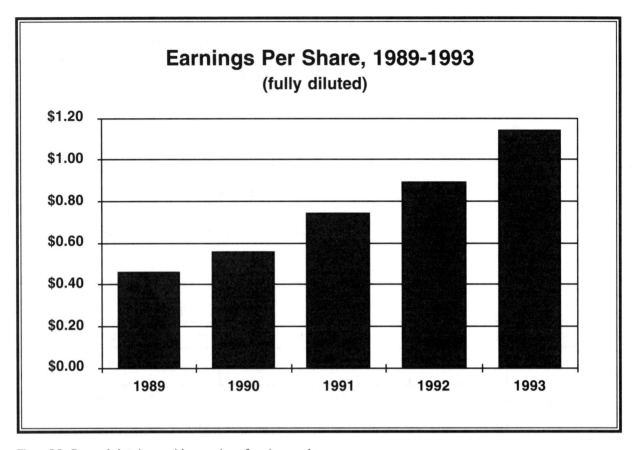

Figure 5.5 Bar graph that gives a quick comparison of earnings per share.

5.6). Bar graphs can be used to show proportion within a whole, comparison to other wholes and parts, and change over a variable (such as time) all in one visual field (see Figure 5.7).

For conveying a sense of both relative quantity and change of variables, bar graphs are always an option.

Although bar graphs can also represent changes in quantities over time, distance, or other variables, they usually do not perform that function as well as line graphs. Still, for conveying a sense of both relative quantity and change of variables, bar graphs are always a viable option. Generally, if bar graphs represent change over time or distance, they are flipped 90° to the right to become horizontal bar graphs (see Figure 5.8). If you wish to give an impression of volume or simply make the graph more dramatic, you can make the bars appear three-dimensional (see Figure 5.9).

If you make the "suppressed zero point mistake," your reader may think you are being deceptive.

Computer programs give you many options for manipulating bar graphs, but they can't decide for you which options will be most effective. The same orientation to audiences, uses, and objectives that has guided your other textual and graphic choices must guide you here. Use labels, colors, orientations, sizes, lengths, grids, unit sizes, and all the other variables to produce bar graphs that your audience will find easy to grasp and that will promote your objectives. As you

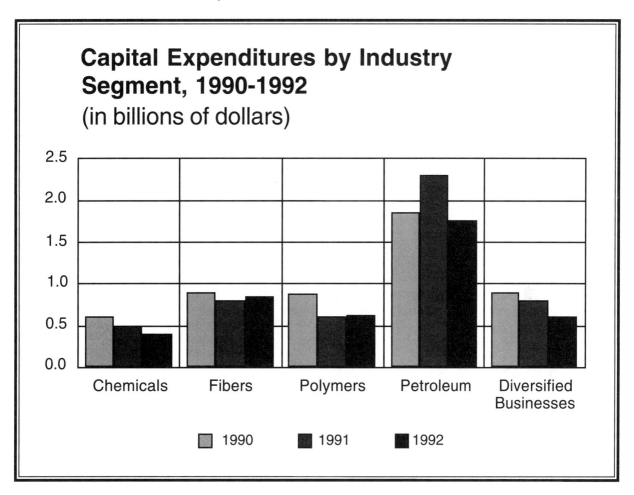

Figure 5.6 Bar graph that allows reader to easily compare expenditures for five industry segments over a three-year period. Adapted from *1992 Annual Report,* DuPont.

manipulate these variables, take care not to create bar graphs that may mislead your audience, such as the "suppressed zero point" mistake shown in Figure 5.10. If done intentionally, such a graph produces fraudulent results. In Figure 5.10, *visual* comparison of shareholders' equity over a five-year period is thrown out of proportion. Earnings per share in 1990, for example, seem to be double those of 1989, when in reality they are only about 20 percent more.

Do not be afraid to experiment with bar graphs. Represent data in the form that will be easiest on the reader's eye and mind. Avoid keys where possible, but use them when they will significantly reduce annoying repetition (see Figure 5.11). Label bars inside the bar when possible; make units and tick marks on axes clear; use color, shading, and hatching that allow readers to see groupings and distinctions at a glance.

Do not simply find a standard bar format and use it every time, unless the regularity of form is actually *helpful* in the report. You might use this regularity of form, for example, if the report calls for a series of bar charts on the same subject

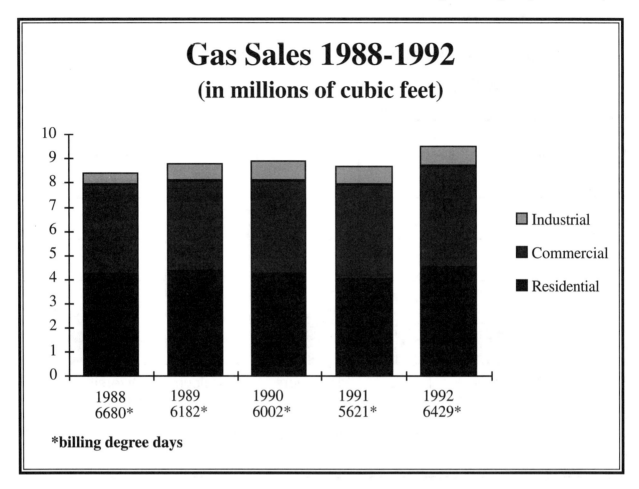

Figure 5.7   Comparison bar graph showing proportion within a whole and change over time. Adapted from *1992 Annual Report,* Central Hudson Gas & Electric Corporation.

and with the same variables, and you have determined that consistency of form, size, and perhaps even placement, will help the reader use the document. But in general, think of variety and adaptability in visual communication as you would in verbal/textual communication: you would not use one invariable sentence pattern in your prose; do not engage in monotonous visual communication, either. Figures 5.12 and 5.13 demonstrate a few alternative ways to style bar graphs.

Bar graphs can also be combined with line graphs to tell two or more stories in one visual. In Figure 5.14, note how Sears depicts the market value of its shares on the left vertical axis and the price earnings (PE) multiple on the right vertical axis.

Pictographs

Pictographs can be effective, but be sure they are accurate and in good taste.

Pictographs, often called "infographs" in journalism graphics, *pictorially* represent data otherwise represented by simple geometric forms—the rectangles of bar graphs, circles of pie charts, lines in line graphs, and other shapes. They are often

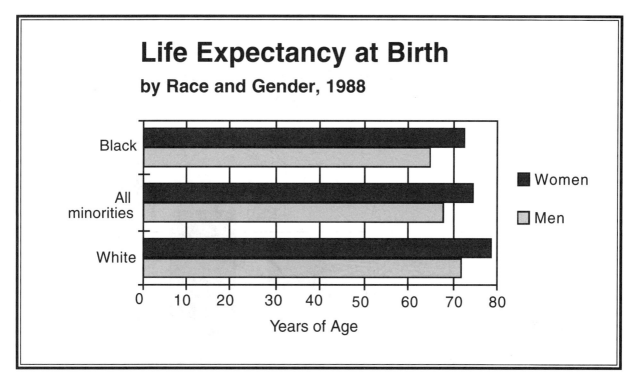

Figure 5.8 Horizontal bar graph comparing life expectancies by race and gender. Adapted from *Advance Report of Final Mortality Statistics, 1988*, U.S. National Center for Health Statistics.

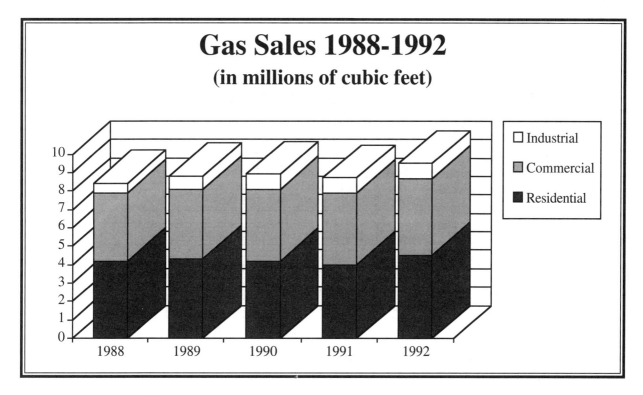

Figure 5.9 3-D bar graph displaying the same data pictured in Figure 5.7. Adapted from *1992 Annual Report,* Central Hudson Gas & Electric Corporation.

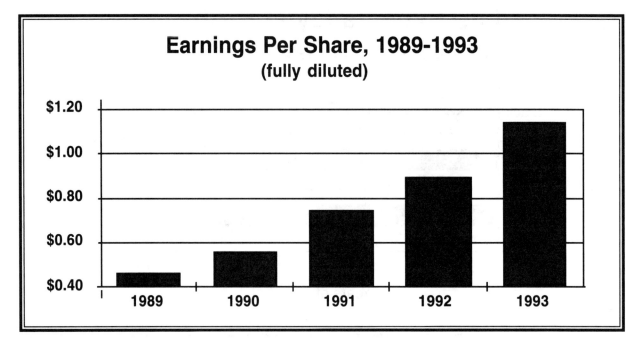

Figure 5.10   Misleading bar graph with suppressed zero point. (Compare this with Figure 5.5.)

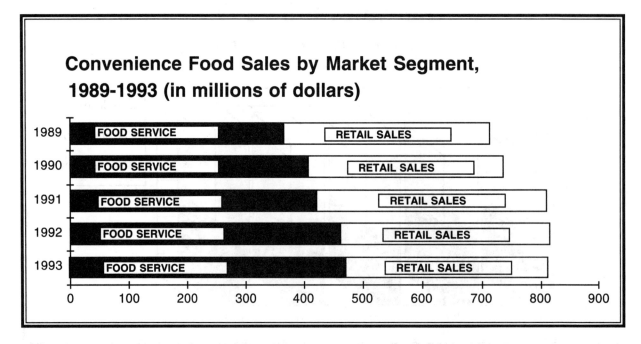

Figure 5.11   This bar graph could reduce visual clutter by using a key to identify dark bars as "Food Service" and light bars as "Retail Sales." (Compare this with the use of a key in Figure 5.8.) Adapted from *1993 Annual Report,* The Quaker Oats Company.

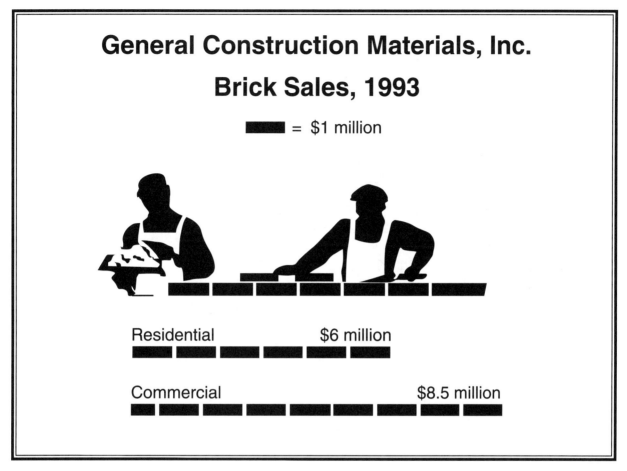

General Construction Materials, Inc.

Brick Sales, 1993

▬▬ = $1 million

Residential $6 million

Commercial $8.5 million

Figure 5.12   Bar graph incorporating "clip art" (commercial art stored on computer disk) that is appropriate for the subject.

a good way to reinforce concepts and make them more memorable, but they can easily be misused. The man whose name is most often associated with pictographs—Nigel Holmes, director of *Time* magazine's graphics—has been widely praised for his pictographs, and widely imitated (most prominently by *USA Today*), but he has also been seriously criticized. It is easy to produce a pictograph that is inappropriate to your audience, or simply in bad taste—such as Holmes' graph of the rise and fall of diamond prices over the years, shown as a red line drawn along the curve of a showgirl's leg.[3] It is also easy to misrepresent data with pictographs, especially those that are modified bar charts.

[3]Stuart Silverstone discusses Holmes' successes and mistakes in "The Picturing of Information," *Aldus Magazine,* Vol. 2, No. 6, September/October 1991.

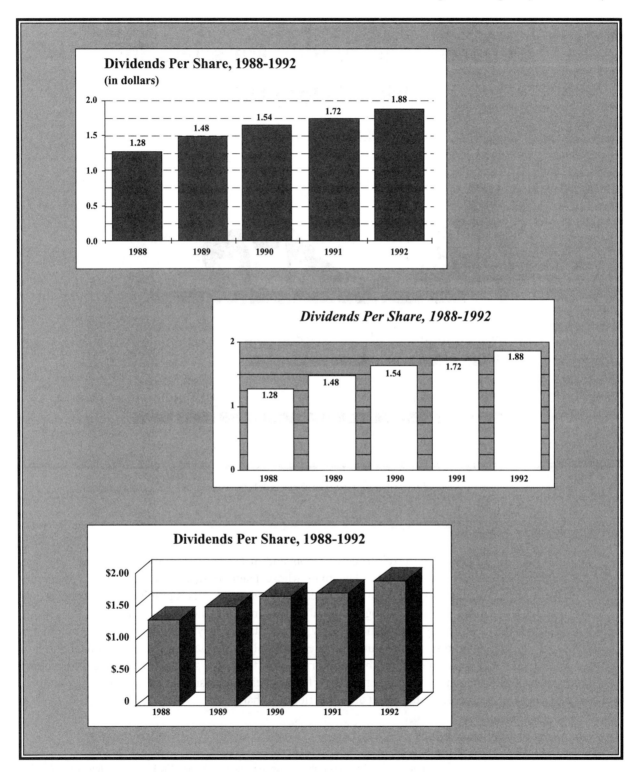

Figure 5.13   The same simple bar graph styled three different ways. Adapted from *1992 Annual Report,* PPG
Industries, Inc.

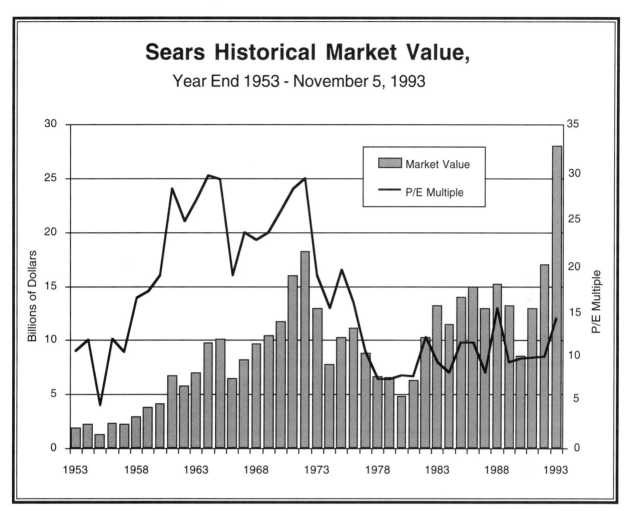

Figure 5.14   Bar graph combined with line graph to show relationships between data. Adapted from *1993 Annual Report,* Sears, Roebuck and Co.

The pictograph in Figure 5.15 is misleading because the overall bulk of the images gives a false impression of volume, which could be more accurately represented by height alone. In some cases, the solution is simple: divide the images into smaller, multiple images stacked on top of, or beside, each other (see Figures 5.16 and 5.17).

Often, though, a better solution is simply to use traditional graphics if you run into trouble. Some quantities may not lend themselves to pictographic representation. A graph of pork and poultry production that shows pigs and chickens stacked on top of each other may look rather absurd and may be inappropriate for your audience and purpose (see Figure 5.18).

Some objects—often those that have or can fit into cylindrical shapes—may lend themselves nicely to pictographs. Pictographs are trickier than most other

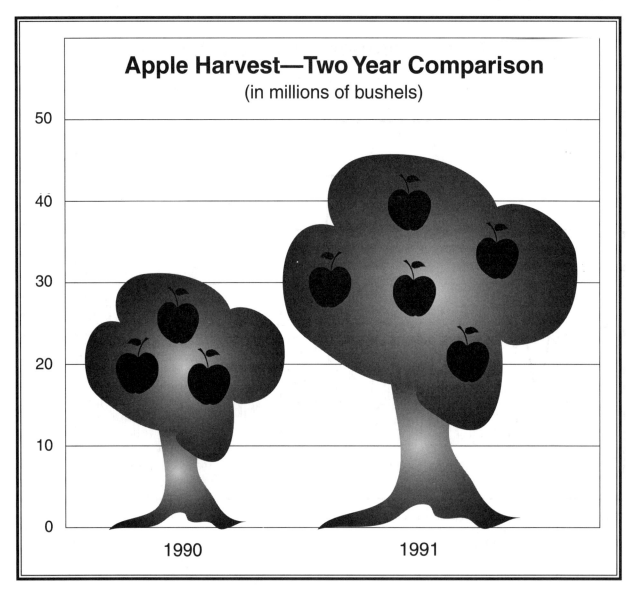

Figure 5.15   Misleading pictograph. Volume of apple harvest in 1991 seems over twice that of 1990, but is in reality less than 70 percent greater.

graphics, and were once almost exclusively the domain of graphic artists. Now, however, with modern computer software and clip art, almost anyone can create them. Used well, they can add interest, emphasis, and memorableness to a report. Used unwisely, they can be ineffective, inappropriate, and even insulting. If you choose to use pictographs, think carefully about how to create them, and consult colleagues for a second opinion whenever you feel doubtful about the propriety of a choice. While computer graphics have made it easier to apply pictures to text, they have not enhanced the supply of artistic talent.

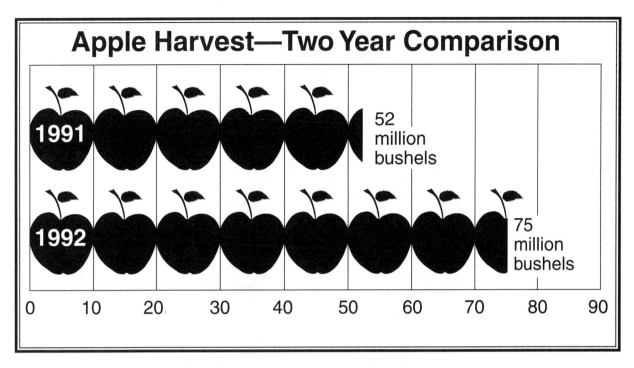

Figure 5.16 A pictograph that works well with its subject, giving an accurate visual impression.

Pie Charts

The human mind quickly perceives wholeness or completion in a circle.

Pie charts are the graphic of choice for representing the parts of a whole. The human mind quickly perceives wholeness or completion in a circle and can roughly estimate at a glance the relative areas of the wedges making up a circle. Label those wedges with titles and percentages, and you have the essential ingredients of a pie chart (see Figure 5.19).

Pie-chart rules of thumb are easy to remember:

- People scan pie charts clockwise or counterclockwise starting from 12 o'clock. Let your biggest wedge start at (or sweep across) 12 o'clock, and then sweep to the right or to the left, with subsequent wedges following in descending order.
- Break the previous rule only to make an element prominent (see Figure 5.23 on p. 82) or if the pie will not look good otherwise.
- Place title and percentage *inside* wedges whenever possible. When labels are too big for the wedge, place them outside but supply callouts[4] to show where they go.
- Do not run labels along the axes of wedges; make labels horizontal, like reg-

---

[4]A "callout" is a label placed outside the portion of the visual it refers to, with a line drawn from it to the appropriate spot in the visual.

Figure 5.17   An alternative pictograph that is effective.

ular text. The aesthetic effect of getting text inside the wedge is not worth sacrificing the readability of horizontal text.

- It is perfectly all right to label some wedges inside and some outside, depending on wedge and label sizes. We also recommend that you depart from descending order when there are multiple categories of very small percentages. That way you will not position two very small slivers of the pie adjacent to one another (see Figure 5.20).

While you should keep these rules in mind when making pie charts, do not let them curtail creativity. For example, you can add pictographic elements to pie charts for reinforcement and visual interest (see Figure 5.21). You can use an exploded effect, especially helpful when some of the pieces are to be considered as separate subtotals (see Figure 5.22). Let us say you wish to emphasize shareholder

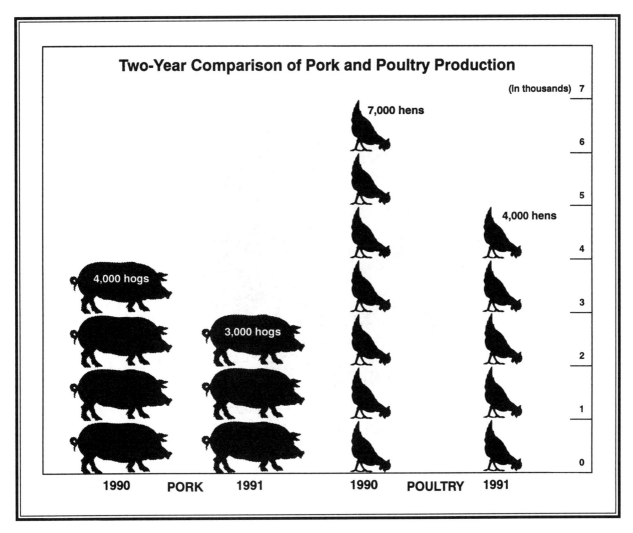

Figure 5.18   An awkward pictograph. The difference in volume between the images of the chickens and pigs is misleading, and the way the animals are stacked makes the graph appear slightly absurd.

dividends in an annual report. You can add a 3-D effect to the exploded pie chart and make the profit wedge stand out strikingly (see Figure 5.23).

Again, construct graphics to serve your purpose; superfluous effects are probably worse than dull graphics. But imaginative and *effective* graphics can add immeasurably to the success of the report.

Line Graphs

Sometimes you will want to design line graphs to do more than show the relationship between variables over time.

The simplest line graphs show how one variable relates to another (see Figure 5.24). Line graphs are also excellent for showing and comparing trends (see Figure 5.25). Line graphs that show multiple trends can be very helpful in a business

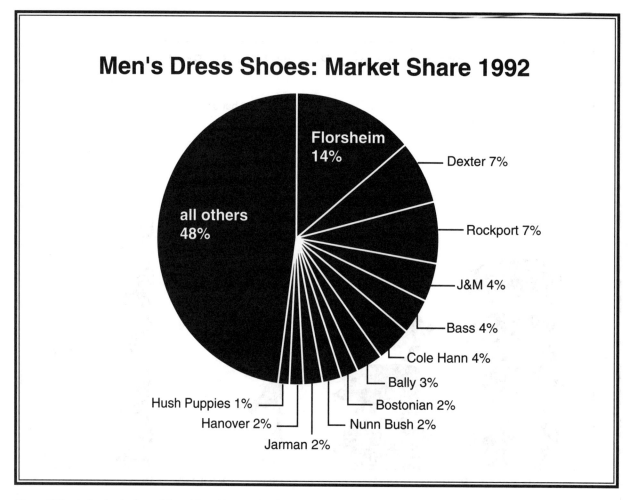

Figure 5.19   A simple pie chart. Adapted from *Footwear Market Insights Annual 1992 Data.*

report, but they must be intelligently designed. Make them readable, and make it as easy as possible for readers to make the comparisons and reach the conclusions you intend. You may want, for example, not only to show trends and suggest how variables affect one another over time, but also to highlight where variables dipped below a zero point (see Figure 5.26).

Here are the most important rules of thumb for line graphs:

- Make lines easily distinguishable from each other. Use different colors if you can. Colors usually work better than varying between "solid line, dashed line, dotted line," and so on. If you can't work with colors in a document, vary the lines in any way that makes them more readable, *especially* in instances when the lines occasionally run close together.
- Use a key to identify lines if that relieves visual clutter (see Figure 5.27).

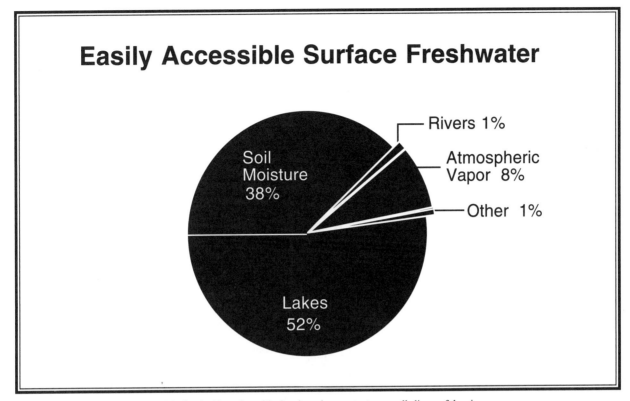

Figure 5.20 A pie chart that uses labeling inside and outside the pie and separates two small slivers of the pie.
Source: *The World Wildlife Atlas of the Environment*, Prentice Hall, 1990.

Figure 5.21 Combining pictograph elements with a pie chart. The missing pieces draw the reader's attention to the expressed loss.

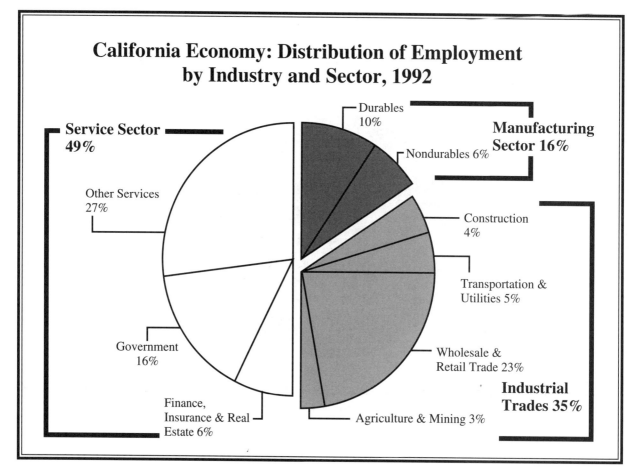

Figure 5.22 An exploded pie chart creates groups of data. Adapted from *1992 Annual Report*, Wells Fargo & Company.

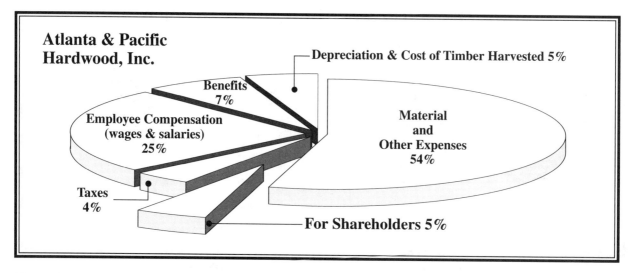

Figure 5.23 3-D pie chart with exploded wedge for emphasis.

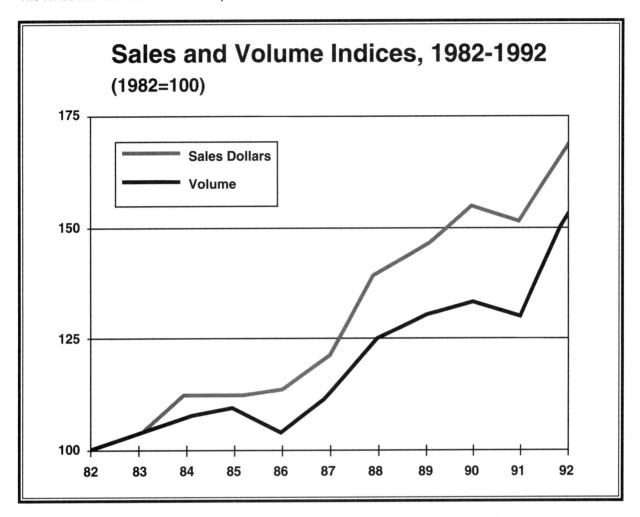

Figure 5.24   A simple line graph showing the relationship of sales (dollars) and volume (units). Adapted from *1992 Annual Report,* Rohm and Haas Company.

- Do not fill the area of the graph with grid lines unless they are really needed (again, do not clutter the visual field). Often, just a few grid lines in one direction, widely spaced, are all you need to orient the reader. If the reader will need to reference specific points on the graph, label those points; if the reader will need to reference many points, supplement the line graph with a table.
- Label axes clearly to indicate the variable being represented even if you think the audience should already understand what the axes represent.
- Provide labeled tick marks at intervals suited to the way you want the graph to be read. If you want to show trends over a period of decades, for example, you do not need to tick off each year. If you want to highlight what happened in a particular year, you may want a tick mark to fall on that year; you may even want to draw a line through the graph at that tick mark.

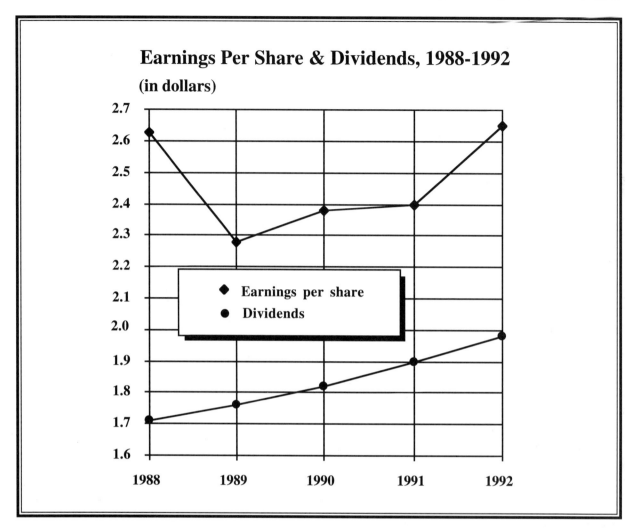

Figure 5.25   A simple line graph comparing two trends (earnings per share and dividends). Adapted from *1992 Annual Report,* Central Hudson Gas & Electric Corporation.

Line graphs can be combined with pictographic elements to enhance a desired effect.

- Do not be afraid to add features to line graphs that will enhance the effect you want. As with pie charts and other visuals, you can add pictographic features (see Figures 5.28 and 5.29).

Surface Graphs

Surface graphs are a type of line graph; rather than using simple lines, they use shading or color between the line and the base, or between lines. Consider using them when you want to emphasize *total amount* rather than changes in amount (see Figure 5.30).

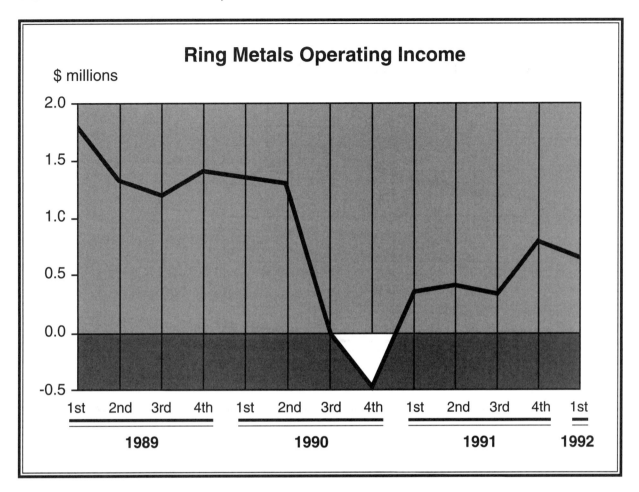

Figure 5.26 Line graph emphasizing data that fall below a zero point. Adapted from *1992 First Quarter Review,* General Binding Corporation.

Flow Charts

Use flow charts to illustrate processes. Rules of thumb for flow charts are:

- Be sure you know how your audience will read the flow chart. Americans read left to right and top to bottom, but not every culture does so.

If you attach meaning to the geometric shapes in a flow chart, be sure that your audience knows how to interpret those shapes.

- If your audience is familiar with certain conventions of geometric representation in flow charts, use those conventions. Flow charts for computer programming, for example, attach specific meanings to squares, diamonds, circles, and other shapes. However, unless you're sure your audience will understand the meaning of symbols in the flow chart, be sure to label each step carefully.

- Label *inside* the shapes wherever possible.

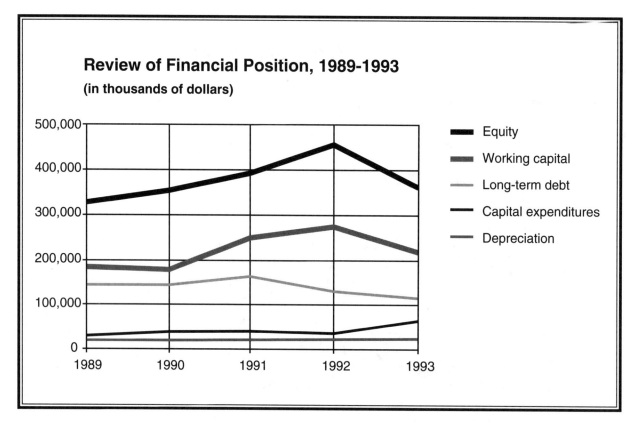

Figure 5.27 Line graph that uses a key to avoid visual clutter. Adapted from *1993 Annual Report*, Gerber Products Company.

- If possible, let the shapes representing steps or phases of the process suggest what is going on at that point (a boxcar shape to suggest transportation, and so on).
- Use arrows to indicate direction. If you must use a callout to label a component of the flow chart, use a plain line, *not* an arrow.
- Use colors in conventional ways (shades of red for heat, shades of blue for cold, and so on).
- *Design the flow chart to serve your purpose.* No graphic is an end in itself. If your audience needs only a general idea of a process, for example, do not feel obliged to represent every substep in the process. (See Figure 5.31.)

Organizational Charts

Organizational charts show the relationship of personnel in an organization, and readers use them to understand the structure of the organization and to guide them in contacting or referring to personnel (see Figure 5.32).

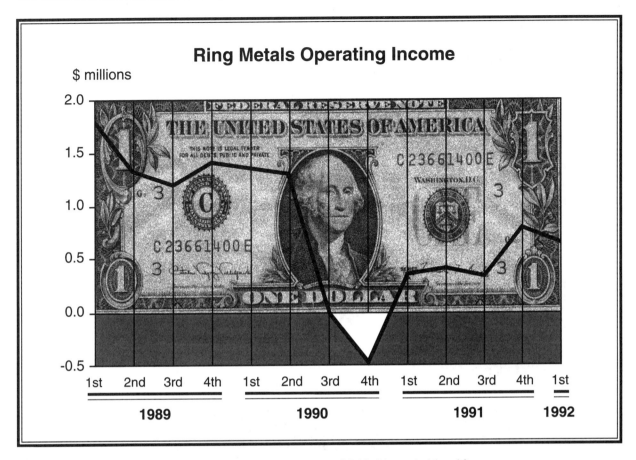

Figure 5.28   Line graph incorporating pictographic element within the visual field of the graph. Adapted from
1992 First Quarter Review, General Binding Corporation. (Compare to Figure 5.26.)

- Design organizational charts so that readers can easily trace lines of responsibility and supervision, as well as areas of cooperation.
- Again, be sure you know the way readers will scan the visual.
- Show only those parts of the organization your readers will need to see.

Don't overdo organizational charts. Show only those parts of the organization your reader needs to see.

Maps

In business reports, maps are particularly useful for comparing quantitative information by geographic areas. The comparative areas should always be clearly outlined by some distinct graphic technique. Figure 5.33 depicts half the globe; however, any size of geographic area can be depicted by a map as suits your purpose. Note the stylized features of the maps shown in Figures 5.34 and 5.35. Lines in both maps have been smoothed and straightened to reduce visual clutter.

Maps need not be exact geographic representations. Stylize them to reduce visual clutter and to emphasize important features.

Maps need not be exact geographic representations. The map of parks in

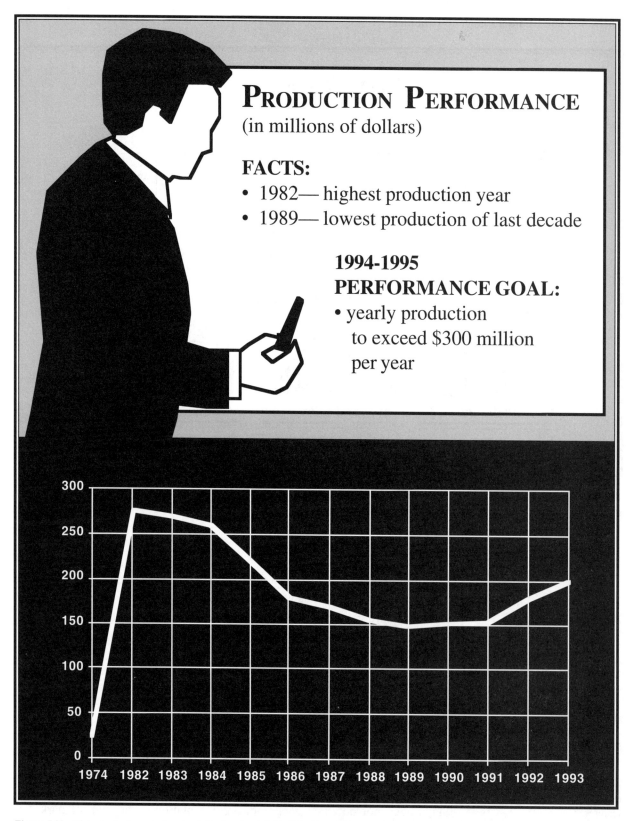

Figure 5.29 Pictograph element placed outside the visual field of the line graph, yet united to the visual as a whole.

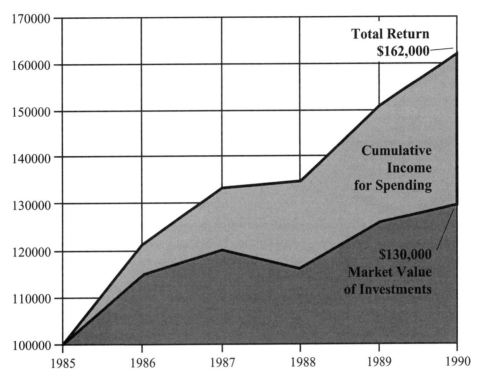

By pooling (instead of seperately investing) 934 separate endowment funds the firm has more than doubled each endowment's income for spending since 1985. Average annual return for the pooled endowment fund was 11.9% for the five years ending June 30, 1990.

The chart above illustrates a typical endowment fund with a market value of $100,000 at June 30, 1985. Assuming that this endowment fund purchased shares in the pooled fund at that date, the current market value of the endowment fund at June 30, 1990 would be $130,000. In addition to the market value appreciation, the fund would have earned $32,000 in income. The cumulative income added to the market value growth yielded a total return represented by the top line of the chart. The total investment return was $62,000 over fifty years on the original investment of $100,000.

Figure 5.30   A simple surface graph. Some graphs require explanatory text, as this one does. Notice that the top area is outlined with a bolder line around the complete area. This is to emphasize the amount of cumulative growth of the investment due to pooling the endowment funds.

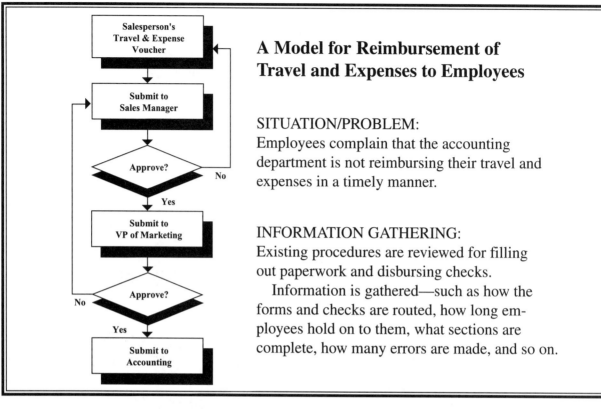

Salesperson's Travel & Expense Voucher

Submit to Sales Manager

Approve? — No

Yes

Submit to VP of Marketing

No — **Approve?**

Yes

Submit to Accounting

A Model for Reimbursement of Travel and Expenses to Employees

SITUATION/PROBLEM:
Employees complain that the accounting department is not reimbursing their travel and expenses in a timely manner.

INFORMATION GATHERING:
Existing procedures are reviewed for filling out paperwork and disbursing checks.

Information is gathered—such as how the forms and checks are routed, how long employees hold on to them, what sections are complete, how many errors are made, and so on.

Figure 5.31   A simple flow chart used for problem solving. Adapted from *Small Business Reports,* July, 1992.

Figure 5.35 is highly stylized, distorting some areas for emphasis and simplifying some lines. Note also its use of icons to signal points of interest, facilities, and activities.

Illustrations

The primary function of the graphics discussed so far is to visually display quantitative data and their relationships. Although, as noted, any graphic can be combined with pictographic elements and therefore become "illustrated," we reserve the term "illustration" for visuals that function more to represent physical objects and configurations than numerical qualities. These visuals fall into four categories: photographs, shaded/colored drawings, line drawings, and cartoons.

Photographs.   Photographs offer the most realistic form of visual communication, and they can add interest and drama. In some cases—a damage report, for example—they may be indispensable. Photographs can be digitized and placed directly into your report (see Figure 5.36).

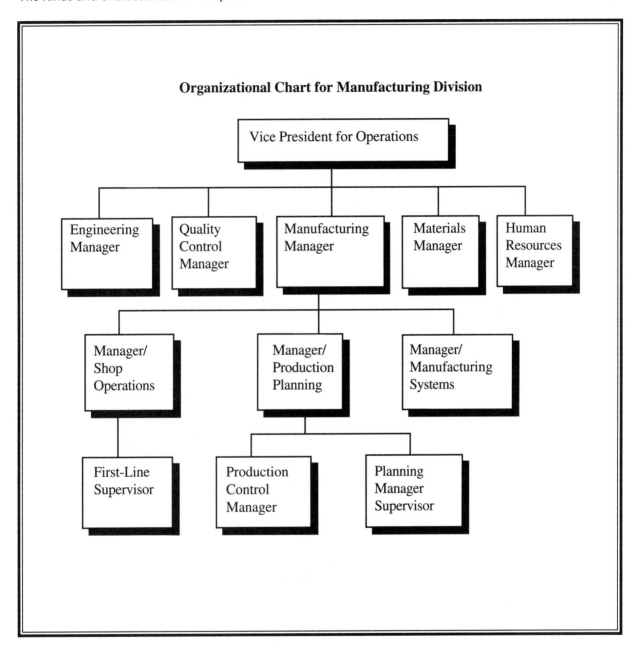

Figure 5.32 Organizational chart showing lines of supervision and coordination.

Diagrams (Shaded/Colored Drawings and Line Drawings).

Although photographs can be excellent visuals, they are often *not* a good choice when you need to separate out components of a visual—that is, when you need a simpler, less cluttered visual field. This situation calls for a drawing, a "diagram." If you have ever looked at a medical textbook, for example, you have seen that

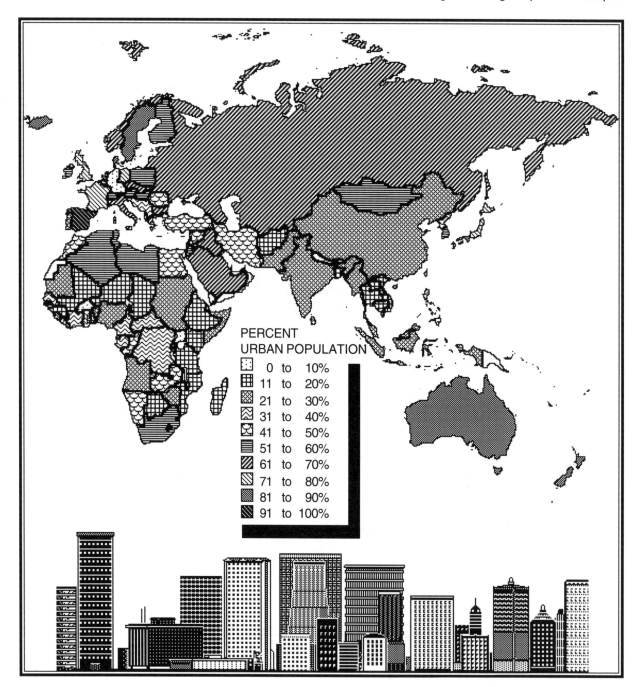

Figure 5.33   Map of eastern hemisphere showing distribution of urban population.

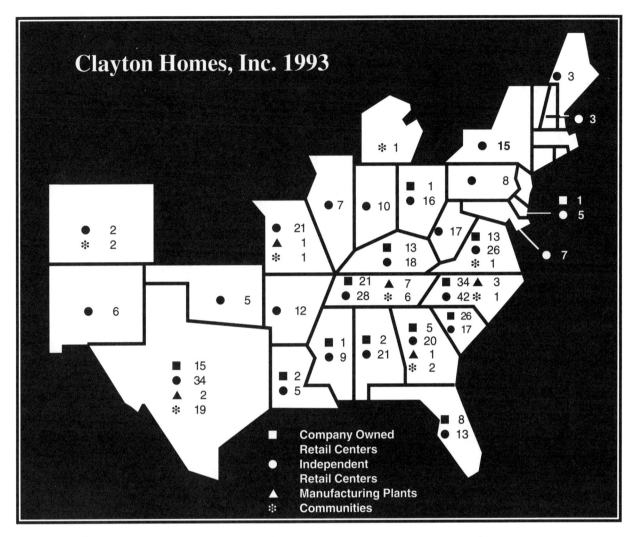

Figure 5.34 A stylized map of a portion of the United States showing locations of company branches. Adapted from *1993 Annual Report,* Clayton Homes, Inc.

Although photographs can be excellent visuals, they are not a good choice when you need to separate out components of a visual—that is, when you need a simpler, less cluttered visual field.

many of the visuals are drawings rather than photos, or photos accompanied by drawings. This is because with a drawing, though less realistic than a photo, you can control the amount of detail presented to the eye, making recognition and learning easier. The same technique applies to drawings of machinery, industrial processes, and other subjects whose complexity might make the use of photos more confusing than enlightening (see Figure 5.37).

Diagrams are the most common type of illustration in reports and have the advantage of versatility and a range of complexity. They can be cut away, exploded,

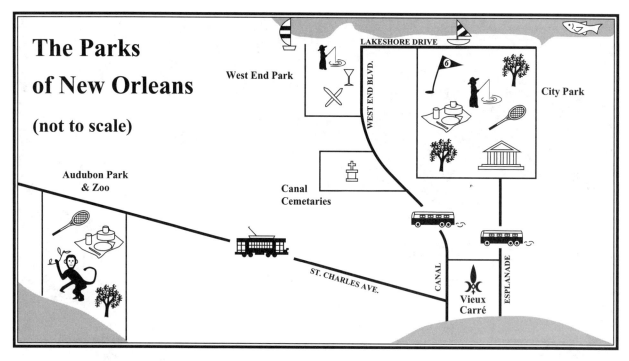

Figure 5.35   A stylized map of parks in New Orleans. Notice use of icons, smoothing of routes. Adapted from
Free Map and Transit Guide, New Orleans Public Services, 1982.

rendered in three dimensions, or in any other format that the hand (or computer) can generate. Here are some rules of thumb for using diagrams in business reports:

- Choose the *orientation* (point of view) that will best accommodate the reader.
- Label parts inside when possible, and label all callouts clearly.
- Use horizontal labels.
- Use color schemes or other visual signals that will help readers see what you want them to see. For example, if you want them to see all the new modifications in an engine, you could shade all those parts in blue.

> Cognitive scientists have confirmed that people learn very quickly, and with excellent retention, from cartoon illustrations.

Cartoons.   This last category of drawings holds an ambiguous status in business reports because some people consider it to be too informal. Sometimes it is, but often a cartoon, or an illustration with cartoon-like features, can provide simple, enjoyable, effective support to a document (see Figure 5.38). Cognitive scientists have confirmed that people learn very quickly, and with excellent retention, from cartoon illustrations.

THE USE OF GRAPHICS

We have already discussed the use of graphics to some degree, suggesting ways you might wish to adapt the various types of graphics to your various objectives and

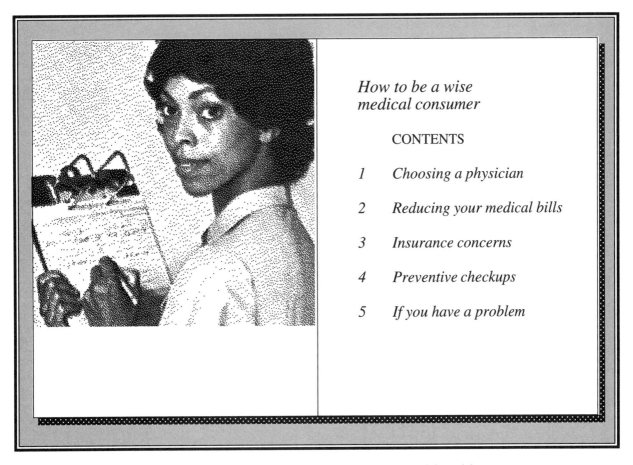

Figure 5.36 A digitized photograph placed into a report to add visual interest. The photo extends beyond the normal margin to "bleed" off the edges of the page. Bleeding photographs off the page is a long-accepted practice of page design.

audiences. There are, however, a few more standard rules for using graphics that you will want to keep in mind.

Titles, Captions, and Numbers

Simplify your labeling system for visuals; a division into "tables" and "figures" usually works best.

Visuals in reports should be labeled "tables" or "figures." Some reports further divide designations for visuals into "charts," "diagrams," "maps," "plates," and so on, but unless there is a large number of one of these things—maps, for instance—this is seldom necessary. The simplest method is to divide all visuals into categories of tables or figures, and number each category consecutively, using Arabic numerals for figures and capital Roman numerals for tables (such as Figure 1, Figure 2, Table I, Table II). If you have more than six tables or figures, provide a "List of Figures" or "List of Tables" in the front material[5] of your report.

[5]The pages that come before the main text starts.

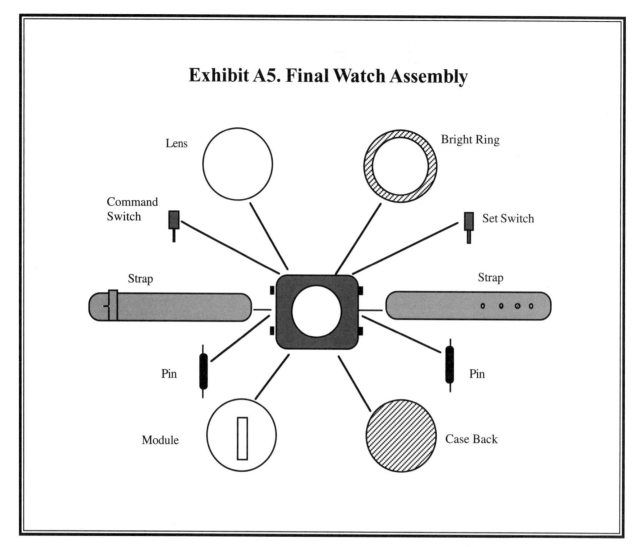

Figure 5.37   A diagram illustrating the parts required for final assembly of a low-cost digital watch. The drawing simplifies the assembly to make recognition and learning easier.

Titles and captions are set up slightly differently in tables and figures. For tables, place the title above (centered on the table) and the caption below (aligned at both left and right margins). (See Figure 5.39.) For figures, put both title and caption below (following the figure number, which is aligned at left margin). When you must attribute a table or figure to a source, place that attribution at the end of the caption, as was done in the caption for Figure 5.38.

If you decide, for design reasons, to depart from these rules, be sure you are consistent throughout the report; do not accustom the reader to looking one place for information and then place it somewhere else.

Most important of all, put helpful *content* into captions. Use captions to give

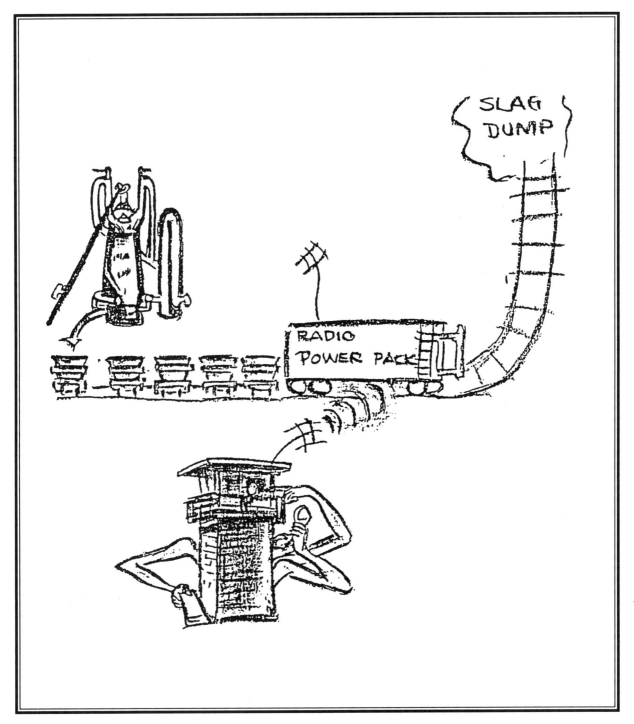

Figure 5.38 Effective drawing with cartoon elements. Source: *The Future of Automated Movement Control in the Iron and Steel Industry,* a report for United States Steel and Union Switch and Signal, 1960. Illustration by Vivienne Bruce.

Table III. Annual Production Volume for Division by Unit, 1976-1994 (in thousands of units)

YEAR	UNIT A	UNIT B	TOTAL	YEAR	UNIT A	UNIT B	TOTAL
1994	370	380	**750**	1985	210	240	**450**
1993	350	360	**710**	1984	200	110	**310**
1992	240	170	**410**	1983	190	110	**300**
1991	300	310	**310**	1982	370	190	**560**
1990	310	290	**500**	1981	360	210	**570**
1989	260	270	**430**	1980	80	160	**240**
1988	290	260	**550**	1979	440	210	**650**
1987	280	240	**520**	1978	290	130	**420**
1986	220	220	**440**		250	120	**370**

Manufacturing production levels tracked over a span of eighteen years, indicating subtotals for individual units within the division, as well as annual total.

Figure 5.39   A table showing the title centered above and the caption set below in justified text (aligned at both margins with no indentation).

• Pareto Chart

While a flowcahrt maps the logical flow of a process, a Pareto chart illustrates the trouble spots. That is why a Pareto chart is ideal when you have several problems but don't know which one needs immediate management attention. Below is an example.

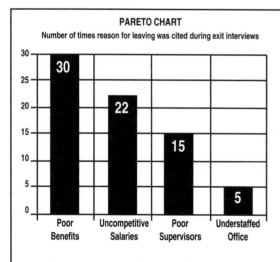

PARETO CHART
Number of times reason for leaving was cited during exit interviews

The management problem you want to analyze is high turnover of support staff. To pinpoint why your business has a revolving door despite good working conditions, collect statistical data regarding how often individuals support employees leave and the reason why (i.e., poor benefits, uncompetitive salaries, poor supervisors, or understaffed office). Use a bar graph to chart the data—the horizontal axis representing the type of problems cited, the vertical axis representing the number of times each has been cited over a specific period of time. *The largest bar represents the principal problem.*

Go back to the statistics to verify when and under what circumstances the problem occurs. This step is necessary to establish the validity of your solution.

Figure 5. An example of a Pareto chart, how to set it up and use it to solve a specific problem. Adapted from the July 1992 issue of Small Business Reports.

Figure 5.40   Labeling and textual integration for a figure.

thorough and accurate labels to visuals and to point out and interpret important features of visuals for your readers.

Textual Integration

One of the biggest mistakes inexperienced report writers make is to insert graphics with little or no textual discussion.

Labeling is part of the verbal integration that you must achieve between graphics and text. We said earlier that "A picture is worth a thousand words," but do not take that too literally: One misleading picture can destroy the effect of a thousand accurate words. One of the biggest mistakes inexperienced report writers make is to insert graphics with little or no verbal discussion of them. The writer who does this is saying one of two things to the reader: "I'm too lazy to discuss this visual with you," or "This visual is self-explanatory; *you* figure out what it means." This is poor service to the customer.

The way to treat visuals is to "nest" them in text. Use words to prepare the reader for an upcoming visual; use words as part of the visual itself (labels, callouts, captions) as in Figure 5.40; and use words after the visual to discuss it, highlight important points, and interpret it.

Perhaps even better than the "nest" image is the common metaphor of "incorporation"; you must *incorporate* graphics into your text, make them integral parts of the body of the document by meshing them with text.

Placement of Graphics

Do not relegate your graphics to an appendix. Place them where they will be most convenient for the reader and most effective in accomplishing your objectives.

An essential part of integrating visuals and text is placement: If a visual must occupy a full page, try to place it on a page facing the text to which it refers. Or if the report does not use facing pages, place it on the page immediately following the page that first referred to it in the text. If a graphic is important to accomplishing your objective in connection with your primary audience, do not banish it to the appendix. (How often do *you* leaf through a report obeying the directive to "see Figure 14, Appendix 3"?) In general, do not relegate visuals to the appendix unless they are merely reference material—nonessential to your objectives—or unless production constraints require it. Figure 5.41 suggests ways to incorporate figures and text into one- and two-column page formats.

CONCLUSION

Graphics can contribute powerfully to your report's success—or failure. Choose and use them wisely. Begin to find or generate them early in the report-writing process. Think about their various functions and consider places in the report where specific kinds of graphics can serve your objectives. Always keep in mind the needs of the reader, and design visuals to serve those needs. Be willing to manipulate graphics until they are in the form that will best serve the customer. Do not look at

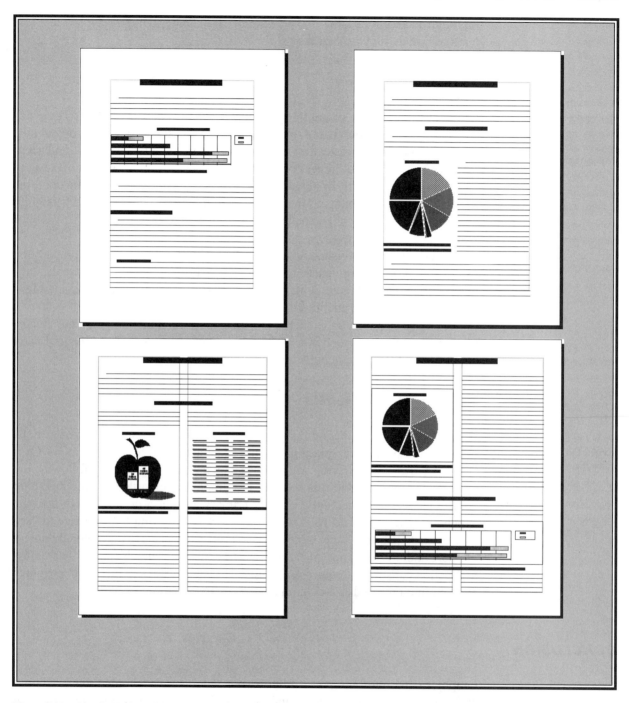

Figure 5.41 "Thumbnail sketches"—rough, small-scale representations of the text block and visual elements of your report—can help you integrate graphics.

graphics as second-class citizens of the report, or as afterthoughts to be stuck into an appendix. Incorporate them into your text, making them integral components of a purposeful body of information.

PRACTICE

You have recently been named manager of a small business unit in the Computer Support Division of a large corporation. Your unit is losing money, and you need to make a presentation to the Division Director to explain why. You need to come up with five visuals on which to base your presentation.

Your unit provides computer support to a well-focused group of internal customers (Graphic Arts, Accounting, Travel, and Personnel), all of whom use PCs connected with LANs. Your unit contains eighteen people, all of whom have at least twelve years with the company and at least four weeks of vacation time; three of them have six weeks of vacation. Your staff's relative seniority also means your unit's salary is 25 percent above that of the division as a whole. Average years of company experience for the larger division is six; average vacation time is two weeks; average sick leave is three days.

Most of your staff enjoy good health and are out sick no more than average, but three have had serious illnesses: One was out three months for surgery, another two months for drug rehabilitation, and a third has legitimate chronic health problems and misses an average of one day a week (not affected by vacations or other absences).

The division of which your unit is a part charges an hourly rate for its services, based on the average salary for staff members throughout the division and the amount of their time (over the course of a year) that they can be working for customers and therefore charging for their time (generating billable hours). The penalties for overcharging (listing too many hours) are severe. The estimate for billable hours is based on these assumptions:

The work year consists of 2080 hours before any time is subtracted.

There are 12 holidays in the year.

There are 5 days off per employee (on average) for training.

There are 3 days off per employee (on average) for sick time.

There are 2 weeks off per employee (on average) for vacation.

Each employee requires (on average) about 4 weeks' time over the course of the year to complete administrative work, time which cannot contribute to billable hours.

The average annual salary throughout the division is $25K.

The company's share of the benefits for each employee costs 20 percent above the salary of each person; the division bears that cost.

The division's hourly billing rate is based on this analysis:

- Total number of working hours in a year: 2080
- Average number of hours unavailable for work
  (from the above):   400
- Difference (available billable hours):   1680
- Average salary (based on local competitive
  pay and number of years of company service): $25,000
- Cost of benefits: 5,000
- Average cost per employee: $30,000
- Rate the division charges
  (cost per employee/billable hours): $17.86

Your task is to come up with five key graphics to explain to Division Director Leslie Burkhardt why your unit is losing money. (To keep this problem manageable, use only the averages provided.) If one or more of your graphics can point to a possible solution, so much the better. Assume that your graphics will be presented to Burkhardt on 8.5" × 11" sheets along with a one-page memo summarizing your thinking. Be sure to integrate your graphics with text in the form of captions, descriptive labels, and explanatory notes. In the meeting, you expect to have the same graphics on overhead transparencies; thus the graphics, not the memo, will be the core of your presentation. Your task here is to come up with the graphics.

6

Revising and Editing Your Report

Jumping from the first draft right into editing wastes valuable resources: time, energy, and judgment.

At this point you should have a preliminary draft of your report, complete with visuals. Having gone this far, many writers make the mistake of immediately starting a line-by-line edit, front to back, fixing the easy and obvious problems first, such as word choice, grammar, spelling, and punctuation. Resist this temptation! That work certainly needs to be done at some point—it is easy to do and it makes quick, visible improvements. Doing it now, however, is the equivalent of applying a superficial fresh coat of paint to a wall that has not been properly prepared and may well have holes, rough spots, or even rotten plaster in it. Jumping right from the first draft into line editing is not a cost-effective method of preparing a report. It ends up wasting resources because it ignores possible fundamental problems ("Is the *content* right?" "Does the *structure* make sense?") in order to deal with more superficial ones ("Should there be a comma here?").

Diving right into a line-by-line edit can actually aggravate serious problems because it gives the report a superficial gloss that can make you reluctant to pursue really necessary substantive changes. Those sentences, paragraphs, or pages you're planning to polish might in fact need to be cut from the document, expanded, or rearranged in ways that will mean all your premature polishing is wasted.

The approach to revising and editing we recommend is consistent with systems thinking: Begin by looking at the document as a whole, then look at progressively smaller divisions: major sections, subsections (including visuals), paragraphs, sentences, words, punctuation, and (finally) other "mechanical" points. Starting with a good first draft, you must now fill out, cut down, reshape, rearrange, and correct the report in order to mold it into the product that will best serve the business system for which you are designing it. Only after you have revisited the draft with these activities specifically in mind can you begin finishing (see Chapter 8).

The most efficient way to improve your entire report is to revise and edit by sweeps:

Preliminary review by a peer should come only *after* these sweeps.

1. **Revise and Edit for Substance**: Make sure that the report has the coverage it needs, that the right elements are covered in the right proportions, and that the material you include is accurate.
2. **Revise and Edit for Structure**: Check the overall structure as well as the structure of each major section, each minor section, and each paragraph.
3. **Revise and Edit for Style**: Make sure the sentences and words you choose are clear, direct, and effective.

When you've finished your three sweeps, the document you print out should be a good, mid-level draft you can show to a peer for a preliminary review. The steps that lead to a final draft (such as deciding on a page design) are discussed in subsequent chapters.

REVISING AND EDITING FOR SUBSTANCE

The best way to discover what needs to be modified on the substantive level is to read quickly through a typed copy of the draft, looking for three things: coverage, proportion, and accuracy.

Coverage

Now is the time to verify that the report really has covered all the ground it should: Does it respond to its circumstances adequately? Does it fulfill its objectives? Does it satisfy its audiences?

Suppose you had written a first draft of a report proposing a new process for infusing innovation into your company, and you realized upon seeing the whole thing on paper that you had two large problems your audience would consider very important: (1) you failed to specify who is responsible for integrating the entire process, and (2) the committee that reviews each innovation project at the end of step one is different from the committee responsible for initiating step two. There is no bridge between the committees.

These realizations are typical of the kinds of problems you may not notice in a piece of writing until you have completed one full draft. Such realizations usually do not call for a major rewrite, just for additions—probably a recommendation about placing "ownership" of the entire innovation process in the hands of one particular vice president (to address the first problem), and a short paragraph about lines of communication (to address the second problem). You can add such details without difficult changes in structure. If writing the new material suggests further gaps that (1) still fall within the scope of your assignment, (2) would advance your objectives, and (3) will help your audience use the document, you are still not finished writing. But as you make each of these adjustments in coverage, you can at least feel good about being well on your way to a much improved second draft. What's really happening is that you're becoming more aware of your assignment, which means you're getting closer to taking control of it.

Proportion

Another aspect of your writing that you can see only when you have completed a draft is *proportion.* While you are checking on coverage, you may see subsections or even whole sections of the report that seem either too large or too small in proportion to one another. Suppose that in an investigative report on production-line problems at a manufacturing plant, you claim in your introduction that three problems affecting production are more or less equally severe: unsanitary conditions, equipment malfunctions, and production bottlenecks. When you come to the headings that expand on each of the problems, however, you notice you've devoted two pages to the first problem, half a page to the second, and two-and-a-half pages to the third. Having attributed equal importance to all three problems, you now find these lengths of their treatment are out of proportion. Now, with the calm and critical eye of an editor, you must ask yourself why the draft turned out as it did and what you're going to do about it.

It may be that you simply know a great deal more about problems 1 and 3 than about problem 2, and writing the draft has revealed your need to gather more information on problem 2. Go do it! Remember the recursive nature of writing; you must go back to research when you need more information. It would be foolish to give short shrift to a point because you failed to research it adequately. It would be worse to pad a section with irrelevancies to make it *look* proportional to the other points.

You may decide, however, that problem 2 does not deserve the treatment 1 and 3 received, either because it is easier to explain, or because it is not as severe as the other two. Aha! Your revising and editing have revealed something to you. Maybe you should add some introductory statement to the effect that problem 2 needs only a brief explanation but remains as severe as the others, or you may decide to rerank the problems. Alternatively, you may decide that all three really do deserve equal treatment, but you just went overboard in writing about 1 and 3, so you will want to prune them back.

One of the biggest problems all writers face is their own closeness to their subject.

Looking at proportion also helps you think about the relationship between sections of text and the important system-responsive character of the report. Suppose one of your major objectives in an 80-page problem-solving report is to convince a very skeptical audience that problem X really does exist and poses a serious threat. No matter how obvious the solution to the problem may have seemed to you when you were writing the first draft, you still have to devote more than a couple of pages to arguing your position to your readers. One of the major problems writers must overcome is their own closeness to what they write. Be willing to expand, contract, or shuffle the elements in your report to make your writing meet the needs of the larger enterprise.

Accuracy

The final part of substantive revising and editing is to find and correct any substantive errors in the text. When that first draft exploded from your fingers onto the computer screen or yellow pad, you probably made a few mistakes of fact, or at least some statements that should be qualified. A common error, for example, is an ambiguous or unqualified statement that should be clarified or qualified. You may have written that customers using your company's new microchip modem are experiencing high failure rates, but now you need to ask yourself some tough questions about that statement. If you do not, your readers will. What is the specific degree of failure, and how is that failure being measured? Are *all* machines using the chips having problems with them, or just *most* of them? Or maybe just *some* of them—or just some of them you have heard about? You are right not to let such qualifications choke your flow of ideas when you are writing the first draft. Now that you've got your ideas on paper, however, it's time to revise and edit its substance for clarity, completeness, and correctness. Read your first draft critically for distortions of fact, emotional excesses, snap judgments, unwarranted claims—all those things that spilled out in the excitement of writing but that should now be cleaned up by the calm of editing.

REVISING AND EDITING FOR STRUCTURE AND FUNCTION

The real test of structure is whether your *readers* understand what you are trying to say.

Structure refers to the way in which the elements of the report support one another, while *function* denotes what each section of the report is designed to accomplish. While structure and function cannot be completely separated from substance, it still makes sense to conduct a second editing and revising sweep that focuses only on these elements. When you revise and edit at the level of structure and function, you should focus on (1) moving from larger to smaller units, (2) making your report coherent, and (3) making your paragraphs effective.

Move from Larger to Smaller Units

First look at the overall organization of your report to be sure that, after being fleshed out and trimmed down, your project still has the structure best suited to the assignment you are trying to fulfill. Make sure you are using the structure that will best accomplish your objectives in connection with your audience(s), that will make the report easy for readers to use, and that allows for the proper scope.

Once you have checked the big picture, look at each section of the report. For example: Does the introduction narrate the history of the problem in an effective sequence? Does it orient the reader to the subject matter of the report? Does it prepare the reader for the conclusions and recommendations that follow? Does it lead the reader to feel about things as you do? Consider each section and subsection and its orientation to the system within which you are working. A full-blown, formal report will usually have the following components (a checklist for the contents of each appears in Chapter 8):

Front matter:	Cover Letter
	Title Page
	Executive Summary
	Table of Contents
	List of Figures and Tables
Body:	Recommendations
	Background
	Conclusions
	Discussion
Back matter:	Bibliography
	Appendices

Within each major section there will also be subsections to review for structure and function. For each subsection, ask yourself whether the organization is still the best it can be (as discussed in Chapter 3). For example, if you are looking at your recommendations, what about that fourth one? Should it really be listed in fourth place, as it is now, or should it be repositioned? Are the recommendations in the best order? Are you proceeding in the order of most important to least important, or easiest to implement to hardest, or least expensive to most expensive—or what? Will this order be obvious to your reader?

One important function of the second sweep is to make sure all the report's parts work together.

Ask yourself, "Is everything where it should be to advance my objectives and best serve my audiences?" That item you planned to relegate to the appendix—is it really that marginal? Perhaps you could at least refer to it briefly in the introduction. Or perhaps you got carried away with some material in the introduction that you see now had best be transferred to the appendix. The point is, during the second sweep you should check your report from the top down, making sure that each section is doing what it is supposed to, is in the place it should be, and is ordered internally so as best to serve your purposes and readers.

Make Your Report Coherent

So far you have largely been checking to make sure that the individual blocks of information in your report are complete, well proportioned, and well ordered; now you must make absolutely sure that they all work together. When you wrote your first draft, you probably wrote in "chunks" of prose triggered by the points in your outline. In a first draft, these chunks will be connected to each other with varying degrees of success. Now that you are editing for coherence, you will need to check the following features more closely.

Table of contents.   You have been making changes in your draft. Make sure the table of contents exactly corresponds to the wording and order of all the headings in your report.

Introduction.   This word means "to draw in." An introduction should orient the readers' thoughts and feelings toward the material they are about to read, and should function as a kind of road map that carries them into the terrain of the document. It should show the reader where each element stands in the report, the order in which the elements appear, and how to recognize them. The introduction creates coherence by reinforcing the logical order of the report. Both your report proper and each major section should have an introduction.

The most important element of an introduction is the overview. An overview states the sequence of main ideas about to be addressed. Here, for example, is the overview of this chapter's section on editing for substance:

> The best way to discover what needs to be modified on the substantive level is to read quickly through a typed copy of the draft looking for three things: coverage, proportion, and accuracy.

Notice that our second-level subheads in the major section on revising and editing for substance correspond exactly to those three points, in that order. When you are revising and editing your own documents, make sure that your introductions include such overviews.

Repetition that helps your audience is *not* foolish.

Conclusion.   Conclusions help coherence by repeating the sequence of your main ideas, often in modified forms. Writers sometimes neglect conclusions at the ends of major sections or other appropriate places because they run out of steam, they think the conclusion is now obvious, or because they do not want to seem repetitious. But repetition that supports your objectives and helps your audience is *not* foolish redundancy. Check your draft to be sure that you have used conclusions helpfully and advantageously.

Headings.   Check to see that all your headings are strong and descriptive and that they correspond closely to the subject matter of the sections. If your report uses too many one-word subheadings, for example, consider expanding them into more functional phrases (either statements or questions).

Also, check on the parallel structure of your headings. For example, in a report on problems with a new line of laptop computers, you may run across a sequence of headings like these:

Small Keys Make Typing Awkward
Screen Brightness Insufficient
Rough Handling of CPU

Revise the headings to make them grammatically parallel:

Small Keys Make Typing Awkward

Dim Screen Tires the Eyes

Rough Handling Easily Damages CPU

Or shorten the headings this way:

Keys Too Small

Screen Too Dim

CPU Too Delicate

Whatever form you choose, make sure that each section's headings are coordinated in tense and parallel in structure; these qualities help readers recognize the relationship between blocks of text and do wonders for coherence.

Transitions.   To improve a report's coherence, make sure you have used enough transitions—those sentences, phrases, and words that show how pieces of text are related. Transitions should provide coherence on every level of the report. Transitions between major and minor sections might require whole sentences or even paragraphs; between smaller blocks of text they may be no more than a word or phrase. Sometimes these are simply repeated words or phrases that connect one sentence to another. Others are explicit connectives such as "moreover," "as a result," "similarly," "later," and "nonetheless."

A transition-poor style of writing is very difficult to read because you have left it to the reader to figure out the textual relationships. We sometimes call this "data dumping." Which of these two paragraphs would you prefer to read?

We call this transition-poor style of writing "data dumping."

1. The contractor is still operating in two shifts. Cleared debris is now being piled. No burning at all is being permitted. The continued dry weather has produced extreme fire hazard conditions. No power equipment is permitted to operate when the relative humidity is below 20 percent.

2. The contractor is still operating in two shifts, and cleared debris is now being piled. Even so, no burning at all is being permitted, since the continued dry weather has produced extreme fire-hazard conditions. Not only is burning prohibited, but no power equipment is permitted to operate when the relative humidity is below 20 percent.

The additional transitional words in the second version make it much easier to read.

There is an adage among good writers: The harder it is to write, the easier it is to read—and vice versa. If you make your reader do mental work that you should have done, such as figuring out how one passage relates to another, you will not have a happy reader.

Make Your Paragraphs Effective

Never present your reader with a solid page of text; always have at least one paragraph break.

Check that every paragraph has a clear topic sentence (one that states explicitly what the paragraph is about), and that you develop (support) that topic adequately. If the topic sentence calls for extensive development, do not worry that you have made a paragraph too long. In fact, long and short paragraphs should be interspersed for variety. If you find that you have created a long, unrelieved block of prose that you think should be broken up into more than one paragraph (say, more than a page), be sure that you link the resulting shorter paragraphs logically. Use transition words to make them cohere.

The effectiveness of your paragraphs often comes from how you use mini-patterns within paragraphs to develop them. For example, if your topic sentence calls for a simple listing of coordinate facts, use simple transitions that show addition or coordination, such as "and," "also," and "in addition." Conceptually, this mini-pattern might look like this:

> We now have excellent reasons for merging with Acme Electronics:
>   A, *and*
>   B, *and*
>   C.
> *In addition*, there is Acme's knowledge of X,
> *and* their record of doing Y.

Fleshed out with words, the mini-pattern might sound like this:

> We now have excellent reasons for merging with Acme Electronics. Their product line complements ours without duplicating it. In addition, placing our products in their outlet stores will nearly double the availability of our products to customers. Most important, the regulatory climate is now extremely favorable for such a merger. As an added plus, there is Acme's knowledge of European markets, and their record of successfully expanding into new countries.

You may even decide to use a bulleted list for these points. However, if your topic calls for another pattern of development—a subordinating pattern, for example—you must be sure the paragraph sends those signals, using all the necessary signposts ("*While* we have some excellent reasons for merging with Acme, there are, *unfortunately*, some drawbacks. *Granted*, A and B favor the merger; *but . . .* ").

Finally, check the first paragraph in your introduction, and the first paragraphs of any introductions you may have written for major sections, to see if they are real beginnings or just "warm-ups." Many writers waste several sentences, or even several paragraphs, making very general introductory remarks that do little to focus the reader on the topic of the report. And *then* only after spinning their wheels do these writers produce a good sentence or paragraph that actually introduces the topic of the report. For example:

Check carefully for "warm-up" paragraphs —throat-clearing verbiage that needs to be deleted.

> Automobiles are a subject on which much has been written. Certainly much of the progress of civilization in the twentieth century has depended increasingly on the

widespread use and manufacture of the automobile. The importance of the automobile to the American economy and way of life hardly needs to be explained to the reader.

This report will discuss the Engineering Department's efforts to develop a new controller design for variable-speed windshield wipers . . .

Clearly, in this example, the first paragraph is much too general to introduce the report, which is about a proposed new controller design for windshield wipers. If you find warm-up paragraphs like these in one of your drafts, remove them. Often, as in this case, the second paragraph opens with a good introductory sentence that can stand very well on its own.

REVISING AND EDITING FOR STYLE

Management's surveys have demonstrated that a large amount of its language has been not only incomprehensible to the people it is trying to reach, but enormously expensive in money, time, and misunderstanding as well. It is high time the American businessman discovered the English language—it would be very useful to him.
—"The Language of Business," *Fortune*

There are a number of general stylistic changes you can make that will improve virtually any business report—usually by about 1,000 percent. Here are eight of the most important:

- Change passive voice to active voice.
- Turn verbs masquerading as nouns back into verbs.
- Cut deadwood.
- Dump jargon.
- Break up long strings of nouns/adjectives.
- Adjust the proportion of prepositional phrases to clauses.
- Use parallel form for parallel ideas.
- Make long sentences readable (usually that means making them shorter).

Change Passive Voice to Active Voice

Normally, the grammatical subject of a sentence is also the *agent* in the sentence. Passive sentence constructions invert the simple order of "agent—verb—object."

Active voice:

Passive voice makes readers work harder.

The customer bought the package.
        Agent   Verb   Object

In this active sentence the agent (which is also the grammatical subject) is in the "normal" or first position. In a passive sentence, that ordering is reversed.

Passive voice:

The package was bought by the customer.
     O   *V*   *A*

In this passive sentence the agent has become the object of a prepositional phrase at the end of the sentence. The object of the verb's action has now moved to the front of the sentence, in the subject position. It has become the grammatical subject of the sentence, but it still receives the verb's action. Thus the "normal" order of "agent—verb—object" has been inverted.

Some passive constructions drop the subject/agent of the sentence entirely, leaving the reader to guess the agent from the context of the prose.

The package deal was approved.
 S but not A   *V*

When you use passive voice, you make your readers work harder; they must mentally invert the pieces of the sentence in order to understand it. If you have omitted the subject/agent in the process of writing your passive construction, the reader must figure that out, too. None of this seems too difficult in the short sentence above, but the difficulty increases with the number and length of passives and the complexity of the material. Consider the following passages, one full of passive voice and one full of active voice:

Poor passage; too many passives

It was found that information concerning readings associated with the reactor drain tank cells was not obtained. These calibrations are needed so that a determination of tank levels can be made and permission can be obtained to resume operations. A system must be established so that prompt readings may be gathered when data is needed on a regular basis.

Better passage; active voice creates natural patterns and discloses subjects and objects

Inspectors found that operators had not yet recorded readings for drain tank cells in the reactor. Plant managers need these readings to determine whether tanks were at safe levels so they can ask permission from inspectors to resume operations. We must establish a regular system whereby operators get readings to managers promptly.

Although passive voice is not the only problem with the first passage, the main thing to notice here is that the active voice version was much easier to read. Why? Mainly because you can tell who did (or did not do) what, and you do not have to read backward.

There are, of course, appropriate places to use passive voice; for example, a passive construction sometimes makes for an effective transition:

Never use passive voice to obscure or hide responsibility when your audience will want to understand *exactly* who deserves credit or blame.

The best feature of this new machine is its simple safety mechanism. This mechanism can be set by inexperienced operators as easily as by experienced personnel.

There may be times when you do not *want* to state the agent of an action, perhaps because it is not important who did something: "The test tubes were washed." But you should never use passive voice to hide responsibility when your audience would want to understand exactly who is to be blamed or credited.

Turn Verbs Masquerading as Nouns Back into Verbs

As you revise and edit for style at the sentence level, you can make sentences shorter, snappier, and more direct by turning some nouns into verbs. (Some editors call this *denominalizing*.) The tip-off to the presence of a verb masquerading as a noun is a noun combined with a "fluff" verb:

Management conducted an investigation into the problem.

The fluff verb, "conducted," sets up "investigation" as a noun. But since *investigation* is really the main idea of the sentence, why not express it as a vigorous, active verb? This change will also make the sentence more *concise*.

Management *investigated* the problem.

In fact, your original prose may have combined passive voice and nominalization.

An investigation into the problem was conducted by management.

Often, denominalizing and switching from passive to active voice work together to create more direct, vigorous, readable sentences. This example is burdened with three nominalizations and passive voice:

There was a review of the proposal and a ruling by the committee, but no explanation was offered for their decision.

Here the fluff elements are the "There was" opening and the "was offered" verb. Passive construction blurs the sentence even further. You should be able to see a good rewrite in a flash:

The committee reviewed and ruled on the proposal but did not explain its decision.

Cut Deadwood

We've learned that "weasel words," those empty or cleverly disguised words and phrases that seem to say one thing but really mean another (or say nothing at all!),

are the common parlance of business writing. . . . We avoid the direct style of state-
ments like, "We should go forward with this venture because it is a moneymaker."
Instead, we have a tendency to write, "It is recommended that this venture be con-
sidered for implementation because of its potential for profit-making returns."
—Carol M. Barnum, Ph.D., "Writing to the Bottom Line," *Sky*, May 1989

Another way to make your writing more concise is by cutting deadwood.
Deadwood refers to all those inflated phrases and unnecessary words—what
Barnum calls "weasel words"—that clog professional writing:

> Due to the fact that we did not possess the data prior to our departure, we were not
> in a position at that point in time to render assistance to the client.

Cut all the deadwood, and you get:

> Because we did not have the data before leaving, we could not help the client.

Many of those unneces-
sary or inflated words and
phrases that clog business
writing today we suspect
are "weasel words":
expressions intended to
confuse the reader,
obscure responsibility, or
avoid confronting an
unpleasant fact.

Here are just a few deadwood words and phrases, along with some of their
shorter, crisper equivalents:

Deadwood	*Better Alternatives*
aggregate (noun)	sum
approximately	about
ascertain	find out, learn
at the present time	now
at this point in time	now
become cognizant with	know, learn, find, realize
construct (verb)	build
deleterious	harmful
demonstrate	show
due to the fact that	because, since
effectuate	do, cause
encounter	find
endeavor (verb)	try
equivalent	equal
facilitate	help
for the purpose of	for, to
forward (verb)	send
in a position to	can, be able
in order to	to
in the event that	if

in the near future	soon
in view of the fact that	because, since
initial	first
initiate	start
it is our opinion	we think, believe
modification	change
occasion (verb)	cause
on the part of	for
optimum	best
prior to the start of	before
procure	get
purchase (verb)	buy
regarding	about
reimburse	repay
subsequent to	after
sufficient	enough
terminate	stop, end
transmit	send
under date of	on
until such time as	until
utilize	use
we are in receipt of	we have
we would appreciate	please

Dump Jargon

Never fear to use little words. Big, long words name little things. All big things have little names, such as life and death, war and peace, dawn, day, night, hope, love, and home. Learn to use little words in a big way.

Most uses of jargon and other buzzwords are unnecessary and annoying.

We use the term "jargon" to refer not so much to big words as to the specialized or technical language of any trade, fellowship, organization, class, or profession. "Etiolate," "reticuloendothelial," "ethology," and "oneiromancy" are jargon terms. While they are, respectively, everyday fare to botanists, microbiologists, animal behaviorists, and those who study dream divination, to the rest of us these "big words" are barriers to communication rather than bridges.

Determining when to use jargon, "buzzwords," or technical vocabulary and nomenclature is a complex issue. In business settings most uses of jargon and buzzwords are really unnecessary—and annoying. Beyond that general principle, here are three guidelines that should be helpful to you in your revising and editing:

1. If you are writing only for your immediate superiors, or for other corporate insiders, use the standard corporate vocabulary and nomenclature you all share. But be sure you use jargon only where it represents the best instrument for making your point. Rookies and newcomers tend to flaunt their use of the "in-group" language to draw attention to their newly acquired membership in the club. Such overuse of jargon may well have the effect of labeling you as a new kid on the block instead of an old hand.

2. When you are writing for outsiders—clients, customers, critics, regulators, environmental or other advocacy organizations—keep jargon and buzzwords to a minimum. You do not want to sound superior or distant, and you especially do not want to be misunderstood—or not understood at all. "Plain English, please" should be your motto in all such situations.

3. Be especially careful to avoid jargon and buzzwords in any communications that go to the general public (including the media). Some people delight in catching—and ridiculing—corporate executives who write about "negative investment outcomes" instead of "losses," or "corporate downsizing" for "selective firing."

"At IBM, the term for firing workers is M.I.A., or management-initiated attrition." New York Times, January 20, 1993.

Break Up Long Strings of Nouns/Adjectives

Usually, the shorter version of a statement saves the reader more energy than the longer one, but in the case of long noun strings, this is not so. Look over your prose for noun/adjective strings, such as this one:

Stacks of nouns and adjectives waste more of the readers' energy than they save of the writer's.

> employee compensation level evaluation procedures

Such strings stack modifiers one on top of another without doing enough to show the relationship among the parts; consequently, they leave the reader to do the work of unpacking and sorting. Consider dividing any such string of four or more nouns or adjectives into several short phrases. For example, the five-word stack above becomes:

> procedures for evaluating the compensation level of employees

Not only are such strings as "employee compensation level evaluation procedures" hard to understand, they are often ambiguous as well. Notice that the following string has two possible (and very different) meanings:

> New motorcycle motor durability equipment engineering tests

This string may mean:

> Engineers are using new equipment to test the durability of motorcycle motors.

Or it may mean:

> Engineers are performing new tests on the equipment that makes motorcycle motors durable.

What exactly is "new" in the original sentence? Motorcycles? Motors? Equipment? Tests? Your writing must clearly show which adjective modifies which noun.

Adjust the Proportion of Prepositional Phrases to Clauses

Using more than two or three prepositional phrases per clause begins to wear on your readers because they are forced to put more and more material on "hold" as they try to figure out what the phrases modify. Try wading through this sentence (prepositional phrases are in brackets):

The combination of deadwood, lack of parallel structure, and overuse of prepositional phrases results in sentences no one will read willingly.

> Aside [from the need] [for adjustment] [of the allocations] [to new heads] [of departments] [in the company], the proper line [of execution] [of all] [of the details] [of the plan] should result [in no further increases] [in the funds] necessary to expend [on the implementation] [of the projects] [under the supervision] [of the various divisions] [of our organization].

While we hope your own prose will not be anywhere near this smothered with prepositional phrases, you should at least do some spot checking for this problem. If you find a number of sentences with three or more prepositional phrases per clause, revise and edit them to reduce that proportion.

Use Parallel Form for Parallel Ideas

The principle of parallelism applies at the phrase level as well as at the heading level. In particular, look for sentences that list items and see if you have used parallel form effectively. If you have written,

> Our plans are to consolidate routes, reduce the number of drivers, and we're also planning on upgrading the computer dispatch system.

change it to:

> We plan to consolidate routes, reduce the number of drivers, and upgrade the computer dispatch system.

Make Long Sentences Readable

Many such problems are caused by the sheer length of the sentences.

In a 1992 memo to its officers and directors, the Railway Supply Association quoted some of the "timely ideas" of its first president nearly a century earlier. See what you can make of the following long and confusing sentence, spoken by "the then president of the Association of Railway Air-brake Men" at the first annual meeting of the association in 1894:

May the pleasures which will be derived from this meeting arise from the consciousness of duties well performed and knowledge gained, and when we have returned to our respective duties, let each, bearing in mind what he has learned, endeavor to perform them in such a manner that when the time of our next convention draws near, those to whom we look for leave of absence and transportation, can grant the same with an assurance that they are pursuing a course, which will be amply justified by the benefits their companies will receive through greater economies and increased efficiencies, due to the educational methods of this Association, and what little, if any, it may cost their respective companies, will be as bread cast upon the waters.

This sentence suffers from half a dozen of the problems described in previous sections. By now you should have no trouble recognizing them. When deadwood, lack of parallel structure, disproportion of prepositional phrases to clauses, and other problems combine in a long sentence, the reader is left to sort out a real tangle.

Here is another example of confusion caused by long sentences riddled with various stylistic problems. This letter from a former Commissioner of Internal Revenue to former Secretary of Defense Melvin R. Laird was distributed as a "fact sheet" by the IRS to answer questions. Draw your own conclusions about its stylistic qualities.

Internal Revenue Service   Fact Sheet
Public Information   November 30, 1970

<u>Moving Expenses of Military Personnel</u>
The Commissioner of Internal Revenue today sent the following letter to the Secretary of Defense:

Dear Mr. Secretary:

In response to your recent questions with respect to reporting and withholding requirements of the Department of Defense under the Tax Reform Act of 1969 for moving expenses of servicemen from one residence to another, we have reached the following conclusions:

1. There will be a moratorium on withholding and reporting by the military services reimbursements of servicemen through December 31, 1971.
2. For at least the 1970 and 1971 taxable years, individual servicemen will not be required to account in their own tax returns for any reimbursements of moving expenses in kind, but will be required to report cash reimbursements of moving expenses, subject in general to an offsetting deduction for expenses actually paid. (I might add that in no event is there any requirement for military personnel to report reimbursements of the expense of government-ordered travel in cash or in kind where no change of residence is involved, as in the case of transfers to and from combat zones, temporary assignments, etc.)

3. Where moving expenses paid by an individual serviceman exceed his reimbursements for such expenses, such excess amounts may be allowable as a deduction. In order for the serviceman to have the opportunity to take advantage of deduction authorized under the Tax Reform Act of 1969 which were not previously allowed, regulations describing such additional deductions will be issued during the coming calendar year.

In reaching these conclusions we are mindful of the fact that military moves are mandatory and at the convenience of the government and allowances for cost of moves are strictly limited. We are advised that there is not provision for reimbursement to servicemen of the type of indirect cost sometimes provided by private industry for which the Tax Reform Act of 1969 imposes dollar limitations on deductibility, with the consequence that military personnel are rarely, if ever, given reimbursements in kind for expenses which, if included in income, they would not be able to deduct.

Again, let me assure you that in your proposed regulations we will make every effort to treat moving expenses in a manner to guarantee fair treatment to all military men and women.

Sincerely yours,

Randolph W. Thrower
Commissioner

An Air Force captain by the name of Richard Koeteeuw sent the following letter to Commissioner Thrower after reading the "fact sheet":

January 22, 1971

Dear Mr. Thrower,

You've *thrown* me! I *think* your letter to Secretary Laird means that servicemen can relax for a year about paying taxes on PCS moving expenses. I *think* you have said you're now aware of the special circumstances of military personnel and their moves. The reason I'm not sure is your sentence length. Assuming it was unintentional, you'd be much clearer if you'd limit your sentences to no more than 25 words (standard English principles).

Just a little note to inform you and to thank you (if you really are aware of what I think you said you were).

Sincerely,

Richard I. Koeteeuw
Capt. USAF

Thrower passed on this letter to William I. Greener, then Director of the IRS's Public Information Division, who replied to the captain with this letter:

February 9, 1971

Dear Captain Koeteeuw:

Thank you for your letter. The Commissioner read it. He sent it to me. I am answering for him. You are right in your recommendations. Taxes, as you know, are very complicated.

As a former Air Force officer, now retired, I thank you for your interest. As a former Captain assigned to Mather [Air Force Base], I envy you.

Sincerely,

William I. Greener, Jr.
Director
Public Information Division

P.S. You figured the letter out correctly.

Greener's reply is humorous because he deliberately goes overboard, making almost all his sentences *very* short and crisp. Still, his prose is undeniably easier to read than Thrower's! Thrower's letter to Laird is full of stylistic problems. The long sentences, in and of themselves, do not cause all these problems, but they certainly make them worse. Captain Koeteeuw could have given a more extensive critique of Thrower's letter, but the flaw he did point out was definitely a major one.

Such excesses do not imply that you should never write long sentences. They do suggest, however, that you should carefully review long sentences throughout your report. Be sure that modifying words and phrases are not too far from the words they modify. Keep an eye on proportion and on parallel structure. Reduce jargon, denominalize, and use active voice. Be sure you have worked in plenty of short and medium-length sentences between the long ones. Do not confront your reader with unbroken stretches of long, needlessly hard to understand sentences.

CONCLUSION

Wherever you work, and at whatever level, clear writing is one sure way to lift your report above the ordinary.

Using active voice rather than passive, bringing nouns out of hiding and changing them into verbs, untangling modifier strings, cutting deadwood and jargon—all such measures will distinguish your report from the ordinary. The question for many business writers is, "Am I *willing* to stand out this much?" Inertia is a powerful force, and sounding the same as everyone else (however bad that is) may seem like pretty safe protective coloration. You may be worried that your superiors will not like your style if it departs too much from what they are used to seeing.

We believe doing something better is a risk worth taking. Here's a true story that illustrates this principle: One of the authors recently edited an annual "Surveillance and Maintenance" report for the Decontamination and Decommissioning (D&D) Program at a major research installation. He edited the report to conform to the principles in this chapter and returned it to the Manager of Risk Assessment for D&D, who had assigned the editing job. This report was important, and the manager was personally delighted at its new look and sound, but he paced the halls worrying that his superiors would not like it—the report was "too different!" Upper management was used to reading passive voice, jargon, and all the rest; would they not consider this report "unprofessional"? After some genuine soul searching, the manager sent the report up the line. A week later, he got a call from a corporate vice president, who enthusiastically told him it was one of the best reports he had ever read. That report helped the manager get some important career recognition. Good writing can help you the same way.

PRACTICE

Revising Headings, Paragraphs, and Sentences

1. Revising headings.   Here are the headings for a short report on the process of innovation at EnerCo, a diversified energy-resource management company. Your task is to rewrite the headings, making them grammatically parallel as appropriate.

The Innovation Process
> What is innovation?
> Why EnerCo needs to improve its innovation process
> Changes that need to be made

Discovering Needs for Innovation
> How does each innovation benefit EnerCo?
> Here's how the process of discovering needs works
> Responsibilities
> The role of integrated problem-solving teams
> One suggested approach for IPS teams to follow

Developing Innovation Ideas
> The Project Development Team
> Process of Innovation Project Development Proposal

How Innovative Projects Are Managed
     Process of Innovation Project Management
     "Fast-Track" Projects Have Right-of-Way
     How Is the Project Turnover Checklist Used?
Market Development is Key to Success
     Key points to account for the Market Development Team
     When does the product marketing cycle begin?

2. Revising paragraphs. Here is a short paragraph in which the sentence order has been scrambled. Your task is to put the sentences in the correct order, inserting transitions where necessary.

In recent years, rising material and energy costs have forced chemical-manufacturing process design toward greater use of heat integration and materials recycling. This trend reduces equipment overdesign. Higher performance demands are placed on the manufacturing process control system. The increasing complexity of today's manufacturing processes has forced designers to consider the entire plant when designing a process control system. Designers can apply steady-state analysis tools to process-gain matrices in order to obtain information about optimum control-system design. Manufacturing process control-system design has historically been based largely on the individual designer's experience and has focused on individual unit operations. The relative importance of various performance objectives must be considered during the design phase. A weighted analysis can represent the relative importance of each variable that needs to be controlled. This trend also reduces the availability of surge capacity that has frequently been used to lessen the impact of process disturbances. The results of applying the weighted analysis can give the designer valuable information about controller pairings, sensor locations, and the relative difficulty of the control problem for various heat-integration and materials-recycling schemes.

3. Revising sentences. The sentences below are poorly written in a number of ways. Revise each sentence to make it clear and effective.

1. It is to be noted that the 30 and 35 polymers almost had similar polydispersity indexes but large differences in molecular weight were exhibited.
2. The visualization of a time line intervalized with three different cycles is represented in Figure 4.
3. The accuracy of this method is far superior to classical sampling techniques since problems in sampling across demographic groups are avoided.
4. Since the beginning of history, aristocracies and governments have taxed the working class. Taxes affect everyone in the United States. A tax avoidance plan is an essential part of any financial portfolio.
5. This report presents a proven theory of successful business acumen through distribution, intuitive management philosophy, entrepreneurial finesse, incredible salesmanship, and intimate knowledge of audience.

6. The exception to this rule is the interest earned on bonds issued by state and local governments and municipalities which is tax exempt.

7. Computer-generated data has the advantage over mechanically produced data in that it is much more flexible in the various possible dimensions of the input as well as ease in *ad hoc* programming flexibility and responsiveness for the input.

8. Thus, by incorporating the seven subregional categories into a broader comparative model, basic assumptions regarding the entire regional status can be generated. In turn, by employing this comparative strategy, unknown status variables which are specific to each area can possibly be identified when the primary assemblages are subsequently isolated in a seven-site rank-order.

9. In most cases, complete temporal use range to index year value correspondence is not possible to achieve, so a degree of temporal underlap and overlap exists within this system as modified here.

10. Any fiscal planning subsystem requires considerable promulgation and synthesis at the division level to ensure efficacy of the resultant algorithm. A policy of redundant standardization performance implies anticipation of future growth dependence and preliminary testing in an evolutionary framework. Subsequent configuration finalization must be functionally concurrent with postulated stepwise interrelationships and full utilization of integral criteria qualifications.

7

Designing Your Pages

Page design refers to the visual appearance of pages. You do not have to make a deep study of graphic design in order to produce well-designed pages for your business reports. If you learn and employ a handful of fundamentals, your reports will be very professional-looking and visually effective. And even if you do have a graphics department to design your report, these fundamentals will give you a big advantage over most business writers, because you will be able to communicate intelligently—and save a great deal of time—when interacting with that department.

The basic principles of page design are simple.

Each page of a business report should be designed with the same considerations that have guided all your other report-writing choices: objectives, audiences, scope, and uses. No one knows these factors better than you. Your job now is to employ visual and graphic criteria that will help your writing balance all four of those considerations. You must create visual flow, balance, and continuity; group your elements logically; make your pages readable; make information easily accessible; emphasize important information; and create a pleasing aesthetic effect. In order to achieve these goals, you need to keep a handful of design principles in mind:

- See each page as a grid that holds moveable elements.
- Coordinate and balance the elements of pages.
- Emphasize important information.
- Make typeface readable and simple.
- Use a helpful heading scheme.
- Be consistent.

SEE EACH PAGE AS A GRID

Thinking of each page as a grid with various moveable elements helps you decide where to place elements and how big to make each one.

On your word-processing or desktop-publishing (DTP) system, or with pencil and paper (or even mentally), mark out borders and zones on your page to create a grid that will orient the various visual elements of the page. If you've ever typed a term paper in school, you know the basics of layout, because you have marked out grids with the tab and space bars to indent for paragraphs and quotations and to put space between headings and text. For the more complex demands of a business report, just extend this thinking to include making grids to accommodate visuals of various kinds and sizes, bulleted lists and other groupings of information, multiple levels of headings, and (at times) multicolumn formats. Figures 7.1 through 7.4 display simple grid layouts for one- and two-column page formats.

Once you are thinking in terms of grids, it is easier to look at each element of a page and consider how big it should be and where to display it in relation to the other elements. There are really only a few elements to think about: text, headings,

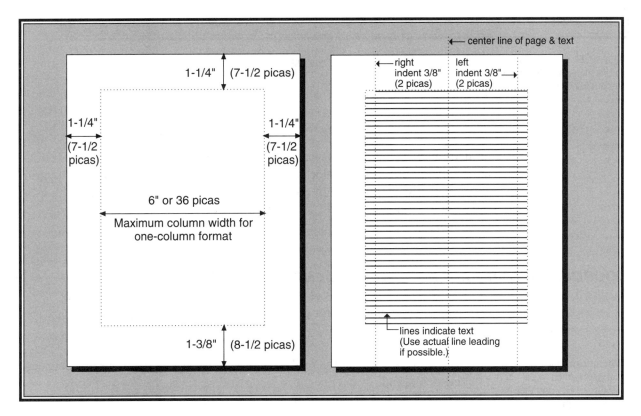

Figure 7.1   One-Column Format. Begin page layout by setting the margins; then establish the first level of left and right indents. Use a center line to center elements such as headings and some graphic elements.

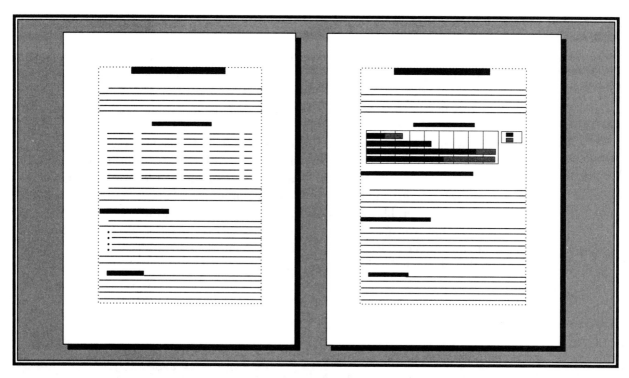

Figure 7.2 One-Column Format. Continue to develop the layout by roughing in headings and simple graphic elements. The left page shows how a table and bulleted list might be organized; the right incorporates a horizontal bar chart enclosed in a box that streches from margin to margin (for better sense of balance).

borders, lists, symbols,[1] visuals, and white space. Imagine the text (as well as almost everything else) as blocks, and be willing to move them around the grid experimentally. It's like one of those Chinese puzzles you used to play with as a kid—you keep moving the blocks around until you get the right pattern. Figure 7.5 shows some blocks you might arrange and rearrange.

COORDINATE AND BALANCE THE ELEMENTS OF PAGES

To a large degree, the rules for good coordination and balance in page design are simple:

Fashion magazines used to advise women to put on their jewelry and then take off one piece, in order to avoid overdoing it. The same applies to page design. *Less* is often *more*.

1. Design pages so that the reader can easily discern the relationships between elements, and
2. Balance the visual weights of elements on the page.

[1]The symbols we refer to fall into several categories, the two most important being "typographic spots" and "dingbats." Typographic spots are the visual signals that accompany a "bulleted list," but they need not always be round. Dingbats can be used as typographic spots or simply for emphasis or aesthetic effect.

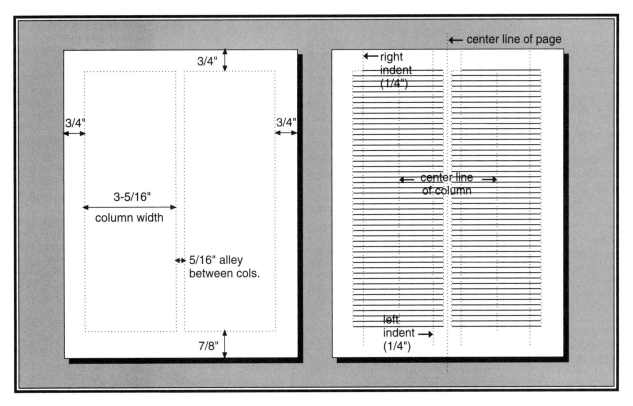

Figure 7.3 Two-Column Format. Begin a two-column page layout in similar fashion, setting margins, establishing the first level of left and right indents, and using center lines.

A simple example is arranging elements according to the way a reader's eye will scan the page—generally, from top to bottom, left to right. Make scanning as easy on the reader as possible, while maintaining a feeling of balance and proportion in the design. Which of the page designs shown in Figure 7.6 do you prefer?

Another example is coordinating visuals and text in a series of related drawings. In a one-column format this would involve a consistent way of nesting the visuals within the text, preparing the reader for each visual, and discussing each one in the same format. There are many possibilities, and they extend beyond simply making a hole in the body of the text to make room for a visual. For example, some text related to each visual might appear in bulleted form, in a "shadowbox" (a shaded-in area as in the lower right-hand corner of the right-hand page in Figure 7.7), or perhaps "boxed in" with the visual. In a two-column format, visuals and text should generally appear opposite each other, with visual clues such as horizontal bars or shading that show the reader when to read *across* and when to read *down* the page. A one-column format can achieve a similar effect by displaying visuals and the text connected with them on facing pages. Align the appropriate headings, visuals, and text. Use plenty of white space. White space is one of the most important organizing and aesthetic elements at your disposal.

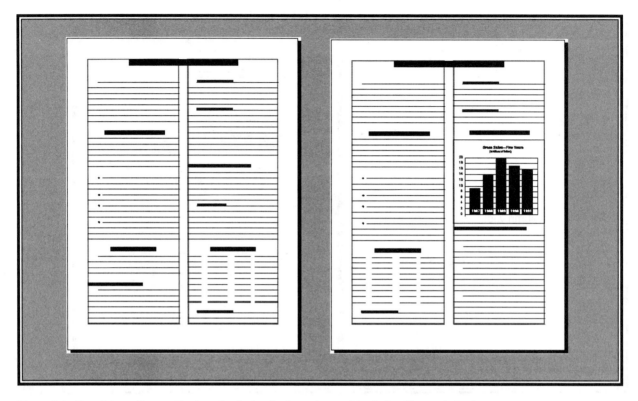

Figure 7.4   Two-Column Format. Continue developing the layout by roughing in headlines and simple graphic elements.

EMPHASIZE IMPORTANT INFORMATION

Successful page design makes important elements stand out automatically.

Remember those little pointing hands once used in advertisements? The printed hand is a cue to draw the reader's attention and emphasize a chunk of information. Emphasis is perhaps the most obvious "rhetorical effect" one can achieve through page design, yet few writers do it competently. The most they can think to do is to make words bigger, or capitalize or underline them in order to emphasize them. These are valid options, but the possibilities are much more extensive. The general rule is to make important information stand out without making it awkward or hard to read. One of the best ways to do this is to surround such information with white space. You can also surround it with borders of various kinds, set it off with bullets or other symbols, shade it, or make it break through lines in your grid for emphasis and aesthetic effect. *Experiment* with page layout until you are satisfied with the result. Consider the difference in emphasis between the two page designs shown in Figure 7.7.

USE READABLE TYPEFACES

Modern word processors offer a generous selection of typefaces, all of which can be produced instantly in a variety of sizes and styles (see Figure 7.8). This range of

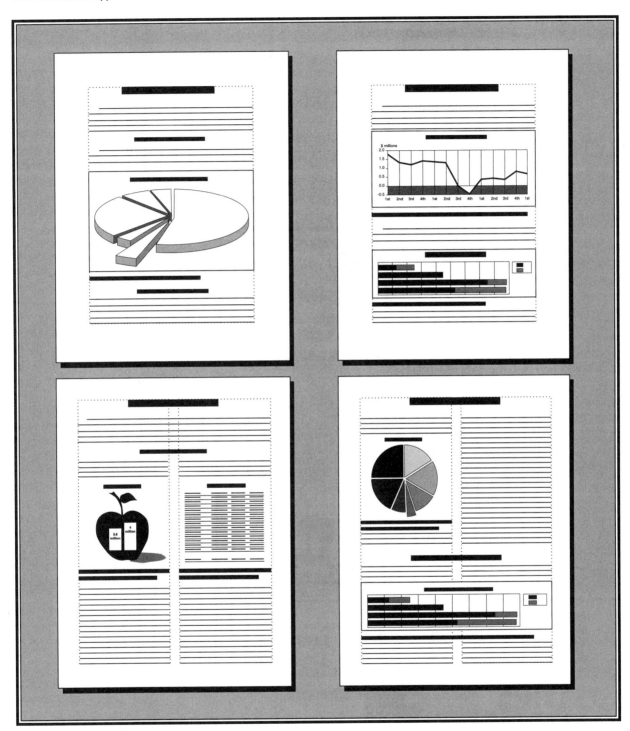

Figure 7.5 Moveable blocks of information on page layout grids in one- and two-column formats.

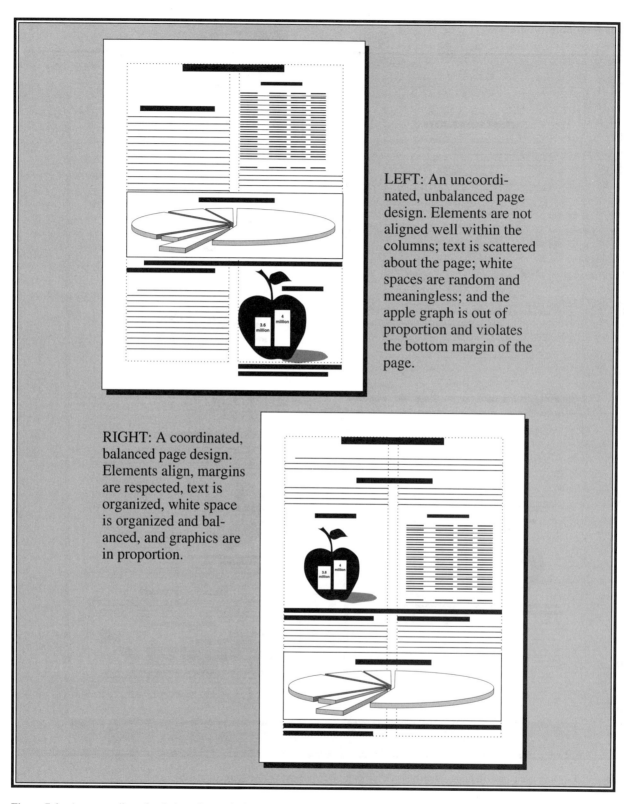

LEFT: An uncoordinated, unbalanced page design. Elements are not aligned well within the columns; text is scattered about the page; white spaces are random and meaningless; and the apple graph is out of proportion and violates the bottom margin of the page.

RIGHT: A coordinated, balanced page design. Elements align, margins are respected, text is organized, white space is organized and balanced, and graphics are in proportion.

Figure 7.6   An uncoordinated, unbalanced page design can make reading difficult.

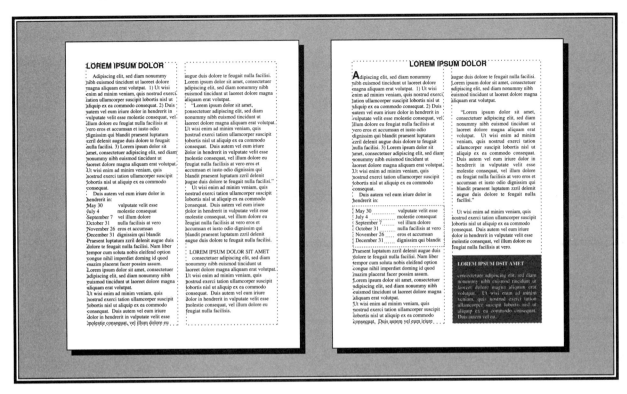

Figure 7.7   Page design that does not differentiate text versus one that does. Both pages may contain the same *words,* but the design on the right emphasizes particular pieces of information in a way that serves the report's objectives. Darkened area at lower right is called a "shadowbox."

choices seems wonderful—until you see the distressing visual mishmash many people produce when turned loose at the word processor. Many reports combine half a dozen or more typefaces and styles in varying sizes, with no discernible rationale behind the choices.

Choosing the typeface that best supports the rhetorical intent of the text is actually a very sophisticated undertaking. You can see why an advertisement for "Tiffany Glassware" may use a different typeface and style than "Anvils for Sale" (see Figure 7.9). But it is not a good idea to go through your report trying to match the subtle differences of typeface to the messages of pieces of text. In fact, we recommend the simplest possible route: Use a standard serif[2] typeface such as Times Roman for the main text and a standard sans serif[3] typeface such as Helvetica for headings. A 12-point[4] Roman is usually ideal for the main text. The same point size

[2]We call a typeface "serif" if its letters have decorative "caps" and "feet," like this "**A**." These cross-strokes are the serifs. The word "serif" is derived from Latin *scribere,* to write, and refers to the chisel marks ancient Romans left on letters while cutting them into monuments. We recommend a serif typeface for the main text because it provides additional visual cues for the reader, making text easier to read. Most *Americans* see it that way, at least.

[3]This of course means "without serif," and describes the entire class of typefaces that are "clean letters," without cross-strokes, such as the Helvetica typeface we recommend for headings.

[4]In printers' jargon, one point = 1/72 inch. A capital letter in an 18-point typeface, therefore, is about 1/4 inch high. Most word-processing software gives you the option of thinking in inches, millimeters, points, or "picas" (one pica = 12 points).

Roman type. **Extra Bold type.** Eras Book typeBookman type.

Helvetica type. **Helvetica Bold type.** Futura type. Futura Condensed type.

Italic. **Bold.** Underline. Shadow. Outline.

Italic, Bold, Underline. Underline, Shadow, Outline.

Figure 7.8 Various typefaces and type styles. Your word processor is loaded with them. Use them judiciously.

Tiffany Glassware

ANVILS FOR SALE

Figure 7.9 Different typefaces and styles deliver different effects. Match them to your purpose.

is fine for footnotes (or endnotes) and captions as well, though many people prefer to go down to 10-point type for those elements. If you want to set off an element—for instance, with boldface—go ahead, but use such type treatments with restraint.

As for *leading* (the space between lines), full double spacing is more convenient for the draft stages of your report; it makes editing easier. But by the time you are working on page design, you can see that something tighter than double spacing will look better. Once again, computers give you a range of choices; you are not restricted to choosing between double and single space. A good rule is to add about 20 percent to the height of the typeface for leading; so 10-point text might need 12 points of leading.

> The space between lines should be about the height of each line plus 20 percent.

USE A HELPFUL HEADING SCHEME

Headings are extremely important in business reports; they are the labels that describe the nature of blocks of information, the signposts that allow the reader to

FIRST-LEVEL HEADING

text text text text text text text text text text text text text text text text text text text text text text text text text text text text text text text text.

SECOND-LEVEL HEADING

text text text text text text text text text text text text text text text text text text text text text text text text text text text text text text text text.

Third-level Heading

text text text text text text text text text text text text text text text text text text text text text text text text text text text text text text text text.

<u>Fourth-level heading</u>. text text text text text text text text text text text text text text text text text text text text text text text text text text text.

Figure 7.10   A simple, four-level heading scheme.

find blocks of information and see their relationship to other blocks. The key to heading design is to make the status of a heading visible *at a glance*—that is, to make it obvious which headings are coordinate to each other, and which are superior or subordinate. You have seen heading schemes that rely on numbers to show rank (1.1, 1.2, 2.1.1.2, and so on). These may be helpful when the document will be used a great deal for reference, but in general, people do not like to deal with numerical headings because they offer so few clues as to the importance of the material following the heading. It is better to decide on a simple heading scheme, such as the one displayed in Figure 7.10, and use it consistently throughout your report.

This scheme differentiates headings by typeface, style, size, and placement:

- Level 1 = 18-point Helvetica bold, centered, all caps, with double space above and below heading.
- Level 2 = 12-point Helvetica bold, centered, all caps, with double space above and single space below heading.
- Level 3 = 12-point Helvetica bold, aligned with left margin, initial caps, with single space above and below heading.
- Level 4 = 12-point Helvetica bold, underlined, indented five spaces from left margin, with period after heading and text beginning on same line.

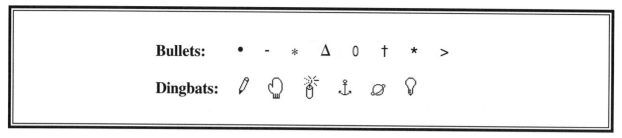

Figure 7.11   Bullets and dingbats come in many shapes and sizes. Use them to mark lists, draw attention to items, and signal types of information.

BE CONSISTENT

Whatever heading scheme you decide on, be consistent. Most word-processing software will allow you to custom tailor an electronic style sheet for margins, headings, footnote text, footnote reference, and other design elements. Take advantage of these tools. You can decide on size, spacing, style, and placement of many design elements for your report and make them part of your computer program. Thereafter, whenever you want to enter a heading or some other element onto the screen, you simply tell the computer which level of heading or what kind of footnote you are about to type in, and it automatically gives your entry the design features you decided on earlier. Pressing the return key (or whatever key your particular program specifies) will return you to normal text and margins. You do not have to think further, and consistency is guaranteed.

However, consistency in page design involves more than organizing headings. It means treating similar material in similar ways at all levels. For example, if you have been using bulleted lists for emphasis in a series of information chunks, do not suddenly drop the bullets and start using shaded boxes to encapsulate the chunks. Do not even change the bullets to asterisks unless you have a good reason to do so and you make that reason obvious to the reader. Readers depend on your page design to orient them to your material; do not confuse them.

There are many other features of page design that make for consistency: you can use running headers or footers,[5] you can use icons[6] or colors to mark related information, and you can spread certain designs over facing pages. It is just a matter of your time, available equipment, and inclination.

CONCLUSION

Modern word-processing systems, DTP software, and 600 dot-per-inch (DPI) laser printers have brought the art of the graphic designer within the lay person's reach.

---

[5] Identical information that appears in the top or bottom margin of each page or section of a report.

[6] Symbolic pictures. For example, you might use a key icon throughout your report to signal "key ideas," a train or airplane icon to symbolize movement of materials, and so on.

You may or may not be inclined to reach very far into that art. Remember, however, that just as you are ill-advised to depend on editors to do all your editing, so you are ill-advised to depend on graphic designers to do all your page design. In the first place, you may not even have access to one. In the second place, you may not have time to use one, or a designer may not be available to work with you within the time frame you require. Finally, there is no reason you yourself cannot learn to understand and then implement the simple principles of page design.

PRACTICE

Pages 40 and 41 in Chapter 3 provide sample text from a report entitled "The Freezing of Raw Materials during Rail Transportation." Use as much of that text as you need in creating the page designs for the documents specified below. *(Note: The point of this activity is to practice creating different page designs, not to write the accompanying text or to create the accompanying visuals. To indicate the places on your pages where text should appear, you can imitate the way the examples in this chapter do it, you can use the text from the report in Chapter 3, you can use lines of dashes, or you can use nonsense words.)*

1. Design a one-page "fact sheet" that your company will distribute to suppliers, freight carriers, customers, and others who may ask for information on the subject. Plan on a two-column layout with two small visuals.

2. Design a one-page executive summary to be distributed to the Board of Directors at its next meeting. You want this to be readable *at a glance*. No visuals are necessary, but displayed lists (and maybe a table) will be used.

3. You need to provide camera-ready copy for a write-up of this research that will go in the Transportation Research Institute's journal. The pages of the journal are 5" wide by 7" high, and you have been allotted a maximum of five pages. Within those limits, you want to be able to fit as much information as possible, whether through words or visuals, but you do not want the pages to look crowded. Design the pages for this article.

8

Checking and Using Your Report

By now your report should look and sound acceptable, and you may be eager to turn it in. We urge you *not* to submit your report until it has been checked at least one more time.

- First, check the report to be sure that all sections are functioning as they should and that footnotes, endnotes, and bibliographic materials are in proper form.
- Next, give your report a final read for grammatical correctness and mechanical accuracy (punctuation, spelling, capitalization, pagination, and so on).
- Finally, test the report on a knowledgeable friend and make any appropriate changes based on his or her evaluation. Only then will you be ready to submit the report—and to use it.

CHECKING YOUR REPORT

Checklists can help you make sure that each section of your report is performing as it should.

The easiest way to ensure that each section of the report is performing its function as it should is to use a checklist. The checklists provided here are for a very complete, very traditional report. You will need to modify them to fit your own writing projects.

Checklist for Front Matter

The front matter of a report consists of all the pages that come before the introduction. Except for the cover letter or letter of transmittal, which is a separate page or pages paper-clipped to the report proper, the pages making up the report's front matter are numbered with Roman numerals. The title page, although it is page "i," does not show its page number; the first page number shown should be on the following page, page "ii." Whether you place page numbers at the top or the bottom of the page, centered or otherwise, is a design choice entirely up to you. Just be sure you follow company standards, if any exist.

Check these points for each component of the front matter:

- Cover Letter

  Does the letter express a clearly formulated purpose?

  Are the letter's format and arrangement appropriate?

  Is the tone courteous and positive?

  Is the letter directed to the appropriate person and signed by the appropriate person? (If the signature will not be your own, the letter may have to wait for supervisory review.)

- Title Page

  Is the subject accurately and specifically indicated in the title?

  Are author name(s), company, place, date, and any other appropriate information included?

  Does the title page create a favorable impression?

- Abstract

  Does the abstract describe the report in a nutshell?

  Does it answer the questions, "What is this report about, and what does it conclude?"

- Copyright

  Is the copyright notice thorough and clear?

- Dedication and Acknowledgments (both optional)

  Is the dedication brief and appropriate?

  Are the acknowledgments arranged in proper order, and do they include all appropriate individuals and groups?

- Summary ("Executive Summary," "Management Summary")

  Does the summary convey only the important conclusions or recommendations that result from the research, analysis, or other work discussed in the body of the document?

  Does it discuss the implications of results/conclusions?

  Does it provide supporting information the reader needs in order to understand the implications of results/conclusions, yet avoid becoming an abridged narrative?

  Does it employ a logical rather than historical organization?

- Table of Contents

  Does the table of contents provide an overall view of the organization (sequence *and* groupings) of the report?

  Are all relevant headings from the text included?

  Do headings correspond exactly to those in the text?

  Is pagination correct in form, and does it correspond accurately with the report page numbers?

- List of Figures, List of Tables

  Do the titles of graphic and tabular materials correspond with pages in text?

  Are they in the correct order?

  Are titles self-explanatory?

- Foreword and Preface (both optional)

  Is the foreword positive, engaging, and written by an appropriate person?

  Does it place the report in the context of other relevant studies?

  Does the preface explain the circumstances surrounding the writing of the report, methods used for research, special problems encountered, and any other appropriate information?

Checklist for Main Text

The main text begins with the introduction and starts the Arabic page numbers. The first page of the introduction does not show the page number. Page numbers begin on the next page with "2."

- Introduction

  Does the introduction orient the reader to the subject matter of the report by providing background, purpose, and scope?

  Does it give main data sources?

  Does it capture the reader's attention?

  Does it avoid unnecessary detail?

  Does it provide a map (overview) of topics to come?

  Does it dispose the reader favorably to the rest of the report, especially recommendations?

- Conclusions

  Do conclusions satisfactorily summarize the major milestones reached in your discussion?

  Are they logically drawn and clearly argued?

- Recommendations

  Do recommendations state categorically what actions should be taken?
  Do they evolve logically from your conclusions?

- Discussion

  Does the discussion restate the objectives of the study?
  Does it make its points as concisely as possible?
  Does it address research methods, equipment, procedures, and results?
  Does it discuss these elements at the appropriate level for the intended audience?
  Do main sections provide maps or overviews to subsections?
  Have graphics been used effectively?
  Are the graphics properly numbered and captioned?
  Are the graphics nested in prose—introduced first in text and then sufficiently discussed?
  Are paragraphs logical and well developed?
  Is language clear, concise, and appropriate for audience?

Checklist for Back Matter

The back matter of a report consists of all the material following the main text: Endnotes (if these are placed at the end of the report rather than following each chapter), Bibliography or References, Suggested Readings, Glossary (though this sometimes appears in the front matter), Appendices, and Index.

- Endnotes

  Does material appearing as endnotes or footnotes really deserve to be in note form, or does it belong in the main text?
  Are notes an appropriate length?
  Are notes in proper form?

- Bibliography, References, Suggested Readings

  Do all entries conform to an appropriate style?
  Are all entries accurate?
  Is the list complete?
  Have unnecessary or inappropriate entries been removed?
  Is the list in alphabetical order?

- Glossary

  Are technical terms adequately defined for your audience?
  Are all necessary terms included?

Is the list in alphabetical order?

If your audience has no knowledge of your subject, have you considered putting the glossary in front instead? In any case, have you told the reader in your introductory material that there *is* a glossary?

• Appendices

Appendices can be a particularly tricky component of the back matter, so they call for a special check. Remember, appendices contain material that is too long to include in the text, or in a footnote, yet too important to cite merely as an outside source in the bibliography. If the report is based on statistical work, for example, you may want to provide the raw data that were analyzed by the statistical procedures, as well as the computer program or printouts for the statistical procedures. Since the computer printouts or the tables involved may be lengthy, it would be awkward for the reader to have to leaf through many pages of numerical data in the middle of the report.

Such material should be placed in an appendix at the end of the report. The text then can state, "The computer program that was used to perform the regression analysis is explained and the resulting printouts are given in Appendix I." If your readers have any question about this program, or if they are interested in computers, they can go to the appendix. On the other hand, they may feel that the computer and statistical work are someone else's department, and they will trust the experts' judgment. In that case, their train of thought has not been interrupted. The following list suggests some suitable material for inclusion in an appendix:

Explanation of computer programs used to do statistical work on which the report is based.

Computer printouts or tables of data on which the report is based.

Pertinent legal opinions used in writing the report.

Earlier reports, or excerpts of reports, that have a bearing on this report.

Visual aids that have some bearing on the report.

Maps.

Equations.

Material that is brief and directly related to the immediate topic of the discussion should, of course, be given as a figure or a table or quoted in the text. As a good rule of thumb, material more than two or three pages long should go into an appendix. Shorter material belongs in the body of the text—*if* it genuinely bears on the text. Do not, in any case, use appendices simply to pad the bulk of the report.

The questions you must answer for appendices, then, are these:

Is the material in the appendices too lengthy?

Are appendices helpfully organized and descriptively named (Appendix I:

Maps; Appendix II: Equations; and so on)?

Is there anything in the appendices that would more appropriately be included in the main text?

- Index

    Have you included the words to which your audience is most likely to refer? Have you cross-indexed in a way that anticipates the likely search patterns of your readers?

- Form for Notes and Bibliographies

    We recommend the *Chicago Manual of Style* for footnote or endnote form, and for bibliographic form. Here we list just a few examples of footnote and bibliographic forms based on the *Chicago Manual*. For complete information, we recommend that you consult the *Chicago Manual* itself.

A Note on Bibliographic Styles

The *Chicago Manual of Style* lists two styles for bibliographic entries, which it calls *A* and *B*. Style *A*, says the *Chicago Manual*, is "favored by writers in literature, history, and the arts," while style *B* is "favored by writers in both the natural and social sciences." However, in the Thirteenth Edition, the *Chicago Manual* asserts, "Either one, and sometimes a variation using elements of each, is acceptable when followed consistently throughout a bibliography" (p. 439).

Where does this leave bibliographic style for business writing? In a wide range of acceptable forms. But this book uses, and we recommend, style *A* because it is more common and more complete than style *B*, even though some form of style *B* is common in business publications.

The essence of style *B* is downsizing. For example, it uses initials for the author's given name; it omits quotation marks around article titles; it often omits subtitles or even whole titles of articles; it restricts capitalization in the title to the first letter of the title, of the subtitle (if included), and proper nouns; it may abbreviate names of publishers and even journals, and so on. The other significant feature of style *B* is is that it lists the date of publication immediately after the author's name (this is sometimes called an "author-date" system). Here is one comparison of styles *A* and *B:*

Chicago Style A

Grunwald, Joseph, and Kenneth Flamm. *The Global Factory: Foreign Assembly in International Trade*. Washington, D.C.: Brookings Institute, 1985.

Chicago Style B

Grunwald, J., and K. Flamm. 1985. *The global factory*. Washington, D.C.: Brookings Inst.

You may decide to use bibliographic style *B* in some cases—for example, space may be at a premium in a report that is to be published. But beware: It is much easier to cut down bibliographic entries than to flesh them out. You don't want to find yourself running back to the library, or even to electronic databases, seeking details you should have noted earlier. Also, if you decide you want to use an "author-date" system—a common bibliographic feature of business publications—don't assume that you must use *all* features of the abbreviated *B* style.

Use of footnotes.   Use footnotes to credit the source of quoted material in the text, to lend authority to a statement not generally accepted, to explain or give additional information, to give an appraisal of the source, or to provide a cross-reference to material presented in some other part of the report. Over the past several decades, there has been a steady movement away from the classic footnote form of a raised number in the text referring the reader to formal documentation at the bottom of the page. *Ibid., loc. cit.,* and *op. cit.* are now seen only in the most formal and stylized academic writing.

The more recent tendency is to incorporate the documentation as much as possible into the body of the text. An acceptable way to document a statement would now be, "According to Bagley (p. 226), nearly half of all private investment in the 1880s and 1890s went into railroad construction." The reference to Bagley can then be looked up in the References. If your references include more than one work by Bagley, and it is not clear in your text which work you are referring to, you can write, "According to Bagley (*History of the Railroad*, p. 226), nearly half of all private investment in the 1880s and 1890s went into railroad construction." This style is comfortable to read, and readers do not need to hunt for the note at the bottom of the page or end of the chapter, section, or report. Thus, their concentration and the flow of the report are less likely to be broken.

Inexperienced writers tend to use too many footnotes, rather than too few. This tendency can be corrected by gaining the self-confidence to let a well-thought-out line of reasoning stand on its own whenever possible. Using too many footnotes (or citations in the text) gives an air of "Look how hard I'm working." It is more businesslike simply to make the point and move on.

At the same time, it is true that footnotes or citations may be considered lines of defense. When you base conclusions on information from respected sources, and cite those sources, you protect yourself. You also give your reader indication of what went into your thought processes as you wrote the report. The bottom line is that you should use footnotes or citations judiciously.

Footnote form

1. For a book with one author, first edition:
John Sibbald, *The Career Makers: America's Top 100 Executive Recruiters* (New York: Harpers Business, 1990), 205.

2. For a book with one author, later edition:
Franklin R. Root, *International Trade & Investment: Theory, Policy, Enterprise*, 3d ed. (Cincinnati: South-Western Pub. Co., 1973), 425.

The contemporary trend is toward incorporating essential documentation into the text itself. John Barrymore is given credit for saying that stopping your reading to look at a footnote is like interrupting your wedding night to answer the doorbell.

One sign of an inexperienced writer is an overabundance of footnotes.

3. For a book with two authors:
   Marius van Nieuwkerk and Robert P. Sparling, *The Netherlands International Direct Investment Position* (Dordrecht: Klower Academic, 1985), 110.

4. For a book with three or more authors:
   Efrem Siget et al., *The Future of Videotext: Worldwide Prospects for Home/Office Electronic Information Services* (White Plains, NY: Knowledge Industry Publications, 1983), 121–25.

5. For an edited book:
   M. H. Bond, ed., *The Cross-cultural Challenge to Social Psychology* (Newbury Park, CA: Sage Publications, 1988), 32.

6. For a book with one or more authors and an editor:
   R. F. Allen and C. Kraft, "Transformations That Last: A Cultural Approach," in *Transforming Work*, ed. J. D. Adams (San Diego: Miles River Press/University Associates, 1984), 53–56.

7. For a book of two or more volumes:
   D. Landis and R. W. Brislin, *Handbook of Intercultural Training* (Elmsford, NY: Pergamon Press, 1983), vol. I, 25.

8. For an article in an encyclopedia:
   Encyclopedia of American Economic History, 1980, s.v. "savings and investment."

9. For a magazine article, author given:
   Ron Lacharite, "Spending Money to Save Money: The Limits and Potential of Cost Justification," *Records Management Quarterly*, October 1991, 3–6.

10. For a magazine article, no author given:
   "Nerves, Indigestion or Worse," *The Economist*, 11 July 1992, 71–72.

11. For a newspaper article, author given:
   Bill Hendrick, "Anecdotal Evidence, Not Just Figures, Paints a Picture of Consumer's Mood," *The Atlanta Journal/The Atlanta Constitution*, 26 July 1992, p. 1.

12. For a newspaper article, no author given:
   "Mall Anchor Stores Replaced Quickly," *The Atlanta Journal/The Atlanta Constitution*, 9 August 1992, p. C2.

13. For an unpublished dissertation:
   Paul Herman Cardwell, "The Effect of Tax Reform on the Ex Ante Variance of Security Prices" (Ph.D. diss., University of Tennessee, 1991), 90–91.

14. For interviews and personal communications:

Sen. Q. T. Flood (R., Minn.), telephone conversation with author, 10 January 1990.

Mr. K. T. Jones, interview with author, Dallas, TX, 26 July 1991.

15. For a government publication:

Senate Special Committee on Aging, *Future Directions in Social Security*, pt. 5, 93d Cong., 1st sess., 26 July 1973, 5.

16. For a book with author's name in title:

Louis Rukeyser's Business Almanac (New York: Simon & Schuster, 1988), 226–30.

Bibliographic Form

The bibliography is an alphabetical listing of all the books, articles, and other sources you used to prepare the report. If footnotes have been de-emphasized in the report's text, the bibliography is proportionately more important. It may be the only place where readers will find the full source information for items cited in the text. The bibliography also suggests to readers the route you took in assembling the report and guides them should they wish to investigate the topic in greater depth.

1. For a book with one author:

Moyer, Reed. *International Business: Issues and Concepts*. New York: Wiley, 1984.

2. For a book with two authors:

Grunwald, Joseph, and Kenneth Flamm. *The Global Factory: Foreign Assembly in International Trade*. Washington, D.C.: Brookings Institute, 1985.

3. For a book with more than two authors:

Kirkpatrick, C. H., N. Lee, and F. I. Nixson. *Industrial Structure and Policy in Less Developed Countries*. Winchester, MA: Allen & Unwin, 1984.

4. For a book in a later edition:

Kolde, Endel Jakob. *Environment of International Business*. 2d ed. Boston: Kent Pub. Co., 1985.

5. For a book with an editor:

Ghosh, Pradip K., ed. *World Development*. Westport, CT: Greenwood Press, 1984.

6. For an article in a periodical:

Labich, Kenneth. "The New Crisis in Business Ethics." *Fortune*, 20 April 1992, 167–76.

7. For successive entries by same author:

Axtell, Roger E. *The Do's and Taboos of Hosting International Visitors*. New York: John Wiley & Sons, 1990.

_____. *Do's and Taboos Around the World: A Guide to International Behavior*. 2d ed. New York: John Wiley & Sons, 1990.

_____. *The Do's and Taboos of International Trade: A Small Business Primer*. New York: John Wiley & Sons, 1989.

8. For a publication that is part of a series:

Acharya, Meena. *Time Use Data & the Living Standards Measurement Study*. LSMS Working Paper, no. 18. World Bank, 1985.

9. For a journal article:

Adler, N. J. "Expecting International Success: Female Managers Overseas," *Columbia Journal of World Business* 19, No. 3 (Fall 1984): 79–86.

10. For government reports:

Executive Office of the President of the United States. *Budget of the United States Government, Fiscal Year 1993*. Washington, D.C.: U.S. Government Printing Office, 1992.

Interstate Commerce Commission. *State-to-State Distribution, All Commodities, Traffic and Revenue: 1948–1956*. Washington, D.C.: Bureau of Trans-port Economics and Statistics, 1948–1956.

Robertson, Almon F. and William J. Dempsey "Investigation of the Shady Valley Manganese District, Johnson County Tennessee," *United States Bureau of Mines*. Washington, D.C.: United States Department of the Interior, December, 1949.

Checking Grammatical and Mechanical Accuracy

You or a proofreader should make a final editing sweep for grammar and mechanical accuracy. Check for correct grammar, spelling, punctuation, capitalization, italics, acronyms, and abbreviations—in short, all the details that any good English-language handbook provides. We have mentioned the *Chicago Manual of Style*, but there are many good handbooks, such as the *Harbrace College Handbook* (see our Suggested Readings in Appendix B for more). Because such handbooks are exhaustive and easy to find, we do not cover the details of mechanical accuracy in this text.

Remember, though, that details of grammatical and mechanical accuracy are important. Even in an otherwise well-written report, mistakes in grammar and mechanics may cause readers to question the reliability of your analysis. Their reasoning goes like this: "If this writer makes mistakes on simple things like grammar, spelling, and punctuation, what *else* might be wrong with this report? I can't trust

Computerized spelling checkers arc remarkably narrow-minded; mistakes such as "sight" versus "site" slip right past them.

it." This reasoning is not strictly logical, but it is a very human reaction. Avoid the problem: Make sure your report is "clean."

You can do this check for grammatical and mechanical accuracy yourself, or you can have an editor do it. So long as your editor is competent and is given enough time, there is every likelihood that all, or nearly all, the mistakes will be caught. Do not rely on a computer's spelling checker alone to clean up your text; such spelling checkers can tell you only whether you have typed any words not included in their "dictionaries." That is why, for example, a recent economic report from a major midwestern bank made the blunder of referring to "hosing figures" rather than "housing figures." Despite the fact that "hosing" is a legitimate dictionary word, it is the wrong word here. We like this poem from Dale Dauten's "Corporate Curmudgeon" column in the *The Chicago Tribune* (September 27, 1993):

To Bee Oar Not Two Be
I have a spelling checker,
It came with my PC,
It plainly marks four my revue
Mistakes witch I can not sea!
I've run this poem threw hit,
I'm sure you wood bee pleased too no,
Its letter perfect in it's weigh,
My checker tolled me sew!

Simple errors in grammar and mechanics can really embarrass you. Imagine the impression given to customers who received the following letter, sent to penthouse passengers who were soon to embark on the luxury cruise ship *Queen Elizabeth 2*. Imagine, too, the reaction of upper management when the letter came to their attention:

Dear Penthouse Passenger:

As a valued Cunard Passenger it is our pleasure to invite you to be part of our PENTHOUSE PRIORITY Embarkation. This procedure will ensure you of a quick and efficient check-in when you arrive to embark the Queen Elizabeth 2. Please check your passage ticket for the embarkation time appropriate to your sailing.

For us to be able to assist you, kindly present your PENTHOUSE PRIORITY Embarkation Card to the Information Desk, and personnel there will direct you to the appropriate area for ticket processing.

To help us in serving you in the most expeditious way, kindly have all necessary documents ready and completed by the time you arrive at the Terminal.

After completing all formalities, a ships's steward will be available to escort your to your suite.

BON VOYAGE

Did you count the mistakes? The letter begins with an error in modification—the *reader* is supposed to be the valued customer, not the staff of *Queen Elizabeth 2*. Queen Elizabeth 2 (sic), by the way, should be italicized or underlined, since it is the name of a ship. The letter ends with a reference to the "ships's" steward, who "will be available to escort *your* (sic) to your suite." Not a very good performance from the world's premiere luxury cruise ship. And if this is how they take care of the little things, how well do they take care of the big ones?

Testing with a Reader

A carefully chosen second reader often can find mistakes you have missed.

As always, *you* are the person with the biggest investment in your report's quality, so be prepared to do some careful checking on your own. The sharpest eyes belong to the reader with the most to gain or lose. Even so, bear in mind that another reader can often find mistakes that you, the author, have missed. We think it is important that you take one final step before submitting your report: test it with a reader. At least one pair of fresh, competent, and friendly eyes should read the report before you submit it. We took our own advice and had the manuscript for this book checked by F. K. Plous, a top professional communicator, resulting in many fine suggestions for improving its clarity and correctness.

Choose this test reader carefully. It should be a person with some knowledge of the subject matter of the report, a good grasp of English, and time to read through the report calmly. Above all, it should be someone whose status is not threatened by your success—that is, someone you can trust. Your test reader will need a briefing about the report's objectives, audiences, uses, and scope. The copy you give to this reader should be one he or she can write on while reading, in order to jot down reactions to the report during the process. Arrange to sit down and talk with your reader immediately afterward. Allow enough time between this test reading and the time you must turn in the report so that you can make appropriate changes based on the reader's reactions.

Choosing Paper, Cover, and Binding

You have worked hard to write an excellent report; now make sure its physical production is as impressive as possible. Specifically:

- Print your report on a good-quality, white bond paper that will withstand handling.
- If your company does not have preprinted covers available, you should use a heavy, good-quality commercial cover stock. Print the cover with most of the material from your title page. There is some variation here, so you should

check to see what is appropriate according to your company's practices. For example, it may not be appropriate to print your name or *anyone's* name on the cover of the report. Most companies include a company logo on the cover, especially if the report is to be distributed outside the company or used in a formal presentation to upper management. Choose a color for the cover stock that is easy on the eyes.

- Bind the report with slip-on, thermal, peg, ring, spiral, or comb binding. You can have this done at a print shop, but this binding is much more convenient to do right in your office. The major U.S. supplier of office binding machines and materials is General Binding Corporation and Subsidiaries.

  If the report is short—ten pages or less—a staple in the upper-left corner may be fine, but anything longer calls for binding. Use ring binding if (1) the report is thick, (2) large sections of the report may be removed or large additions made, or (3) changes may be made frequently. However, spiral or comb binding generally gives a better impression—certainly a better impression of *completion*. Also, an office comb binding machine will permit you to remove and add material if necessary.

USING YOUR REPORT

Once you have your final product printed and bound, it's a good idea to celebrate in some way, but it's a bad idea to entertain the feeling that you are completely finished. We all want that feeling of closure after working hard on a long project. But the hard work you have put into the project is also the best reason not to drop the ball now. Your relationship with that report is far from over.

Even a well written and attractive report must be promoted to some degree. Like any other new product, a report is no use to anyone if it languishes on the shelf or in a desk drawer. It must be read in order to be used. That means you may have to use sales techniques to insure its consumption in some quarters. For example, you may want to hand-deliver copies of the report to certain members of your audience, taking the opportunity to impress on the recipients the ways in which the report will serve them. This personal element can sharpen the reader's orientation to the report and make its consumption more likely.

Reports are soft goods, not hard ones. The resulting limited shelf life means you have a short time to take advantage of what you have written.

But "using the report" means much more than just making sure it gets read by the right people. You should now use the report, in various forms and various contexts, to serve the business system and *promote your own career.* You have been researching and writing on your subject for weeks or even months. You have become a bit of an expert on heat transfer in railroad cars, or high-speed adhesives used in assembly-line packaging, or the market for exporting farm machinery to Russia. For a short time, you "glow." You are in the know about something important to your business system. The need, opportunity, or problem that originally called for the report to be written is still there—but for how long? The time to step forward to serve the system, even beyond the parameters of the original assignment, is *now*. The report, the currency of your understanding, the business situation itself, all have a limited shelf life. For a time, you can turn the convergence of those elements into career capital. But that shelf life is all the shorter because reports and knowledge and situations are soft goods, not hard. You need to sell your product, in multiple forms and markets, before it gets stale.

Use your imagination—and systems thinking. Keep your eyes and ears open; look for places where your report or your newly gained knowledge are natural fits. Come up with ideas about how the report might be used to serve the system beyond the essential service for which it was designed. Develop a usage plan and put it into memorandum form to submit to supervisors. They will usually listen—because you will be showing them how to save money and capitalize on opportunity. Remember that when you produce excellent reports, presentations, publications, or do any kind of good work, you make your boss look good. That kind of success—success that spills over onto the people who work with you—is a potent means of advancing your career.

Utilization of reports is an enormously underdeveloped resource in business today. Millions of dollars are wasted in fees, salaries, and material because reports are authorized with a single purpose in mind when the same report could serve other uses as well, or because reports disappear onto someone's back bookshelf rather than being widely circulated. Here are just a few ways reports can be used:

- **Advertising.** Some parts of the report might be used for promotional brochures, flyers, or posters, or even as a basis for radio or television commercials.
- **Education.** The material in the report could be adapted for educational seminars to bring employees, clients, the public, even children, up to date on various subjects, opportunities, situations, and problems.
- **Publication.** Beyond the in-house publication of the report itself, there may be other publication possibilities, such as magazine articles and academic monographs.
- **Oral Presentations.** The materials of the report may be used for oral presentations in a variety of forms and for a variety of audiences and purposes. The report might become part of a national sales or management meeting program. It might be presented to a board of directors. You may want to develop an oral presentation as part of a strategy for persuading management to adopt the recommendations you've proposed in the report, or for persuading clients to invest in or buy a product or service.

Consider this: Your brain is buzzing with the contents of the report, and as you begin to brainstorm about additional uses for your document, ideas will come fast and furiously. You are ripe for invention, and this time, you already have a wealth of well organized and illustrated material *on computer disk*. Now you can easily manipulate that material in any number of ways: You can create shortened versions of the report; you can extract sections of particular interest to particular audiences; you can make outlines of the report's contents and turn subheads into bulleted lists, perhaps with brief explanations of each section and subsection. There are even

Utilization of reports is an enormously underdeveloped resource.

Preparedness creates opportunity.

computer programs to help you, such as *Persuasion* and *Powerpoint*. These programs will allow you to make handouts and colorful, well designed slides from the material of your report.

The visual components of your report are especially valuable. Sometimes visuals must be simplified or otherwise modified in order to adapt them for an oral presentation; you must take care that any text projected onto a screen is legible from the back of the room, reasonably simple and uncluttered, and adjusted to the oral component of the presentation. Often, though, you can use visuals just as they appear in the report, turning them into slides or transparencies for overhead projection. If your company has the resources, you can even incorporate the visuals into multimedia presentations.

Prepare as many versions of the report as you think you can use. Doors of opportunity open when you are ready and waiting to hear the knock. If you have prepared, for example, 10-, 30-, and 45-minute oral presentations of the report, and if you have prepared yourself to speak to supervisors, upper management, clients, and the public, you will be ready for just about anything. You may not get the chance to deliver presentations to each of these audiences, but you may be pleasantly surprised at the way preparedness seems to *create* opportunity. When people see that you are ready to speak on something important, you are very often called on to do so. And there will be a vast difference between you and those who fumble and bumble when giving a business presentation.

You have added authority if you have just written a report or had a major role in writing one. *Use* your momentary status to get your ideas a hearing, get your efforts recognized, and get something done. Do not grandstand, but do not be a nonplayer, either. You will never have a better opportunity to serve the business system with the knowledge you gained through the report-writing process, or a better opportunity to advance your own career on the basis of that effort, than you will have when the report first appears.

Of course you should also plan to use the report in its most fundamental way: as a basis for further work. Once you have done something successfully, you will most likely be called on to do it (or something very much like it) again. Never erase the computer files containing your report. You can expand, reformat, and reuse parts of the report in future reports.

Even if you never reuse any of that material verbatim, you will still take the report with you wherever you go, both in the form of your increased understanding of its subject matter, and in the ways your report-writing ability shapes your reputation. In these senses, the report transcends the boundaries of its immediate use, your current position, and your present employer—even if you do not recycle the report for advertising, education, broader publication, or oral presentations.

PRACTICE

An Inventory for Finishing

This chapter provides a number of checklists to use when you are finishing a report. Here is one final ten-point checklist:

Have you given the report an appropriate title?

By the end of the first page of the report, will the reader know both the purpose of the report and why he or she is being asked to read it?

By the end of the first page of the report, will the reader have a clear idea of what the report's structure is?

Does your report fulfill its stated purpose?

Has your report been successfully adapted to meet the needs of its real audience?

Have you included the appropriate amount of detail in each section of your report?

Has the report gone through a finishing process that is as thorough as its planning, research, and writing processes were?

Have your company's or client's *formal* requirements for the report been met or exceeded?

Have you paged through the completed report one final time to make sure all of the pages are there, in order, and that all visuals and other relevant materials have been included?

Have you made your own plan for exploiting the report, both by recycling its materials into other projects and by taking advantage of the corporate "glow" that develops whenever a strong report begins to circulate?

Part Two

SPECIAL PROJECTS

9

Writing and Delivering Speeches

Most of the speeches top executives give stink.
—The Wall Street Journal, *August 2, 1993*

Speechwriting is certainly not the most common writing task you will face in business. You might well write twenty reports, five hundred letters, and one thousand memos for every speech you create. If you prove to be good at it, you might create ten speeches for other people for every one you give yourself. But those statistical probabilities should never be taken as a reason to ignore speech writing and delivery. The opportunity to create or deliver a speech, when it comes, can be one of the most crucial events in the development of your career.

Writing effective speeches can be one of the best ways to move up the career ladder.

When executives are asked to name turning points in their careers—times from which they can identify a dramatic change in their fortune within an organization—they often cite a speech or presentation. *The right speech at the right time can dramatically boost any executive's career.* And the wrong speech—or even poor delivery of a good speech—can have a strong negative effect.

Speeches differ fundamentally from reports in that virtually every other form of corporate document is intended for the eye alone, but speeches must reach human consciousness primarily through the ear. Because eyes and ears perceive reality differently, someone writing or delivering a speech must act on several principles that have little application to documents intended solely to be read. So before you write or deliver a speech, prepare to change your approach.

That is the focus of this chapter: how writing and delivering speeches differs from preparing and presenting other kinds of documents. We assume that your career will offer increasing opportunities for speechwriting as you advance—speechwriting not just for yourself, but also for your boss. In fact, writing effective speeches for corporate officers can be one of the most important ways your writing ability can help you move up the career ladder.

SPEAKING VERSUS WRITING

The distinctions between words for the eye and words for the ear can best be summarized in terms of three problems: We call them the *audience problem*, the *speaker problem*, and the *language problem*.

The Audience Problem

Unlike readers, listeners who once lose the thread seldom pick it up again.

Because people listening to a speech usually have no written copy to refer to, the material presented in a speech must be simple enough, colorful enough, and coherent enough for the audience to remember it unaided by text. When you are reading a printed document, if you let your attention lapse momentarily you can simply refer back to what you missed and reread it at your leisure until the words make sense. Those who listen to a speech, however, enjoy no such luxury. Words fly by and cannot be recaptured. The speaker must make an impression on the first pass or risk not making an impression at all—or worse, risk making a bad impression. Speechwriters, therefore, are under intense pressure to present their material in the clearest, tightest, most coherent way possible. Once listeners are put off by an unclear thought, or by a set of thoughts that are not crisp and naturally flowing, their attention is likely to wander for the remainder of the speech. Only the most dramatic recapitulation by the speaker is likely to win back the listeners' attention.

The Speaker Problem

Effective speeches are written not just for the listener's ear, but also for the speaker's mouth. To be effective, a speech must be capable of being *spoken*. Writing that kind of speech is not always as easy as it would appear. Sentences that read perfectly well on paper may be too long to be recited effectively by a speaker (or absorbed effectively by a listener). A speaker who must pause—or gasp—for breath cannot present ideas effectively. Moreover, most speeches are still read from a text rather than memorized. If the sentences are too long, the speaker will too often be forced to refer back to the written text in mid-sentence, rather than at the end of a sentence (or, even better, of a paragraph). That kind of interruption is doubly disruptive: It forces the speaker to stop speaking at an inappropriate time and to break off eye contact with the audience as well. Audiences almost always perceive this withdrawal of attention negatively and, as a result, begin to withdraw their own attention from the speaker.

The Language Problem

Finally, there is the problem of spoken language itself—the actual structure of the sounds. English is not the easiest language in the world to pronounce. Unlike many other languages, English is plagued by consonant clusters, clumps of consonants that must be pronounced together without a vowel sound to separate them. Words like "judgment," "twelfth," and "strength" are difficult for many native speakers of

English to pronounce. Former President Gerald Ford never has been able to pronounce "judgment" properly; he inserts an extra syllable, making it "judge-a-ment." Listen closely, and you will notice many people actually say something closer to "strenth" than "strength."

Add an "s" to make such a word plural, and you are really asking for trouble. Perhaps only a few prime-time newscasters can say "twelfths," "strengths," or "facts" correctly and easily on the first try. And a word many speeches in business cannot easily do without—"products"—usually ends up being pronounced "prodix."

In ordinary conversation these lapses are overlooked because our physical proximity to the speaker allows us to hear more clearly, as well as to ask politely for a repetition or clarification of any words we might not have caught. But when people are trying to follow a speaker's thoughts in a noisy conference room or banquet room, the same sloppy pronunciation can become annoying enough to cause many in the audience simply to tune the speaker out.

The second language hazard in English is our huge and growing vocabulary, particularly scientific and technical terms based on Latin or Greek models. "Nuclear" is a typical example: The "-clear" part of the word should be pronounced in two syllables—"klee-yur." But many public officials still pronounce it "nu-kyuh-ler" or "nu-kler," and many of them stumble as they say it. They sense they are doing something wrong, but they are not sure what it is, so they hesitate. The mispronunciations, in fact, do not matter as much as the stumbling and hesitation, which send a clear negative message to the listeners about the speaker's general competence.

Given the size of the audience problem, the speaker problem, and especially the language problem, no speechwriter can expect to write a first draft without encountering one or another of them. So to protect yourself and the person giving the speech, remember speechwriter's rule number one: *Before you turn over a speech to the person who commissioned it, stand up and read it out loud yourself.* If you find yourself stumbling over certain words or phrases, change them to something more pronounceable. In fact, if anything about the speech does not sound right when you read it aloud, go back and change it even if it appears perfect when read silently. In speechwriting, the mouth and the ear—not the eye—are the ultimate arbiters.

> Listeners have to sort through enough distractions without also having to deal with a speaker's consistently sloppy pronunciation.

WRITING THE SPEECH

Of course there are entire books and college courses on speechwriting (see the Suggested Readings at the end of this book). This chapter covers six of the most important things to do when you are writing a speech and preparing for its delivery, whether the speech is for you or for someone else:

1. Think of last things first.
2. Focus on the essentials.

3. Ask for help.
4. Protect your speech.
5. Prepare a readable final copy.
6. Do not leave your audience in the dark.

The chapter ends with guidelines for delivering the speech.

Think of Last Things First

As a speechwriter, the first questions to ask are "by whom," "to whom," "where," and "when."

Before you begin writing a speech, give some thought to its ultimate delivery. Who is going to deliver the speech? Is the person an accomplished public speaker, a talented amateur, or a complete novice? And who is the audience? What do they expect to hear, and under what circumstances will they be listening to the speech? Is the occasion a solemn, commemorative one, such as a college commencement or an awards dinner? Is it part of a long-anticipated annual event, such as a professional convention, or part of a regular speaker's series that members of a club attend once a month?

Where in the proceedings is the speech to occur? Is it to be the climax of the event, or just one more obligation for people attending a series of workshops, seminars, and other speeches crammed into a busy day? Will the speech occur in the presence of food or drink? Audiences behave one way when they are seated in an orderly theater or conference-room format and another way in a banquet setting, where clinking glassware, scurrying waiters, and guests slipping out to the washroom create intermittent noise and distraction, and poor sightlines often obscure the speaker from those seated at the more distant corner tables.

Banquet-room configurations, moreover, are less likely to be congenial to the use of graphics. Slides and overhead projections cannot be seen clearly or comfortably by many of those seated at the eight-guest circular tables standard in hotel banquet and ball rooms. Most often, the speaker's words, thoughts, and delivery must carry the speech unassisted. Graphics should be confined to rooms where all listeners sit in rows facing the front and food and drink are served only during breaks at the rear of the room or in an adjacent room.

Focus on the Essentials—Speaker, Audience, Idea

Any of the considerations discussed in the previous section can impact the success of a speech for good or ill. But once you have figured out how to deal with the specifics of setting and surroundings, the real essentials of the speech come into play, essentials that have not changed in the twenty-one centuries since Cicero stood up and declaimed before the Roman Senate. Those essentials are the *speaker*, the *audience*, and the *ideas* the speaker wants to communicate.

Veteran Chicago-based communications consultants Joan McGrath and Myrna Pedersen developed a four-point scheme to help them create memorable speeches for their corporate and association clients. Known as the "Mindset for

Take-Charge Presentations,"© their scheme helps the speechwriter focus both the content and the speaker on the ultimate target—the mind of the audience. We offer here our interpretation of their ideas:

a. Content is key; it must meet the audience's need for information.
b. The best presentation is conversation.
c. Your *real* audience is very specific.
d. Perception is reality.

Most business audiences are looking for practical information and fresh approaches—not "fluff."

Content is key.   Audiences really crave a speech that *says something*. "You must have something substantial, new, interesting, and innovative that fulfills your audience's need for information," reads the Pedersen/McGrath Associates' handbook for clients. Giving an audience old material is as insulting as giving them new material so poorly presented as to be incomprehensible. Most people, especially the kinds of professionals who attend business speeches, are looking for practical information and fresh approaches to old problems that they can apply in their work. They have already heard all the platitudes, and they will head for the exits if they hear them again. But give them meaningful, challenging material that offers them a refreshing new way of looking at themselves and their work, and you will usually win both their attention and their gratitude.

The best presentation is conversation, not testimony.   The single biggest problem with most speeches is overformality, the misconception that anything worthy of being called a "speech" must be composed in some sort of high-blown, formal language. Not true. There was a time, a century or so ago, when sermons and political speeches generally were more flowery and more formal than we find acceptable today. But today's effective speeches sound very much like all other forms of contemporary verbal communication, written or oral, in the world of business: The sentences are shorter, punchier, and less complex, with fewer commas and dependent clauses and less self-conscious ornateness. The vocabulary tends to mimic conversational speech as well.

"Even if your material suggests a highly formal presentation, like reciting the company's end-of-year financial results, you don't have to cling slavishly to a formula in everything you say," says Myrna Pedersen. "Once you've finished reciting all the obligatory facts and figures you can personalize the speech by offering your own interpretation of the numbers, or perhaps by suggesting some ways they could be improved during the next quarter. We always urge our clients to look for opportunities to enhance the materials they're presenting. We tell them, 'You're going to be up there speaking anyway, so you may as well use the opportunity to tell people what you want them to know.'"

Any good speech must be *authentic for the speaker*.

Two important elements in keeping speeches conversational are *personality* and *personalization*. The speech should not only sound like conversation, but should sound like the conversation normally used by *this* speaker. Each person has a distinctive conversational style. The conversational style you write the speech in needs to be the same as that of the speaker.

Making the speech authentic to the speaker may require that you forget some of the so-called "rules" for good speeches. Take humor, for example—is it essential for every speaker to "relax" the audience by opening with a funny story? Absolutely not. If the speaker is not an accomplished joke teller or raconteur, any attempt to sound like one will start off the speech on a false note. The best guarantee of establishing rapport with the audience comes from the speaker's sincerity, demeanor, and knowledge of the subject.

The same goes for efforts to insert colorful quotes or illustrations into a speech. To be effective, they must sound authentic in the mouth of the person who uses them. Do not insert words of wisdom from Thomas Aquinas and St. Augustine into the mouth of a speaker who has no familiarity with the church fathers, or maxims from Patton or Clausewitz into the speech of someone with no background in military affairs. No matter how powerful those words look on paper, they will come out sounding hollow if the wrong person says them. By the same token, if the speaker is crazy about football, you may want to use gridiron metaphors to illustrate important points (provided the audience will understand the references). The speaker will feel natural, and the audience will usually grasp the concept the speaker is trying to illustrate.

Remember that every speech—even the most formal speech before the largest and most distinguished audience—is a matter of *talking*. Somebody is telling something to somebody else, and because the spoken word is fleeting, the speaker gets only one chance to make an impression. That is why Pedersen and McGrath emphasize that a speech should sound like a normal person talking, rather than like someone taking an oath of office. A speech today is not supposed to sound as if it were being "read into the record" for reassimilation in literary form. A speech's impact comes when it is given—or (usually) not at all. When you write a speech, assume that the speaker has only one chance to get the speech's points across.

Your real audience is very specific.   In the reality of today's business world, effective speeches are tailored to the needs of specific audiences with specific information needs. These are people with very little time to listen. Before preparing a speech, learn as much as you can about the people making up the audience so you can tailor the speech to their needs.

What are the audience's interests, and which of their interests are they going to be concerned with at the particular meeting, convention, or luncheon to which they have invited the speaker? What are their values, and how do they assert them? Are they currently engaged in any lobbying campaigns to advance their interests? Do they feel under pressure from an adversary or competitor? Are they the current darlings of the media, legislators, or public-interest groups? Are they looking for reassurance and encouragement, or simply for information?

What kind of speech are these people interested in hearing at this time, and why? Are they looking for advice from a sagelike figure who will clarify for them a world grown complex? Are they simply seeking a better understanding of the speaker's own industry or company?

"Insiders" and "outsiders" must give different kinds of speeches.

Is the speaker addressing people from his or her own industry, or from a different one? Is the speaker, in other words, an insider or an outsider? Insiders normally can take a more familiar tone with their listeners. Outsiders, unless preceded by a prominent and favorable reputation, typically begin their addresses with expressions of deference and respect designed to close the insider-outsider gap before the real speech begins.

The important point is to know your audience, and thus to write a speech that appeals to their specific needs and interests. The speech that works on auto salespeople is likely to fall flat with a conclave of bishops, just as a speech that informs and interests lawyers may be a yawn to manufacturers of garden supplies. But when you are tailoring a speech to an audience, be careful not to pander. If a speaker is addressing a gathering of physicians, do not assume the talk must be peppered with medical metaphors or with stories about doctors in order to establish rapport. That is patronizing, for one thing. And unless the speechwriter is extremely careful, references to the listeners' specialty will probably contain some embarrassing errors. Stick with what the speaker, not the audience, knows.

Probably the most important part about knowing your audience is to ascertain whether it includes any special individuals who need to be targeted as a select "audience-within-an-audience" for your remarks. Pederson and McGrath point out that some of the most effective speeches have a hidden agenda: They're actually addressed only to a few selected members of the audience—perhaps even an audience-of-one—from whom the speaker is seeking a particular response.

For example, a speech purportedly addressed to a room full of product reps and distributors might actually be pitched to the handful of trade-magazine editors also in the room whose editorial support is essential to a successful launch of your company's exciting new product. The reps may not be able to grasp the full impact of your remarks during your speech. But when they see the same information enthusiastically explained later by a trade-journal columnist who really understands your industry, they'll be eager for the rollout and for the chance to start selling your new line.

Or you might take on an otherwise ho-hum speaking engagement, knowing that the audience will include a researcher from the staff of a legislator whose understanding is essential to your organization. Telling your story to Congressman Sludgepump could cost you time and money if you traveled the classic lobbying route. But an exciting speech followed by a brisk Q-&-A session could convince a congressional aide that his boss needs to meet with you.

The most rewarding audience-of-one, of course, is the listener who liked your speech so much that he or she approaches you directly afterward with business for your company (or a job offer for you). It may not happen often, but when it does it's because speaker and speechwriter have done their audience homework.

The atmospherics of a speech are as important as the speech itself.

The best way to ascertain the audience's preferences is simply to ask. Telephone or sit down with the meeting planner who is organizing the function at which your speaker is to appear. Find out who the guests are and what their concerns are. Find out what other speakers they have heard in the last year or so—and how the speeches were received. You may get valuable clues as to what kinds of speaking styles and subjects press this group's buttons. Equally important, the meeting planner should be able to provide you with many of those circumstantial details that can affect the speech's reception—the size and configuration of the hall, the presence or absence of a meal, and availability of lighting, electrical outlets and other technical support systems you may need to display graphics. Pull all these details together before you put pen to paper.

Perception is reality.   If the audience *perceives* the speaker to be confident, well-informed, and authoritative on the subject, then the speaker *is*, say Pedersen and McGrath. Part of the audience's perception of the speaker's professionalism comes from how well (or poorly) the physical surroundings of the speech are controlled so as to support the speech. That is, the atmosphere of a speech—including proper management of the audience's environment and proper presentation of the speaker—is as important as the content of the speech itself. A speech may be factual, accurate and pertinent, yet still be perceived as boring if the speaker, audience, occasion, surroundings, material, and presentation have not been properly coordinated. Get control of as many of these elements as you can before you agree to write or deliver a speech.

Ask for Help—from the Speaker

If you have taken care of the important advance details properly, you will probably find that *writing* the speech itself is the easiest part. It will probably be the fastest part, too. The actual writing of a speech usually does not take much time because speeches themselves do not take much time—no more than twenty-five to thirty minutes for even the most serious and complex message in the most formal setting, such as a theater or amphitheater. Less formal speeches in less formal settings—the typical after-lunch address to a business or professional group in a hotel banquet hall—should run no more than twenty minutes. A full stomach, a full bladder, and a full appointment book for the rest of the afternoon make extended concentration difficult for the audience. The head will absorb no more than the "tail" can endure.

Another factor that shortens the speechwriting task is that very often only a single source need be consulted—the speaker. Although composing a speech typically will involve some research among the same types of printed or on-line reference materials used in the preparation of corporate reports, the bulk of the material used in the speech will likely come directly out of an interview with the person who is going to be doing the speaking. In fact, holding a solid interview with the speaker before writing a word is so critical that you should insist on it.

A serious but relaxed get-together with the speaker will help your effort in two ways: It will enable you to establish precisely what it is the speaker wants to say and how the speaker wants to say it, and it will give you a chance to familiarize yourself with the speaker's conversational style so that the phrases, expressions, and syntax you create will sound authentic and natural.

When you go in to interview the speaker, remember these four tips:

Probe gently but firmly to determine whether the speaker already has a serious theme in mind. Many speakers do not. They have received an invitation to speak but have not been instructed to address a particular subject. If your speaker is not yet committed to a theme, feel free to suggest some possibilities. If he or she already has a theme in mind—and, in particular, has already promised the organizers of the event that he or she will discuss it—proceed as directed.

Once you get into speech-writing, you may find it pays to keep a file of ideas for talks your company's executives might give.

If you have been asked to write a speech for an executive who does not know what to say, you might try this technique: If asked to develop some possible speech themes, slip into brainstorm mode, and whenever a possible subject for a speech pops into your head, quickly scrawl out a title on a piece of paper, briefly outline the subject in three or four points, and then stuff the sheet of paper into an envelope and move on to the next subject. In short order you will have outlines for half a dozen speeches, each filed in a labeled envelope, each available for further development once the speaker approves a topic.

Be discreet in asking questions of the speaker, and beware in particular of probing too deeply into areas where the speaker is likely to be ignorant. Make the best use of your limited interview time by focusing on what the speaker really wants to discuss. Do not overload the speaker with questions that might create discomfort. Be aware of when you might be starting to waste the speaker's time.

Do not expect to walk out of the first interview with the notes for a complete speech in hand. More likely, you will have a series of ideas for an outline that, once submitted, will be approved for further development. It may take several interviews before the speaker gives you all the information you need. As you become more experienced, you will be able to interview more efficiently. Ultimately, you and your speaker may develop such good chemistry that you will be able to get all the information you need in a single interview.

Make sure that you and your speaker develop good chemistry. One trick is to get on good terms with the speaker's secretary or other assistants and reassure them that the speechwriting relationship you have entered into with their boss is a temporary—or, at least, intermittent—one that in no way threatens their own functions.

Once you have put the speaker's ideas on paper, be sure to label your work "Draft 1," to assure all concerned that criticisms and revisions are anticipated, even welcomed. If you have done your work well, little revising should be needed.

Protect Your Speech

Do not be caught off guard when all sorts of extraneous people start to horn in on your speech.

For a variety of reasons, speeches activate office politics to an unusual degree, attracting all sorts of peripheral personalities into checking, critiquing, vetoing, and often radically rewriting (usually at the last minute) speech texts that both the speechwriter and the speaker mistakenly believed to be finished. The problem of extraneous employees horning into a speech is particularly intense in large, hierarchical organizations where each department expects to have its own piece of the action when a top official ventures out to make a speech. The vice president of public relations or media relations may demand to review any material prior to its disclosure to the public—whether by written or oral means. Expect the legal department to get involved, too. After all, one of its jobs is to protect the organization against lawsuits and prosecutions, either of which can be ignited by the inadvertent disclosure of information that should have been embargoed.

However necessary it may be to have a speech reviewed by other parts of the organization, the experience can still be frustrating for those who have to write and deliver the speech. The reason: In their well-intentioned effort to protect the organization, public relations people and lawyers change language, including that all-important conversational style you have worked so hard at crafting. "Lawyers are the worst of all," says a former speechwriter for a very large professional association whose president and vice president are on the road year-round making major policy speeches. "The trouble with lawyers is they all think they can write, but everything they write comes out in legalese. Legal-sounding language is exactly what you don't want in a speech. Nobody actually talks that way, and audiences can tell immediately when a speaker slips out of his own natural style and starts talking like a lawyer. Nobody's fooled, but the lawyers keep insisting on injecting their kind of language into other people's speeches."

It is up to the highest authority involved—usually the speaker—to define clearly who has the right to review and/or change the speech.

The cure for this sort of interference is to develop in advance a firm set of ground rules to be observed by all parties contributing to the preparation of a speech. The highest authority—usually the speaker—should clearly define what the other participants can and cannot do and should make sure everybody understands the rules. As the speechwriter, you can make your job easier by familiarizing your "client" from the outset with the organizational problems likely to arise in connection with his or her speech. While deferring to the legitimate interests of other departments, you should insist on final control over stylistic matters. And when submitting your speech draft for approval by other departments, be sure to include a clause stating that unless the recipient's comments and suggested changes are returned to you within a specified time, you will consider the speech to have been approved.

Prepare a Readable Final Copy

At last your speech is finished and approved. All necessary revisions have been made, all errors eliminated, all facts checked. The speaker is pleased and ready to present what you have written. But wait. One final step remains—putting the text in the best form for easy reading at the rostrum. Fortunately, most word-processing systems can easily handle this once formidable task. The rules to follow are common sense:

For easy-to-read speeches

- Use a bigger type face than you normally would—double or triple the size.
- Set the line spacing at the equivalent of triple spacing.
- Do not let a paragraph (much less a sentence!) be carried over from one page to another. Each page should begin with a fresh paragraph.
- Number each page prominently.

The large type and additional spacing will enable the speaker to look up and away from the text more frequently, and to return to the text with more assurance. Of course, the large type and spacing will also result in more pages and a thicker and heavier stack of paper. The size of this stack of paper should not intimidate the speaker, however, because the whole point is to make the speaker's delivery look and sound more natural.

Most novice speakers flip their pages over as they read a speech, thus restoring the stack of pages to its original order. Experienced speakers, however, know that flipping pages is distracting, both visually and audibly. So instruct your speaker to move the pages the way the pros do: Simply slide each used page silently to the side, and slide the next page on top of it. (The speech text ends up in reverse order, but since the speech is not going to be read a second time right away, this does not matter.) The audience will appreciate the smooth and seamless delivery uncluttered by background noise.

> Flipping pages is a distraction you can easily prevent.

Do Not Leave Your Audience in the Dark

Has this ever happened to you? The speaker has had the lights dimmed so slides can be displayed, and when the slides are finished the speaker says "May we have the lights, please?" There is a pause. "May we have the lights, please?" Pause. "Ahem. I'm sure we'll have the lights back up momentarily." Somewhere someone may be trying frantically to find a switch, but the same control panel that was so easy to find before has now disappeared. What had been a really solid presentation has now been ruined by human failure.

All of us have had that experience. And we have all wondered, "Why don't they ever check these things out before the presentation?" Far too many otherwise well-planned speeches are spoiled by poor control of the immediate speaking environment—the room where the speech is to be given, the availability of food and drink, and the audio-video technology. This last category is especially inexcusable. *If you are using technical support of any kind, from a microphone to a computer-driven video display, make sure you test the equipment in the room well in advance of your speech.* Use this checklist:

Light and darkness.   Learn the location and function of the light switches. You may need an assistant to work them. Are there curtains or shades that will need to be drawn? Where are their pull cords?

> When preparing for a speech in a hotel conference room, be sure to have a way to page the appropriate technician if there is technical trouble.

For slide projectors.   Load the slide tray yourself, and run through the entire tray to make sure all slides are in proper sequence and facing the right direction. Personally make sure the projector is positioned accurately and that the remote changer is functioning properly. If you are using a large hotel ballroom or an auditorium, make sure the slide projector has a lens and bulb adequate to throw a large, undistorted image on a very large screen. If viewers are going to be seated at circular tables, make sure the screen is elevated and positioned properly so that everyone can see it. If you want to show document pages, either use a computer program designed for the job or have a graphics studio prepare the slides. Finally, secure the name and pager number of the technician who will be on duty during your presentation so you can get immediate help if a breakdown occurs.

Other visual aids.   Do not throw high-tech solutions at low-tech problems. If you are in a small room, an overhead projector or an easel with illustration cards may well be more appropriate, more flexible, and more foolproof than slides. The military-style shadow box, or a simple flip chart, can be useful as well.

The only way you can make the right decision about visual aids is to make sure the meeting planner is absolutely definite and reliable about the size, seating capacity, and configuration of the room in which you will appear. Then, as soon as you arrive at the location, recheck the room to make sure that the facilities and the visual aids do indeed match.

Be careful not to overuse the pointer.   Most speakers who have not had formal training will, if given the chance, overuse the pointer. Proper use is to point it once at your target, then *lay it down*. Nervous speakers will always transmit their anxiety to whatever is in their hands—a paper clip, a spoon, a pencil, or a pointer. Poking, waving, and wiggling of a hand-held object are always annoying to the audience, and pointers, being the most conspicuous instruments, are also the most likely to be abused. This continues to be true for the recent innovation of laser pointers.

General.   Check the room for possible hazards and foul-ups. Where are the electrical outlets? Will they take grounded (three-pronged) plugs? Where will power cords run? Will they be taped down? Can you, or anyone else you need to introduce, make it up to the dais without tripping over chairs, electrical equipment, and cords?

"Remarks prepared for presentation."   Even if the speaker is a natural raconteur who works without a printed text, have one on hand anyway to pass out to the media. Providing this copy will make the reporter's job easier, and it will protect you against possible misquotation.

DELIVERING THE SPEECH

When asked to name their greatest fear, most Americans say, "Speaking before a group."

Once you have a well written speech and are in control of the setting and technology, you have solved *half* the problem. The other half is the speaker and how he or she delivers the speech. Even if you have written the perfect speech and had it printed in the largest and most legible type, one possible hazard still lurks. Is the person scheduled to deliver your speech—whether that means you or someone else—a trained public speaker? Chances are, the speaker is not. Surveys taken year after year reveal that when asked to name their greatest fear, most Americans check the box labeled "Getting up and speaking before a group." Training in public speaking has all but disappeared from the curriculum of U.S. schools and colleges. And

Figure 9.1. Simple flip charts can be highly effective. Drawing by Matthew Atkinson.

even people who do not suffer from this fear will seldom display all the arts of the trained speaker. Almost all of us could use some speaker training.

Fortunately, help is available. If the person for whom you are preparing speeches (including yourself) is deficient in speaking skills, help may not be as far away as you think. Your local college or university probably includes a speech, theater, or drama department. If so, one or more of the instructors probably is experienced in coaching business speakers and is willing to do so on a consulting basis. Just call and ask.

Even if the institution does not have a full-fledged drama department, it may have drama courses within the English department. Schools of journalism can also be useful. A curriculum in radio-TV journalism inevitably includes at least one instructor who trains students in on-air announcing and newsreading, a specialty even closer to business speaking than theater. Feel free to call on such an institution if you or someone in your organization needs preparation for public speaking.

Such preparation also is available commercially. The larger public-relations firms offer speaker training to their business clients, and most of the larger metropolitan areas have one or more small consulting firms that specialize in training business speakers. Do not let the additional time and expense of training stop you from bringing in professional help at the start. The payoff usually comes quickly, and it can have an enormous impact on a company's fortunes. Powerful speakers backed by strong speechwriters give an organization a presence that few other kinds of exposure can match.

Finally, there is a resource that has proven helpful to thousands of would-be speakers, particularly those who suffer from stagefright. Toastmasters International, which has chapters in most metropolitan areas, offers instruction and support in a clublike atmosphere. In addition to formal instruction, members pick up those little tricks of the trade that can really help anyone become a much more successful speaker. Here are just a few of them:

- Remember that *practice makes perfect*. The best way to become a good speaker is to take every speaking opportunity that is offered. It does not have to be a major address in a formal business setting. Work your way up from simple to more challenging assignments by talking to local service organizations, church groups, community organizations, and special-interest groups —even your local country club or PTA. You will be less nervous in these comparatively low-pressure settings, and any slips you make will be observed by a relatively small number of easygoing people. The more of this practice you get, the better a speaker you will become.

- Does your nervousness make your mouth dry? Try slipping a "Lifesaver Hole" into your mouth as you are being introduced. It will be dissolved by the time you rise to speak, and the dryness in your mouth will be gone.

- Remember to go to the bathroom before joining the group for dinner, and while at the mirror be sure to check your appearance one last time. Did the swirl of wind as you entered the hotel put your hair into a topknot? You don't want to look anything but your best when you speak.

Being an "after-dinner speaker" usually means you should eat your own dinner *after* you speak.

- When dinner is served, pass it up. If you're scheduled to speak at the conclusion of a meal, remember that your consumption of food and drink will make speaking more difficult. Your blood supply goes to your stomach, not to your head, after you eat. The feeling of satiety that accompanies a full stomach can lead to a sense of self-satisfaction and complacency that could make you careless just when you need to be sharp. And if eating before a speech is risky, drinking alcohol is downright dangerous. Even if the alcohol doesn't make you tipsy, it will act as a diuretic, bringing up the possibility of a steadily growing sense of discomfort and urgency just when you most need to feel alert and focused. The recommended menu for an after-dinner speaker is unbuttered bread or crackers and a little water. This *ad hoc* diet may require discipline while the other guests plow their way through the filet mignon or broiled grouper, but you will be rewarded for the discipline twice: once when your speech is warmly appreciated, and again when you gratify your stifled appetite by going out to a real restaurant after the program and savoring your favorite dish in an atmosphere conducive to its complete enjoyment.

"Audiences rarely care how witty or amusing you are. They have two goals in mind. They want to hear your points as directly and simply as posible, and they want to get the hell out of there." *Wall Street Journal*, August 2, 1993.

- The same eating and drinking that may complicate your delivery will also shorten your listeners' attention span. For after-dinner speeches, speak no more than twenty minutes and try to keep the speech on the lighter side. Keep your talk short and punchy.

Dealing with Stagefright

Staying away from prespeech food and drink, along with other sensible practices like getting a good night's sleep, will help every speaker focus more successfully on the performance at hand. But for some people, these little tricks of the trade are not enough. If the task of facing an audience causes you such pathological anxiety that you experience nausea, diarrhea, sleeplessness, irritability, or loss of the capacity to focus on your everyday work tasks, it is only realistic to admit that you are not yet ready for public speaking as a part of your career. Some writers suggest that people experiencing such symptoms try meditation or aerobic exercise to relieve prespeech anxiety. We respectfully disagree. Exercise and meditation are serious disciplines, not one-shot quick fixes to be applied opportunistically to a temporary problem. The wiser course of action is to seek professional help as detailed earlier in this chapter. Until you can do that, it only makes sense not to risk a fiasco by accepting a speaking engagement for which you clearly are not prepared.

The Overconfident Speaker

Actually, people who are terrified of public speaking are not the real problem. They are in fact a very small minority, and they know who they are. The real problem in the corporate world is the large number of executives whose self-confidence (i.e., *ego*) prevents them from recognizing what everybody else knows: They are not that good at making speeches.

Watching a videotape of their own rehearsal can help most executives identify their weaknesses.

How do you suggest to a would-be speaker that he or she could use a little training—without injuring that all-important corporate vanity? A few years ago, such suggestions would have been difficult to make. But today's ubiquitous video cameras and videocassette players make the job a lot easier. Pedersen and McGrath suggest that the speechwriter arrange a brief private rehearsal, a read-through of the speech by the speaker with the video camera running. Afterward, the tape can be replayed and the speaker allowed to make his or her own critique.

Most will immediately spot their weaknesses and, after a brief moment of embarrassment, admit they need help. When the speechwriter suggests the name of a firm or individual that trains speakers, the executive immediately feels relief and authorizes retention of the consultant.

A few executives, of course, remain too vain to admit in front of their subordinates that they need assistance. But Pedersen and McGrath offer an ingenious technique for handling that problem. "Ask the executive to take the tape home and view it with his or her spouse," they say. "What the speaker won't notice, the spouse will. It never fails. They come back to the office and ask for speaker training."

PRACTICE

Writing a Speech for Your Boss

Your boss has been invited by the local Chamber of Commerce to give a brief (ten to fifteen minute) after-lunch address on "The Importance of Clear Communication in Business." The boss has asked you, as a new college graduate with good communication skills, to write the speech. When you asked the Chamber of Commerce's Program Manager if she had anything particular in mind beyond what the simple title suggests, she said, "No, you can take it in any direction you want, as long as it has to do with communication and with business." Your task, then, is to write the text for that speech, using whatever variation or slant on the subject looks best to you. If you need some basic material to work with, feel free to borrow anything you want from the Introduction and Chapter 1 of this book. Your boss will be flying in from Washington at 9:00 A.M. on the morning of the luncheon and will be seeing the speech for the first time then. Your assignment is to produce exactly what you will have placed on your boss's desk by 9:00 that morning.

10

Letters and Memos

*Often the best letter or memo
is the one you* didn't *write.*

LETTERS, MEMOS, PHONES, AND FAXES

Lines of communication
are essential; pieces of
paper are not.

- One currently popular business-writing textbook devotes almost a third of its eight hundred pages to how to write letters and memos. Anyone reading that material has got to ask, "Is there really all that much to this subject?"
- If you talk with any business executive about the paperwork aspect of the job, you will probably hear quite a bit of complaining about the sheer number of incoming letters and memos that person has to deal with every day. (Of course you may be talking with someone who sends out just as many memos as he or she receives.)

Our position is somewhat radical: We believe that the *lines of communication* are essential, but most of the *pieces of paper* are not. Most of what goes on in letters and memos in business today should be handled in person or on the phone. Most of the letters and memos that get sent are, quite frankly, clerical matters, not executive ones. Did the order get sent on time? Does the bill need adjustment? What day does the conference in Las Vegas start? Your secretary should handle those things. If you do not have a secretary, you should handle such minutiae by phone. We see four major arguments against the steady downpour of letters and memos:

- Most of the paper is unnecessary—the issues raised are sufficiently routine to be handled by phone or in person.
- Most of the remaining paper is routine enough to be handled clerically.
- In today's litigious climate, the decision of whether to put something on paper, or even in the computer, should always be accompanied by a consideration of potential legal ramifications six months, a year, and five years down the road. Too many of the letters and memos that plague executives today are

being sent "for the record" or written "for the files," and on a clearer-thinking day would never have been written, much less sent.

- The same arguments are true for faxes. Ease of transmission holds potential trouble.

"E-mail is a dangerous time bomb in every corporation that uses it because trial lawyers can argue that more than any other kind of written communication, E-mail reflects the real, unedited thoughts of the writers."
Hemispheres, June, 1993.

In general, before you send a letter, a memo, or even E-mail, you should think, think, and think again. Is this really a message that needs to be sent at all? If so, is this something *you* should be handling instead of your secretary? If so, should the matter be handled on paper (or on computer screen via E-mail) instead of with a brief phone call or personal visit? Only if the answer to all of those questions is *yes* do you really need to think about writing a memo or a letter. Let us illustrate our point with a few examples:

Example One—Bad Pipe: The pipe supplier for a construction project your firm is managing continues to send flawed pipe. Approximately 20 percent of the pipe you have received is judged unusable by the people on the site. During repeated phone conversations, the supplier has stressed that the unusable pipe should be returned, after which it will be replaced with new pipe. Your concerns are, first, that the quality of material you are paying for continues to be shoddy; second, that pipe whose defects are not apparent to the naked eye may be slipping into your construction; third, that waiting for replacement pipe is starting to slow down construction; and fourth, that your supplier seems to be complacent. Should you write a letter?

Discussion: You have talked with the supplier on the phone many times, and the negative situation continues unaltered. There are potential legal ramifications, from which you can protect yourself and your employer with a letter. So yes, you write a letter, and of course you keep a copy. And you accelerate your search for a new supplier.

Example Two—Personnel Evaluation: You have an employee who consistently shows up for work late, leaves early, and generally seems to expect others to pick up enough of the slack to raise his effort from "not quite passing" to "barely passing." This is the third person in this position this year, so you do not want to dismiss the employee outright—at least not right now. When you did the employee's evaluation (orally) at the end of the six-week trial period, this problem was barely visible, and you mentioned it only in passing. Three months have now passed, and the situation is getting worse. It is time for another evaluation. Do you put this negative personnel evaluation on paper, either as a letter to the employee, or as a memo to yourself for your files, so that you will have a good "paper trail" in case termination becomes necessary?

Discussion: You have talked with the employee only once about this problem, and then only in passing. What your instinct is having you do here is create a paper trail just for the sake of creating a paper trail. We think the letter you are considering writing would be a difficult one, and that what you really need to do is to have a very frank, confidential session in your office with that employee. If you are worried about the paper trail, keep your dated notes from that meeting. A more meaningful paper trail to have, however, would be a daily log of specific instances. But once you start down that road, you know firing is imminent. The situation has not yet gone that far, but it might if no turnaround in behavior is apparent after your heart-to-heart three-months' evaluation. At this point, there is no need for a letter or a memo.

Example Three—The Program for the Board Meeting: You need to know if Bob Harris, Production Manager for the El Centro plant, will be including *updated* production figures for your division in his presentation to the Board next month. Should you write a letter?

Discussion: Pick up the phone instead.

We prefer a *minimalist* view of letter and memo writing.

If you think along these lines about situations that *might* require a letter or memo, you should be able to put an effective limit on the amount of paper or computer files you generate. Do remember, though, that we are not talking about limiting your lines of communication, only about limiting the amount of written words that flow along them. What we present in this chapter, then, is a *minimalist* view of letter and memo writing. For more information, refer to one of the excellent sources in our Suggested Readings list at the end of the book.

Recent unfortunate events in the business world only reemphasize our advice that writers choose carefully what to commit to paper (or to E-mail), as well as what to disclose orally, in situations where matters of consequence are being made part of a formal record or are likely to find their way into the media. In a number of recent cases, both the mass media and the specialized business press have turned what were supposed to be private, internal corporate documents into script material for highly speculative and overpersonalized boardroom dramas masquerading as "business news." Many of these unanticipated disclosures have gone on to serve as fodder for multimillion-dollar lawsuits charging management with the illegal firing of an executive, with marketing a product known to be dangerous, or with arranging a less-than-arms-length sale of a valuable corporate property to a well connected buyer. In other cases, filched memoranda and careless remarks to outsiders have revealed internecine tensions between differing corporate factions, a normal fact of life in any company made up of many individuals, but also a fact of life that can be made to look bizarre and dangerous in the hands of a reporter who has decided that a nice, juicy chronicle of corporate backstabbing could be the fastest way to advance his or her career.

Instead of piling up printed correspondence and oral disclosures that only whet the media's appetite for stories of executive intrigue, we prefer to err on the side of discretion, much as Barry Diller, chairman of the QVC Network, Inc., did when his company lost its bid to take over Viacom. When reporters tried tempting Diller to explain, complain, or blame, he refused to take the bait, saying only, "We lost. They won. Next." Why say more?

MATTERS OF FORM

Letters, faxes, and memos have important elements of form in common:

- All of them should have at least a one-inch margin all around.
- All of them should be produced with a printer that makes fully formed characters; no nine-pin dot matrix work should be sent out under your name.

- All of them need to designate clearly exactly who the sender is and who the receiver is, although in terms of form each does it differently. Second and subsequent pages of all of them need to carry the sender's name as well, either by itself (or together with the date) in the upper left-hand corner.

Form in Letters

All letters need an *inside heading*, giving the sender's full address. Many times company letterhead serves this function. It has become common to include the sender's name on the top line of the inside heading, but that is not required. If you are not using letterhead stationery, the easiest page layout to use is to put the sender's name (and every other element of the letter's form) flush left—beginning at the left-hand margin.

The easiest placement on the page for letters, memos, and faxes is to start everything at the left margin.

All letters also need an *inside address*, giving the recipient's full address. If you do not know a specific name to address the letter to, use a corporate title instead. Two spaces below the inside address, put the correct *date* on the letter.

The next formal element of a letter is either the *subject line* or the *salutation* (or both). The subject line is an element borrowed from memos: a clear and succinct statement of the purpose of the letter. Especially when you do not know whom to address the letter to, the subject line can substitute for the salutation. If you are using only a title in the salutation, the subject line will help whoever receives the letter in that department to route it to the correct individual. Unless the recipient is a close friend, the salutation is always followed by a colon.

After the body of the letter, there needs to be a *closing* and *signature*, with your signed name and your typed name. If you put any more lines after your typed name (such as specification of who gets copies or of enclosures), those are called *supplement lines*; they are frequently printed in either italics or a smaller type size, or both.

Here is an example of a typical letter form using each of the elements discussed above.

Benton Products
1223 Center Park Road
Dallas, TX 75230

Mr. Ed McElway
Director of Conference Planning
Roman Holdings, Corp.
824 State Street
Calumet City, IL 60409

January 12, 1994

SUBJECT: Requested information on custom advertising displays

Dear Mr. McElway:

Thank you for your interest in our new line of custom advertising displays. We have had a terrific response to this product line since its introduction last year. As you requested, I am enclosing with this letter materials describing the entire line, along with an up-to-date price list.

The "Signet" model that you were particularly interested in is one of our best sellers. I'm happy to say those are currently in stock; our policy is to keep all of our products in stock all the time. If you request it with your order, we can ship your displays the same day. Please note also that there is a 10% discount on orders of six or more.

I will have our customer service representative, Sharon Cantor, call you next week to answer any other questions you may have about our products. Thank you again for your interest in Benton Products.

Sincerely,

Thomas L. Cooley
Director of Merchandising
Benton Products

c: Sharon Cantor
encl: product brochures
price list

Form in Memos

"There is no such thing as a confidential memo. Even if you write the most secret memo in the CIA, you can be sure that within 24 hours it's going to be front-page news in Moscow." *The Miami Herald,* March 16, 1989.

Caution: Remember that no memo typed at the office is confidential, no matter how you label it.

Letting your readers know whether this is an INFORMATION memo or an ACTION memo is a nice touch.

If you are communicating with someone in your company, especially someone subordinate in rank, you would normally use a memorandum instead of a letter. The memo's formal elements consist of the heading "Memorandum" or "Memo" and the familiar four opening headings (TO, FROM, SUBJECT, and DATE). Because one of the primary aggravations of people who receive memos is that they do not know whether the memo writer really expects them to *do* something based on the memo or merely to read it and file it, a nice addition to those elements is a fifth line that says simply "This is an INFORMATION memo" or "This is an ACTION memo." Traditionally, memo writers put their initials next to their name on the "FROM" line, but that serves no real purpose today; anyone who would forge a memo would quite obviously also forge your initials. As with letters, memos that run more than one page should carry the sender's name on the top of each subsequent page.

Form in Faxes

Caution: Remember before you send a fax that there is no such thing as a "confidential" fax. Unless you know the receiver's machine is a personal one in a private office or home, do not assume that material in your transmission will remain confidential.

There is no reason to use a different form in faxes than you use in letters and memos as long as you also use a cover sheet. The *fax cover sheet* must provide the following information:

Every fax needs a cover sheet.

- The sender's name, address, phone number, and fax number.
- The number of pages being transmitted.
- The receiver's name, address, phone number, and fax number.

The cover sheet helps keep the fax pages together, helps route the document to the right person, and does so without making the first page immediately and easily visible. For really important faxes, someone should call the recipient's office to verify receipt.

IMPORTANT INTERNAL STRUCTURES

Because certain kinds of writing situations occur so frequently in business, it is worth remembering a few basic patterns that address them. Those patterns include sending neutral information or good news, sending bad news, and making a request.

Sending Neutral Information or Good News

Often the message you need to send is either neutral or good news. In such situations, you can use a very straightforward pattern: purpose, news, and implications.

Purpose: State briefly and explicitly what the purpose of this letter, memo, or fax is. You may think that the next element, "news," makes the purpose clear, but given the number of times people read correspondence and respond with "why are they *telling* me this?" it is better to be explicit about your purpose. There is no reason to avoid beginning with "The purpose of this letter is. . . ."

News: Explain your news in appropriate detail. If you omit key facts for brevity's sake, state where those facts may be found. A good check on your completeness in this section is to make sure you have covered as many of the journalist's questions as appropriate: *Who* is involved; *what* is occurring; *when* is it taking place; *where* is it happening; *why* is it happening; and *how* is it to be done?

Even when sending neutral information or good news, you need to include an "implications" paragraph.

Implications: Be careful also to let the people who receive this news know its implications for them. If you are telling people the new building security system is to be activated April 10th, remind them that this means they will need to wear their employee IDs or building passes at all times beginning April 10th. Do not rely on your readers to think up the key implications of your news; spell out those implications for them.

The sample letter on page 174–175 is a good example of this kind of letter. The first paragraph makes the letter's purpose clear: It is a response to a potential customer's request for information. The second paragraph adds critical details to the requested information: The requested item is in stock, it is readily available, and there is a discount for multiple orders. The final paragraph gives the implications of this news: Since this particular letter is also a sales letter, the last paragraph paves the way for a sales call.

Sending Bad News

There are going to be times when you have to send bad news: the bid was too high, the contract has been cancelled, or the position has been eliminated. In these situations, use a standard pattern: buffer, bad news, and explanation/alternatives.

Bad news letters require an *indirect* structure.

Buffer: The opening of bad-news correspondence needs to be *indirect*. While you do not want to beat around the bush, or begin on a rosy note that will be directly contradicted in the next paragraph, using a buffer can soften bad news if done carefully. Bad news about a bid can be softened by information about how many bids were received or how competitive the bids were. News of cancellation of a contract can be softened by a reminder of a history of continuing problems on the contract. News of elimination of a position can perhaps be softened by background information on corporate reorganization, industry-wide slumping sales, or the disappointing results of last year's new-product introductions.

Bad News: State the bad news clearly and succinctly. If there are relevant facts to support the bad news, be sure to include them. Be careful neither to understate nor to overstate the news.

Explanation/Alternatives: The last piece of this pattern consists of adding any clarifying information that may be relevant. If there are alternative courses of action for the recipient to consider, list them here. If you want to invite the recipient to contact you for further explanation, you can do so here also.

Dear Miss Williams:

Thank you for your application for employment with the Neal Smith Agency. Many of our current employees are also graduates of the management program at State University. The opening you applied for drew a particularly large number of applications, including at least 25 from your classmates and another 25 from graduates of other equally fine programs.

Because we had so many good applicants from other programs, we have decided to fill the position with a graduate of St. Charles University who has also had two years' prior work experience. We felt that her somewhat different education would bring valuable diversity into our operation; the additional work experience was a bonus.

This year's job market is difficult for everyone. Locally, I know a number of the other large agencies like ours are also heavily staffed with State University graduates. In light of that, may I suggest that you consider focusing your applications this year on some of the newer (and thus smaller) local agencies, ones that may still be expanding and may not have quite so many of your classmates currently on staff? And of course, as you gain more experience and the economy improves, I invite you to send us another application whenever you see that we have another opening.

Best of luck in your continued search.

Sincerely,

Monique Henderson
Senior Vice President,
Development and Planning

Making Requests

One other situation occurs often enough to merit discussion. There will be times when you need to make a written request—for information, action, goods, or services. In this situation, you can use this simple pattern: request, elaboration, action.

Request: In this letter, put your statement of purpose up front. Doing so will help route your letter to the right person.

Elaboration: You may want to explain why you need a particular action taken, or how you intend to use a requested service or product once it has been provided. The "elaboration" section helps make sure that your letter produces exactly what you are looking for. The letter's recipient can usually do a better job of fulfilling your request if you include relevant background information.

Letters of request need *both* an "elaboration" and an "action" paragraph.

Action: Close your document with a clear statement of what you expect will happen next—receipt of an order form, a confirming phone call, shipment of goods, or whatever is appropriate.

The following letter is an example of this simple pattern.

Mr. Thomas Cooley
Benton Products
1223 Center Park Road
Dallas, TX 75230

January 5, 1994

Dear Mr. Cooley:

I saw the ad for your company's new line of custom advertising displays in *Sky* magazine, and I am interested in learning more about them. Will you please send me product information on the entire line, together with a current price list?

My company often finds itself needing such displays in substantial quantities with very little notice. In the past we have had difficulty finding a supplier who can provide next-day shipment; for us, shipment in 4-6 weeks just will not do. What is your availability and shipment situation in general? In particular, how readily available is your Signet model?

I look forward to receiving the product information from you soon.

Sincerely,

Edward McElway
Director of Conference Planning
Roman Holdings

SPECIFIC TYPES OF LETTERS

Employment Letters

In essence, job application letters are letters of request.

At one time or another, everybody must write a job-application letter. Such letters are basically letters of request. As a letter of request, the underlying pattern for each job application letter will be some variation on the pattern presented above: request, elaboration, action. So if you were to write a three-paragraph letter, the first paragraph would be a specific request: "I would like to apply for the position of . . ." or "I am submitting my application for the position of . . . ." We would add to that request a one-sentence statement of your biggest claim on the job— typically, either that you have the right experience for the position, or (for entry-level jobs) that you have the right education for the position, or both. The second paragraph would elaborate on that claim. How much detail you put into that paragraph depends on whether the letter is accompanied by a résumé, a Portfolio of Accomplishments, or both (see Chapter 11 for more on these documents). The third, or "action," paragraph would spell out what you hope will happen as a result of this letter. Are you going to phone for an interview? Are you waiting for the recipient to contact you? Just what do you want to happen next?

Dear Mr. Wright:

I would like to apply for the position of management trainee that you have advertised through the State University Placement Office. This May I will receive my B.A. in Accounting from the University, with an English minor specializing in writing. In addition, I have worked each of the last three summers as an intern at public accounting firms. Last summer I worked in your company's Nashville office.

My course work at State University gives me a strong background in public accounting. As the enclosed résumé shows, I have also taken two extra statistics courses and two extra tax courses, making me especially qualified in the quantitative area. The English Writing minor required me to take four upper-division expository writing classes from the English Department and two writing-intensive classes in business, which makes me confident that I can perform strongly in the area of communication. Brief samples of my writing, as well as fuller descriptions of my summer internship accomplishments, are available in my Portfolio of Accomplishments, which I will be happy to show you upon request.

I will be visiting relatives in Chicago the week of April 4-11. Is it possible to arrange an interview with you or a representative of your firm at that time? I look forward to hearing from you and discussing the ways I can contribute to your company's continued growth.

Sincerely,

James Patrick Mulhern

This letter conforms to the general pattern of "request, elaboration, action." The first paragraph makes it clear that the letter is a job application. Since the employer has advertised the job, there is no need for any kind of indirect opening sentence. The first paragraph also *names* the applicant's main qualifications for this position. The second paragraph *elaborates* on those claims. The final paragraph makes it clear what action the writer hopes the reader will take.

The decision to use the phrase "Is it possible to arrange an interview" is important. Someone who wanted to push just a little harder might say "I will call your secretary to request an interview," and someone who wanted to push a little less might say "I look forward to hearing from you." Each applicant will need to make the decision about how hard to push this "action" statement for each letter written; the right answer for one letter, or one applicant, may not be the right answer for another.

Letters of Agreement

A letter of agreement is generally sent to confirm the results (the substantive content) of a conversation, usually in situations where a contract would not be an appropriate instrument or where the discussions have not yet reached the contract stage. Thus the information in a letter of agreement is either neutral or good news to the recipient, and the letter can be handled within the general "purpose, news, application" framework.

Note the level of detail in this letter of agreement; the point of the letter is to confirm that the details are right.

Dear Mr. Schwarz:

The purpose of this letter is to review the terms of the contract we discussed at our meeting in Boston last week. Before we decide whether to accept your offer, we want to make sure we understand it correctly.

As we understand it, you are offering advances of $75,000, divided equally between the two authors, to be paid incrementally as follows: $7,500 each upon signing and $10,000 each upon receipt of finished manuscript for each of the three parts. In addition, there will be a $5,000 grant to each author for word processing, payable upon request, and an additional $5,000 available for the authors' travel in connection with finishing this project, payable upon your receipt of appropriate documentation of expenses. The advances will also be paid back incrementally: no more than 50% out of the first year's royalties, 25% out of the second, and 25% out of the third. Royalties are to be 6.5% for each author on sales up to 50,000 copies, with an escalator clause up to 7.5% if the sales go above 50,000 in any calendar year. If you as publisher decide at any time to assign a different editor to this project, the authors have the right to withdraw the project for cause (which would of course require return of any advances already received). There is also a $5,000 bonus for each author upon successful completion of the project by August 1995; otherwise the completion deadline is January 1996.

If we have misunderstood or omitted any key parts of your offer, please let us know immediately. If we fail to hear from you, we will assume this letter faithfully reflects the terms you are offering us and will make our decision accordingly. We expect to be able to give you our decision within two weeks.

Sincerely,

Sebastian DeMeglio

Complaint Letters

There is not much pur-
pose in sending a com-
plaint letter unless you
are also requesting some
kind of adjustment or
compensation.

Because no one likes to receive a complaint letter, complaint letters fall into the
"bad news" category, with the general pattern "buffer, bad news, explanation/alter-
natives." Depending on how strongly you want your complaint to register, you may
downplay or emphasize the initial, "buffer" paragraph. If you want your letter to be
a letter of complaint *and* adjustment (really the only reason you would ever *send*
such a letter), you will need to explain the desired adjustment in the last, "explana-
tion/alternatives" paragraph. In fact, if you want to receive an adjustment, the first
and last paragraph's length are connected; what better way to persuade someone to
replace a faulty product or improve unsatisfactory service (in the last paragraph)
than by using a portion of the first paragraph to stress how pleased your company
has been with that product or service in the past?

SUBJECT: Construction during annual meeting

Dear Mr. Nunzio:

For the last five years our organization, the Plastics Retailers of America
(PRA), has held its annual meeting at your hotel. We have always enjoyed
the many facilities you offer and the friendliness and competence of your
employees. Thus, it was a shock to us to arrive for our meeting this year
and discover major construction going on directly above the main
ballroom, which we use for all of our meetings. Not only did the frequent
jackhammering repeatedly disrupt our speakers, the many air-condition-
ing shutdowns made it impossible to carry out an effective or pleasant
meeting.

In my role as conference planner, I was in touch with your facilities planner, Mr. Dick Thompson, as late as one week before the beginning of the
conference. He never mentioned construction of any kind. I clearly remember at one point saying, "So we look forward to using the same excellent facilities as before," and he said, "Absolutely. We plan on your
group having another first-rate stay." Nothing could be farther from what
we experienced. As soon as I got to the hotel and saw what was happening, I sought out Mr. Thompson and asked him what was going on, and I
found him uncommunicative, uncooperative, and basically unwilling to say
anything other than, "We're doing the best we can."

You must understand that your hotel's failure to provide the standard of
service you advertise not only disappointed and angered all of the 200 retail and marketing managers who attended this meeting, but it also re-
flected poorly on me as conference planner. Conditions were so bad that
we actually had people at your registration desk demanding refunds on

their rooms! Others made it very clear to me we will not be back to your hotel next year. I am reluctant to cancel a longstanding and successful relationship based on one bad experience, however, so I propose this: Our organization normally receives a 10-15% reduction in the room rate because so many of us stay at your hotel. The only way I can recommend we come back next year is if you offer us a substantially increased reduction in our rate for next year, something in the neighborhood of 30%. If I can go to our Directors with that offer, based on your recognition that neither the facilities nor the service this year were anything like your standard, I may be able to bring the meeting back to your hotel next year. Failing that, I feel you will have given your hotel a black eye in front of 200 influential business people and, in doing so, lost an important professional organization that has been a customer for a long time.

I look forward to hearing from you.

Sincerely,

Harrison Blackstone

TYPICAL PROBLEMS

As we discussed at the beginning of this chapter, one of the biggest problems with many letters, memos, and faxes in business today is that they never should have been sent. Either the writer is using the writing only to try to protect his or her own position, which makes the document meaningless for the reader, or the writer could quite easily have accomplished the same task with a phone call or quick personal visit.

Assuming that writing something down really is necessary, here is a short list of the most common problems that afflict business correspondence:

- The document offers no clear idea of its purpose. Remember, the recipient will always ask, "Why am I being told this?" Make sure you explicitly answer that question.

Of course, this list of key problems can apply to any kind of business writing.

- The organization of the document makes no sense to the reader. Some people write letters of request where the request comes only in the last line, or bad-news letters with such a positive first paragraph that the bad news comes as much more of a shock than it should. Remember that the test of "organization," like that of "purpose," is in the eyes of the reader. If the reader does not "get it," you have wasted both your reader's time and your own.
- Key information is fuzzily stated or missing. In all three kinds of basic situations, make sure that you have included all the necessary information. Ask

yourself, "What will my reader need to know in order to act on this document in the appropriate way?"

- Key generalizations are not supported with relevant facts. Make sure that the important generalizations in your letter—"the group's consistently sub-par performance," "a sufficient quantity of diesel fuel," or "a replacement for the current DEC mainframe"—are supported with the exact details your reader will need or want to know.

- The appearance is unattractive or makes the document hard to read. Your letter, memo, or fax is an extension of you, and it represents you, just as you represent your company. Thus you need to make sure that all documents you produce are suitably dressed out for business. Just as you would probably not come to work in sandals, torn cutoffs, and a Spuds McKenzie T-shirt, so you do not want to send out correspondence that suggests by its appearance that you are anything less than a real professional in your field.

- The document suffers from too many overly long sentences, too much jargon, and too many obscure words. (See Chapter 6 on revising and editing.)

PRACTICE

One of the most important letters you will ever write is your own job-application letter. For this practice session, we want you to write one now. (If you read on into the next chapter, you will be able to combine your letter with a résumé and a Portfolio of Accomplishments.) Once you have written your letter, test it against the standards suggested in this chapter. If you already have done such a letter, test it against our standards and consider rewriting it.

11

The Most Important Report You'll Ever Write: Your Portfolio of Accomplishments

*O wad some Power the giftie gie us
To see oursels as ithers see us!
It wad frae mony a blunder free us,
An' foolish notion. . . .*
— *Robert Burns*

SEEING OURSELVES AS OTHERS SEE US

The power to take an objective look at oneself, "To see ourselves as others see us," remains one of the most elusive and useful of human character traits. Few people have it; fewer still really want it. But those who can stand the rigors of rating themselves objectively have a real edge in life—and especially in business.

As the poet suggests, learning to see ourselves through the other person's eyes acts as a kind of safety measure: It helps us catch details of our behavior that get blurred by the distorting lenses of our own egos. Taking an objective look at ourselves frees us from many a blunder and foolish notion. Not from all blunders, perhaps, but from "mony" of them. We all have opportunities to learn how others see us:

Totaling up your own business performance record on paper may well be the most important writing you ever do.

- In college we are graded regularly on our ability to assimilate course material.

185

- On the job, we receive annual or semiannual performance reviews in which others measure how much we are contributing to the enterprise that employs us. Corporate life contains a number of mechanisms that more or less force us to examine our professional performance—if not our entire selves—from the viewpoint of the outsider.
- Even people who are self-employed are forced to see themselves as others see them. The bottom line is the ultimate measure of performance, and no amount of denial and excuses can overturn the income statement's objective judgment of how the business was run.

None of those objective measures, however, is quite as powerful as what happens when we voluntarily subject ourselves to the discipline of looking objectively at ourselves—*and write down what we find.*

When self-examination is conducted on paper, it can be especially transformative. In that sense, totaling up your own business performance record on paper may well be the most important report writing you will ever do. It can identify for you, in private, both strengths and weaknesses of which you were unaware. When the outcome of that self-examination is properly edited and submitted to an employer, it could lead directly to your next job. It could mean the difference between getting your "dream position" or getting "just another job." All that is required, of course, is that you present what you learn about your professional background to prospective employers in an appropriate document. Traditionally, that document has been a résumé. But that is changing.

THE RÉSUMÉ: USEFUL BUT LIMITED

Yesterday the standard way for Americans in business to document their professional performance on paper and to use the results to get a new job with a different organization was the résumé. All of us know what it looks like and how it reads:

A traditional résumé:

Block 1:
Your name (in all caps)
Your address
Your phone number

Block 2:
Your availability date
Whether you will relocate

Block 3:
Your college degree(s) and date(s)
Your major, with a list of important coursework
Your minor, with a list of important coursework
Any other important coursework
Applicable extracurricular activity, volunteer or military service

Block 4:
Your previous employment record, with brief descriptions
of your role in each position

Block 5:
Any awards, honors, or other recognitions you may have received

Block 6:
Where the employer can find the names, addresses, and phone numbers
of your references

For entry-level employees, traditional résumés may be only one or two pages long. Especially at that level, one résumé looks pretty much like the next. Here is an example of a good, entry-level résumé.

JUDY JEFFERSON

1403 Forest Avenue   Available May 15, 1994
Knoxville, TN 37916   Will relocate
(615) 555-0483

EDUCATION   University of Tennessee, Knoxville, Tenn. **MBA—Management**, May, 1994.

University of Tennessee, Knoxville, Tenn. **BS—Accounting**, May, 1992.
Earned 100% of college expenses through part- and full-time employment.

HONORS   Dean's List: 1989-1992. Outstanding Leadership Award, UTK Intramural Board, 1991.

EXPERIENCE
1/93-present   Blake and Co., Inc., Knoxville, Tenn. **Insurance Adjuster.**
• Act as financial liaison between private/commercial clients and insurance companies.
• Evaluate financial losses; estimate replacement costs; conduct financial analyses.

9/90-9/92   University of Tennessee Affirmative Action. **Student Assistant.**
• Developed computer databases for affirmative action searches.

- Conducted library research, supported administrative functions.

6/88-8/90   East Tennessee Coca-Cola, Knoxville, Tenn.
College Marketing Representative.
- Served as Strategy Chair of committee that created and implemented a $10,000 interactive sales promotion on the UTK campus.
- Developed and presented to corporate executives a plan for a national advertising format based on the success of the UTK promotion.

ACTIVITIES   Tennessee Organization of MBAs; American Marketing Association; Student Government Association.

REFERENCES   Letters of recommendation available on request from UTK Placement Office.

Variations on the traditional résumé can individualize it a little. Perhaps the most common is the *skills inventory*, in which the compiler of the résumé lists relevant technical abilities that may not come out in the other traditional entries. That section of the résumé printed above would look like this:

COMPUTER SKILLS   Proficient with Microsoft Excel, Lotus 1-2-3, Word, Wordperfect, DOS, and Windows on IBM hardware.

LANGUAGES   Proficient in conversational Spanish.

In the current flood, even the most well written résumé may not get a good reading.

Different individuals would record different skills in this section. Although "computer skills" is becoming almost a universal item, "languages" may not be relevant for some people, while an expanded listing of "statistical analysis skills" or Total Quality Management skills might be. It is important in this kind of listing on your résumé to include only those things that you have direct experience with; simply having read the DOS manual does not qualify you to claim DOS proficiency here. You should expect readers of your résumé to ask your basis for claiming each of these skills; in fact, you should hope they *will* ask that question.

The Limitations of the Résumé

"Everybody [standing in line at the job fair] was my age, wearing the same clothes as me and *carrying the same laser-printed résumé*." *Wall Street Journal*, September 20, 1993.

Despite the fact that anyone entering the job market must have and use a résumé, there are a number of limitations to the form today. Résumé language has grown so formulaic that a modern résumé can be almost as stilted and ritualized as a petition to the Emperor of Cathay. Beyond that, résumés have become too common, too likely to be mass produced, too easy to mislead people with, and—for all those reasons—too easy for employers to disregard.

Résumés have become too common.   The corporate career résumé is actually a relatively recent creation. Until about 1960, résumés were not widely used in the United States. In the late 1960s and early 1970s, however, due to fundamental changes in the way U.S. citizens live, work, and travel, corporate personnel departments found themselves often hiring strangers—including managers—from thousands of miles away, rather than the sons or daughters of veteran employees. When strangers began employing strangers, written documentation replaced the testimony of friends and relatives. For managers, the résumé became an essential part of the job-switch process. Beginning in the mid 1980s, another set of forces, notably corporate downsizing, augmented the growing trend to job-switching, and a résumé became as essential to a manager as a rifle to an infantryman.

Today, résumés have become so common that many managers responsible for hiring feel swamped by a flood of them (Figure 11.1). Mr. Richard U. De Schutter,

"Résumés over there."

Figure 11.1.   The fate of today's résumés. Copyright *The New Yorker,* October 5, 1992.

President and Chief Operating Officer of G. D. Searle & Company, commented on this state of affairs:

> I've received over 2,000 résumés since the first of the year. It's a shame, but my secretary throws them all in the trash. Formerly we forwarded unsolicited résumés to the human resources department. These days, that's absolutely a waste of money. (Interview with De Schutter, October 15, 1993)

This practice of throwing out stacks of unsolicited résumés is now common.

Résumés are too likely to be mass produced.   Today it is not uncommon to see résumé preparation advertised in newspaper classified columns right along with income-tax preparation, or to find storefront "consultants" offering to prepare a résumé for $25 or $30. You can even buy customized computer software that will give you a "very professional-looking" résumé (i.e., *just like everyone else's*). Is it any wonder employers increasingly ignore résumés? In about a quarter century, the résumé has gone from a cutting-edge career placement instrument to a cliché.

"The best résumé is a homemade résumé."

On June 16, 1992, *The Wall Street Journal* discussed the résumé problem in William M. Bulkeley's "Information Age" column. "Computer entrepreneurs are waking up to the potential market of desperate job-seekers and offering a growing number of computer products for PC users," Bulkeley wrote. One computer program he cited actually helps turn plain English into bureaucratese to make an applicant's résumé more attractive to government hiring officers. Another provides a sample cover letter, sample margins and paragraphs, and a list of essential buzzwords to restrain users who might become too creative. Employment professionals who reviewed the new computerized résumé products, however, told Bulkeley they held them in low esteem.

"The idea that a computer can properly express and elicit the correct information seems not in the realm of reality," said Frank Fox, executive director of the Professional Association of Résumé Writers. New York-based executive recruiter Dwight Foster told Bulkeley, "The best résumé is a homemade résumé, as far as I'm concerned. Everyone recognizes the store-bought résumé."

Résumés are too easy to mislead people with.   The problem goes beyond the fact that résumés are too common and too similar. If recent stories in the *Wall Street Journal* are to be believed, today's typical business résumé no longer holds credibility with the decision-makers responsible for hiring middle and upper managers. The language of résumés can conceal as much as it reveals, and in a business climate of mass layoffs and job buyouts, carefully screening a tidal wave of résumés for bogus claims, titles, and histories—as well as for "innocent" omissions—is beyond the resources of all but a handful of firms.

A June 17, 1992 article by Joan E. Rigdon in the "Marketplace" section of the *Wall Street Journal* suggested the scope of the résumé-authentication problem. "Deceptive Résumés Can Be Door-Openers But Can Become an Employee's Undoing," the headline barked. Ms. Rigdon then went on to cite a 1988 study by the security unit of Equifax, Inc.:

> Almost one-third of 200 randomly chosen résumés misstated dates of employment by three months or more—presumably to cover up unemployment or unpleasant stints at companies omitted from the résumé. The survey also found that 11% of applicants lied about why they left previous jobs, 4% fudged job titles, 3% listed fake employers, 3% fabricated jobs, and 3% pretended to have a college degree.

In a business climate of mass layoffs and buyouts, carefully screening a tidal wave of résumés is beyond the resources of most companies.

A particularly embarrassing case cited by Ms. Rigdon was that of James Fang, director of international trade for the city of San Francisco. "Most people thought he was a lawyer because his résumé included the words 'Hastings College of the Law (1987),'" the *Journal* reported. "But Mr. Fang wasn't a lawyer and says that those who thought otherwise must have misread his résumé." Mr. Fang, it turned out, had *attended* the law school, but he had not actually *graduated* (nor, in all fairness, had he claimed to; but the formalized language of his résumé made it easy to miss this detail). And though he had passed the California bar examination, Mr. Fang was not actually a member of the bar, which requires another, shorter exam before granting admission. The résumé did not say that, either. "Before the brouhaha began to die down in March," Ms. Rigdon wrote, "a weekly newspaper dubbed the document 'the résumé that ate San Francisco.'"

That should have been the last word on résumés, but it was not. Only a week later, on June 23, 1992, Bulkeley took up the problem once more in a column titled: "Job Hunters Turn to Software and Databases to Get an Edge." So vast is the wave of résumés swamping corporate employers, Bulkeley wrote, that several large corporations have installed electronic "résumé banks" to store them. The corporations use optical-character equipment to scan résumés and pick the ones that look most promising. At the same time, Bulkeley noted, other companies have sprung up to help job applicants circulate their résumés electronically to assure maximum exposure:

> Some services try a hard sell. "Career Database," Boston, which is free to employers and costs $50 a year for job hunters, advertises that "your résumé is made available to thousands of recruiters and millions of companies." How many actually call? Philip Weiss, president, declines to say. "Your name may never come up," he concedes.

Résumés are too easy to disregard. One of the strongest observations about résumés comes from Detroit-based outplacement counselor Pamela Crossett, who has taught thousands of buyout-stricken middle managers to reconstruct their employment histories and weave the details into effective résumés: She says even a well-written résumé may not get a good reading:

> We know from experience that nobody spends more than five or six seconds reading a résumé. It's a sales brochure—that's all. The titles and dates of employment mean nothing. In some companies the title of president may even be misleading.

Experienced corporate executives know the pitfalls of résumés, Ms. Crossett says, which is why they so often ignore these increasingly useless documents in favor of a serious interview and a background check. "People hire people, not résumés," Ms. Crossett says.

BEYOND THE RÉSUMÉ: YOUR PERSONAL PORTFOLIO OF ACCOMPLISHMENTS

"White-collar workers today should feel greater insecurity and vulnerability than they have at any point in recent times."

"It's very risky. People think they can just go out and take their technical skills and be successful. But they have to learn how to market their product."
—James L. Medoff, Harvard economist, and Peter Longini, recently laid off worker, quoted in the *Wall Street Journal*, August 24, 1992.

"Individuals will move up and down the income ladder at faster rates. 'Careers' will increasingly become portfolios of jobs, *on and off numerous firms' payrolls at various times. And companies—including members of the Fortune 500—will appear and disappear, leap forward and tumble backward at a furious pace."*
—Tom Peters, "There's Method to Seeming Madness of Job Churn," *The Chicago Tribune*, August 31, 1992.

If even the best-written résumés are being discounted as so much boilerplate, how is an eager, well-qualified applicant supposed to make his or her abilities known to corporate management?

Writing a POA requires a level of discipline not generally necessary in compiling a résumé.

The good news is that there *is* a way: A new kind of professional dossier, called the Portfolio of Accomplishments, or POA, can tell corporate managers what an ordinary résumé cannot. The bad news—if anything about the POA can actually be termed "bad"—is that this new document actually has to be *written*, rather than merely *compiled* as a résumé is. And the best time to begin this writing process is early in your career. We recommend you begin today.

The POA uses the same skills presented throughout this book to solve the most important business problem—getting a good position.

For someone who has already embraced the challenge of business writing, however, having to write the document rather than merely compile it is no problem: The other chapters of this book have shown you how to organize your thoughts and put them on paper so as to solve specific business problems. In the POA, you use these same skills to solve the most important business problem of all: getting yourself a position.

How does the POA help you solve your employment problem? Unlike a résumé, the POA is not just a tabular listing of your past job titles and dates of employment. It is a work of prose that uses chronological order, complete sentences, and a narrative, past-tense construction to describe the work you did and the results you achieved.

A typical POA reads more like a personal memoir or a magazine interview than like a résumé. The pronoun "I," which never appears in a typical résumé, is not only permissible, but obligatory, in a POA. Telegram-style sentences ("Directed six employees in telemarketing department") are out. Complete sentences, starting with the pronoun "I," are in. The emphasis is on *showing the unfolding of developments over time*:

> On November 1, 1988, I was directed to hire and train six employees to conduct a telemarketing campaign. I organized the employees into a team and helped them develop daily, weekly, and monthly targets, along with a measurement system designed to track individual and group performance. At the end of the first six months this team had accounted for a 36-percent increase in sales.

When employers consider hiring you, they want to see evidence of concrete improvements you brought about in your previous positions.

A strong POA focuses on the writer's demonstration of how he or she *made a difference* on the job. "Placeholding"—merely occupying a position and carrying out its duties in the way they were historically understood—is a negative in the POA. The traditional résumé lets people hide behind placeholding and offers no way to feature making a difference. (The only exceptions to the POA focus on making a difference might be if the applicant is a teenage summer employee, a trainee, or an intern; such novices are generally not expected to innovate or overturn accepted practice.) When employers look at your POA, they want to see evidence that you were able to bring about positive change in your past positions. Businesses thrive by finding ways to do things better, not by doing the same old things in the same old ways.

POA Format: Tell Your Story So They Will Remember Your Results

Travis Tully developed a strong record for making positive changes at the companies where he worked during his thirty-year managerial career. So he designed a POA format in which all elements—page layout, titles, paragraph and sentence structure, even typography—would lead readers quickly to a perception of his effectiveness in each job he held.

Mr. Tully's twenty-page POA treats each job with each company much like a chapter in a book, with each chapter title (each new position) starting at the top of a right-hand page. The title is written in modified newspaper-headline style: At the very top of the page, a complete sentence in uppercase, bold type succinctly states the substance of the writer's accomplishment:

FIRST DISTRIBUTION DEPARTMENT IN THE CHEMICAL INDUSTRY SAVES OVER $2 MILLION PER YEAR PLUS IMMEASURABLE BENEFITS

Director, Distribution—Unexcelled Chemical Company

That is how Mr. Tully opens the "chapter" of his POA covering his five years as the Director of Distribution for Unexcelled Chemical Company. Note that the actual job title he held appears two lines below the headline in lowercase type. This way the title does not usurp the headline's function, which is to summarize Mr. Tully's main accomplishment in dollars.

Rule Number 1 for the POA writer, therefore, is *Put your results, not your job title, up front.* Not much like a résumé, is it? The job title is followed by a horizontal rule, under which appears a brief paragraph of what screenwriters call "exposition," that is, a sort of preamble designed to help the audience understand the action that follows. Here is how Mr. Tully wrote his:

> The Unexcelled Chemical Company was planning to diversify and acquire firms for corporate growth and expansion. I joined them in December 1989 in an executive capacity so as to gain operational experience until a general-management opportunity in an acquired subsidiary became available.
>
> Because of my extensive background in transportation and distribution, I was assigned to organize and develop the newly created Distribution Department. As Director of Distribution, I reported directly to the Vice President-Logistics.
>
> Four managers reported to me: (1) The <u>Director of Distribution Operations</u>, responsible for production planning, and scheduling shipments; (2) the <u>Director of Traffic</u>, responsible for handling the rates and routes of shipments, who occasionally appeared before the ICC on hearings regarding rates and product classifications; (3) the <u>Director of Distribution Planning</u>, responsible for developing the Distribution Division's Annual Plan, for handling the inventory problems (related to various chemicals' instability) at plant and distributor levels, and for assigning over thirty Distribution Centers to handle the distribution patterns of the nine Unexcelled plants; and (4) the <u>Director of Distribution Engineering</u>, responsible for materials handling and the analysis of transportation equipment. Through these directors, a total of fifty people were under my supervision.

At this point, the real narrative begins. To guide the reader securely from opening premise to conclusion, Mr. Tully breaks the narrative into three subsections, each preceded by its own subhead, set in lowercase and boldface, and underlined. These subheads adhere strictly to formula and appear in this order:

<u>What I found:</u>
<u>What was done:</u>
<u>Results:</u>

The three-subhead system benefits both writer and reader. It helps you as writer to organize your thoughts about your accomplishments, and it entices your reader to be alert for the differences between the situation that prevailed when you took the job and the much-improved situation that prevailed when you finished it. These headings set up a narrative that makes the reader anticipate the exciting results but still maintains interest in the process that produced the results.

Make sure your **<u>Results</u>** paragraphs include documentation expressed in dollars whenever possible. Numbers almost always make a business report more authentic, and dollars are the most convincing numbers of all. Be as accurate as possible; prospective employers will almost always check out claims of dollarized results.

Writing a POA chapter requires a level of discipline you are not likely to encounter in compiling a résumé. Because there is no rigid limit on length, it is up to you to use your writing skills to keep each entry as succinct, clear, and cohesive as possible. Because you are writing complete sentences and using a chronological, narrative format, you may be tempted to ramble. Do not give in to that temptation! Keep your prose brief. Do not write anything that does not relate to the headline and the subheads—what you found, what you did, what you accomplished (in dollars!).

Now read Travis Tully's entire POA entry for his three years in the Distribution Department at Unexcelled. Though it occupies only three printed pages, it tells a definite story in a simple, digestible form. Note in particular the **Results** section: In very few lines of prose—loaded with dollar numbers—it testifies eloquently to the positive changes this executive made.

FIRST DISTRIBUTION DEPARTMENT IN THE CHEMICAL INDUSTRY SAVES OVER $2 MILLION PER YEAR PLUS IMMEASURABLE BENEFITS

Director, Distribution – Unexcelled Chemical Company

The Unexcelled Chemical Company was planning to diversify and acquire firms for corporate growth and expansion. I joined them in December 1989 in an executive capacity so as to gain operational experience until a general-management opportunity in an acquired subsidiary became available.

Because of my extensive background in transportation and distribution, I was assigned to organize and develop the newly created Distribution Department. As Director of Distribution, I reported directly to the Vice President-Logistics.

Four managers reported to me: (1) The <u>Director of Distribution Operations</u>, responsible for production planning, and scheduling shipments; (2) the <u>Director of Traffic</u>, responsible for handling the rates and routes of shipments, who occasionally appeared before the ICC on hearings regarding rates and product classifications; (3) the <u>Director of Distribution Planning</u>, responsible for developing the Distribution Division's Annual Plan, for handling the inventory problems (related to various chemicals' instability) at plant and distributor levels, and for assigning over thirty Distribution Centers to handle the distribution patterns of the nine Unexcelled plants; and (4) the <u>Director of Distribution Engineering</u>, responsible for materials handling and the analysis of transportation equipment. Through these directors, a total of fifty people were under my supervision.

What I found:

1. Although the Distribution Department was being staffed with bright young college graduates with good educational background, few had experience in the field of distribution.

2. The Traffic Division was headed by an unimaginative Director who was close to retirement and had nominated an equally unimaginative Chief Clerk as his successor.

3. The Distribution Operations Division did not have a division head and had not been examining essential issues.

4. The Distribution Planning Division was attempting to make contact with other departments within the Company and with Unexcelled distributors to improve unacceptable inventory levels.

5. The Belgian subsidiary was floundering badly. The international Vice President had convinced the President of Unexcelled that he could turn the Company around if he had a distribution system.

What was done:

1. Concurrent with internal training programs on the basics of distribution, which I started for the young MBAs, a total departmental strategic plan was developed and implemented. Each division head within Distribution was required to establish a Management by Quality Objectives System based on the total departmental program, which incorporated broad goals I had outlined. Each member of the Distribution organization was reviewed semiannually in relation to performance against the objectives.

2. I hired a General Traffic Manager with twenty years' proven experience and instructed him to organize a viable traffic function that would include rate activity planning in order to put Unexcelled in the forefront of rate negotiation within the chemical industry.

3. I hired a Manager of Distribution Operations who had a proven record of accomplishment in distribution-center operations. He was instructed to work with the Plant Distribution Managers to develop plans for Distribution Center layout, stock rotation, order cycling and transport-equipment loading.

4. In the domestic market, distribution "out-of-stock" situations were occurring with greater frequency, especially in the areas of new products and low-volume markets. A private trucking fleet, the first in the industry, was established with sixteen trucks operating on a break-even basis. The objective: assuring the Marketing Department that customer out-of-stock occurrences would be eliminated.

Because little or no attention was given to inbound raw-materials order cycling, demurrage expense was amounting to over $150,000 per year throughout the system. To avoid unnecessary penalties, the plants were instructed in the proper techniques for ordering rail cars into the plant.

5. After reviewing the problems of the Belgian subsidiary, I reported to management that a distribution function should be established, but that the subsidiary's primary problem was the total lack of a market base. In the final analysis, this proved to be true, and the subsidiary was liquidated the following year.

After its establishment, the Belgian Distribution Department was staffed with a few key people. The Director of Distribution (whom I selected) reported directly to the Plant Manager and on a dotted-line basis to me. Although savings through better distribution methods exceeded $300,000, the improvement in product distribution was not by itself sufficient to salvage what had become a moribund operation. As the story goes, "the operation was a success, but the patient died."

Results:

The distribution contribution to profit in 1990 was approximately $1,500,000 through greater intensity in rate negotiations with commercial carriers.

- Elimination of inefficient heating devices of all types in rail cars resulted in annual savings of $100,000.
- Savings from the operation of the private truck fleet amounted to $85,000.
- Demurrage expense was reduced to $10,000 from $150,000.
- Reallocation of chemical production to primary plant patterns resulted in transshipment savings of $265,000 per year.

Unquantifiable accomplishments: Projection of packaging-materials requirements in 1990 was undertaken for the first time by the Distribution Department. These projections served as a guide in determining the amount and timing of ordering packaging materials from suppliers.

A freight-cost matrix we developed allowed evaluation of interplant and interpattern shipments, making it easier to identify a least-cost solution for product availability at the distributor's location.

A contingency plan for distribution in the event of work stoppage at various plants was laid out. If a work stoppage had occurred at any of the plants, this plan would have made it possible for the Distribution Department to continue shipments to distributors who otherwise would be affected.

A production scheduling program was completed. It became a useful tool in short-range forecasting and resulted in improved forecasting accuracy.

A computerized rail-car control system was developed to improve management of the assigned fleet of 1,800 rail cars throughout the system.

YOUR POA: IT'S NEVER TOO EARLY TO START

Do you have to be a high-powered executive with a string of successful jobs behind you to create a powerful Portfolio of Accomplishments? Absolutely not. At the University of Notre Dame during 1992–1994, Professor of Career Communications Eugene D. Fanning trained his seniors in business administration to put together POAs, even though the only jobs they may have held were unpaid internships, summer work, or part-time, entry-level positions. Fanning, who runs a Chicago investment firm when he is not teaching, says almost any kind of job history can appear in a POA, provided it shows the writer's ability to grow and develop as part of the work experience.

For example, if you were an employer with the opportunity to hire a young graduate fresh out of college—or perhaps still taking courses—wouldn't you be pleased to interview the student of Fanning's who wrote the following entry in his POA about a summer job? (Names have been changed.)

Stacy's Department Store

In the summer of 1990, I was hired by Stacy's Department Store as a stockboy. During the summer, I was attending the University in the morning, taking six credits. Therefore, I needed a job that would allow me to work nights and still allow time for me to study. My responsibilities included receiving invoices, checking merchandise, maintaining the stock, and supplying departments.

What I found:
The "dock" was where I did most of my work. Many of the employees had been there for a long period and were not as motivated as I was to do their job efficiently. Many of the veterans were content to let the new people work as hard as they could while the veterans loafed. That really fired me up, and I channeled my frustrations into working hard and doing a good job.

What was done:
  1. Using my best skills, I quickly learned the ropes of the trade. It was important to learn all the call numbers for the various departments to efficiently supply them.
  2. I earned the trust of management—after a week, I was given the responsibility of closing the store and securing the stock.
  3. I organized the stock rooms in an orderly fashion in order to get the customer a product as fast as possible.
  4. I met some good people who worked at the store.
  5. Working at night allowed me to go to school during the day—I earned six credits that I transferred to Notre Dame.

Results:

I learned early the value of hard work. This hard work ethic helped me tremendously on the job; for one thing, it gave my co-workers and me extra time to rearrange and reorganize other departments and stock rooms. It came to my attention that our store was throwing away a lot of cardboard. I proposed to the store manager that we should think about recycling to earn a little revenue as well as promote our store as environmentally smart. Projected contribution was $500/year, while immediate results achieved critical acclaim in the *Daily Bugle*.

Hard work is a key to success. No matter how small your job may seem, I think it is important to be dedicated to the job and the company. I really cared about this job and put a lot of effort into it. This work ethic carried over into my academics that summer and the following year as well as into my summer cross-country training.

As is typical for a student working part-time in an entry-level job, this POA writer could not point to a set of results in terms of dollars such as a skilled manager might produce after a year or two in a critical position. Yet the results this young student achieved were real and bore definite value. Any manager reading such a POA would be struck by the freshness and sincerity of the writer's realization of the importance of hard work. The more perceptive manager would probably note with pleasure how this student reacted to the poor work ethic of his older colleagues: While restraining himself from condemning them, he nonetheless recognized their attitude and used it to spur his own efforts. Nor would a manager be surprised that the skills and awareness this student developed on the job proved useful in academic work and athletics: All types of effort tend to be mutually reinforcing, and shrewd employers know that applicants with a good record for applying themselves in off-the-job pursuits are likely to succeed in business as well.

No wonder Professor Fanning reports that some of his students have already used POAs composed in his undergraduate classes to land jobs on graduation. Says Fanning,

> The POA, in my judgment, gives these young men and women a tremendous edge. The first thing it does is to indicate to a prospective employer how well organized that job candidate is. Then it tells the employer, "Here's where I've been. Here are the problems I encountered. Here's what I accomplished. Here's what I was unable to do."
>
> So after a year's trial, the POA is a course requirement. By the fall of the year, my seniors in marketing, accounting, finance, or whatever are already in the job-interview process. If they have a POA, they can conclude the interview by saying something like, "Well, Mr. Smith, I'm very grateful for the opportunity to hear something about your company and tell you something about myself. If you find yourself with a few spare moments later on, I'd like you to look at my Portfolio of Accomplishments. It may give you a better idea of what I could contribute to your company."

The POA becomes even more important at the MBA level, where graduates are often getting ready to move directly into managerial positions, or, as Figure 11.2 says, getting "ready for market."

Additional Examples of Student POAs

You have already seen how one student handled a POA entry for a summer job. Here are two additional excerpts from student POAs, selected to show you good ways to handle other typical (student, entry-level) experiences—one as a marketing assistant, and one as a bookkeeper and general manager. Once again, the names have been changed.

NEW IDEAS GENERATED TO INCREASE ATTENDANCE AND FAN PARTICIPATION AT STATE COLLEGE BASEBALL GAMES
Sports Marketing Assistant, State College

In January of 1992 I joined the Sports Marketing staff at State College. This unit is part of the Athletics Department and handles the marketing and promotion for various varsity sports. I was assigned to men's baseball.

What I found:

Upon arriving, I looked at the previous year's attendance figures and found that much needed to be done to increase the paid attendance for the upcoming season.

- We wanted to get more student involvement, but this was difficult because most of our home games were played at a ballpark ten minutes from campus.
- Records from past events were scarce, so I had to start from scratch with new ideas and new insights.

What was done:

1. I introduced new ideas into marketing the games, including fresh ideas to get the students more involved. Because student involvement was a major goal, I planned activities specifically to increase it, such as dorm visits by the coach, off-campus nights at the games, and other specials (including letting students pick starting line-ups).

2. Another major focus was grade-school children, so I worked with various Little League baseball teams in the area to promote the games. I also came up with the idea of an egg hunt for Easter weekend, which tied into Family Day, another new promotion.

3. I organized each game to have an individual marketing report, which enabled me to keep tabs on the various marketing schemes for each game and its corresponding attendance sheets. I made it a point to keep clear records of everything, and the records were stored in the computer so that all information could easily be accessed in the future.

"In six more weeks, these M.B.A.s will be ready for market."

Figure 11.2. These folks had better have their POAs ready when they hit the market. Copyright *The New Yorker,* March 30, 1992.

Results:

The preseason response was phenomenal. My ideas generated a lot of energy around the athletic department, and I received outstanding positive feedback from the Director of Sports Marketing. Despite frequent bad weather, we did show an increase in total attendance, and the fans enthusiastically participated in the activities during the games. Through this experience I have learned both positive and negative aspects of the sports marketing business. I have learned how frustrating it can be to plan a great game-day promotion, only to have it rain all day. I also learned that by working hard and by keeping open communication with all those involved, success does come.

SMALL FIRM'S ACCOUNTING, INVENTORY, AND CLAIMS PROCEDURES BROUGHT UNDER CONTROL FOR THE FIRST TIME
Bookkeeper and Management Assistant, Jennings Associates

In May of 1991 I joined Jennings Associates, an agency supplying book-keeping and office procedures to small firms. Crown Cleaners, a small dry-cleaning chain in St. Louis composed of three drop-off and pick-up stores and one plant, was a client. I worked on the company's internal books and performed other internal management duties.

What I found:

Because I had worked for Crown Cleaners for two summers, I was familiar with the company's everyday activities. However, I was unaware of the state of the accounting records. The owner, who had very little accounting knowledge, had tried to keep the books to the best of her abilities, so all of the data were stored in accountant columnar paper binders, with daily receipt reports handwritten into these binders by the owner. There had not been an inventory check in over seven years, which made keeping accurate inventory counts difficult, if not impossible. And there were no records on claims that had to be paid to customers as a result of lost or damaged clothing, which made it difficult to get claims processed and paid out promptly.

What was done:

1. I prioritized the work that needed to be done, and as a result of this process decided the accounting books needed to be taken care of first. I persuaded the owner to acquire a computer to make organization of the accounting material easier and less complicated, and I wrote a simple, user-friendly program that would enable all relevant information to be entered on Macintosh Excel spreadsheets.

2. Next I implemented an inventory tracking system that could be directly incorporated with the existing paper files in the pick-up and drop-off stores. A physical inventory check was made at each store, and any existing discrepancies were noted. Once the physical count was completed, I implemented a program that would keep a perpetual inventory count, allowing the owner to see exactly how many pieces of clothing were taken in or picked up each day. With this system in place, for the first time daily receipts could be verified against each day's actual activity as revealed by the ongoing inventory data.

3. With the inventory problem taken care of, I then updated and organized the claim forms. To ensure that true claims were being made, each customer claim had to be tracked carefully. Determining replacement costs for lost or damaged articles required direct communication with retail clothing stores. In addition, I established contact with the Inter-

national Fabricare Institute (IFI), which makes rulings about whether or not items have been damaged by cleaners, or whether a problem may have been caused by faulty clothing manufacture. That way, if IFI determined our firm was not at fault, the customer would be entitled to return the item to the retail store for a full refund.

4. Finally, I made sure that the owner and other key employees of Crown Cleaners were adept at the systems I had set up, so that the successful functioning of accounting, inventory, and claims handling would not depend on the presence or continued employment of any one individual.

Results:

Crown Cleaners became a better organized and more efficiently run small business as a result of my work. I was able to use computer knowledge I had learned in school to implement real-world programs that helped Crown Cleaners, and to introduce the owner to the advantages of computers in the business world, increasing her receptiveness to further computer-based improvements.

I was able to put the owner in much better command of the firm's accounting, inventory, and claims-handling practices than had ever been the case before. This allowed daily receipts to be checked more efficiently, inventory to be regulated more tightly, and customer claims to be processed more quickly.

WRITING YOUR POA: A CAREER-LONG JOB

When Pamela Crossett advises bought-out managers on how to compile a résumé, she suggests they allocate a month to the project. Even though a résumé is a simple tabular document running no more than two pages, compiling it can be a formidable task for someone who has never done it before (and never expected to lose his or her job).

Compiling a good POA is really a career-long effort.

How much time, then, should you expect to invest in preparing your more extensive and more detailed POA? Much longer than a month, obviously. But there is a trick to making the job easier: Do not try to do it all at once. Make the compiling of your POA a career-long effort. Instead of waiting until you lose a job or grow dissatisfied with a job, start compiling your POA *now*, and keep adding to it periodically—at least twice a year.

Naturally, you cannot compose and recompose your entire POA each week. But you should be making timely notes of your professional progress in a diary. These notes can be updated at longer intervals and woven into a tighter narrative that reveals where you have actually gone in your job and what kinds of effort got you there.

"It's a recession when your neighbor loses his job; it's a depression when you lose your own." Harry S Truman.

The biggest payoff you will get from writing a POA is what it does for you as you write it. Staring your career history in the face—perhaps for the first time—forces you to appraise your skills and your performance as an outsider would. The insights you gain from the experience may not all be pleasant, but you will be better off professionally for what you have learned about yourself. Taking a serious longitudinal look at your accomplishments in business (or in college) can be a sobering experience that helps you refocus on the essentials of your career. Long before the first prospective employer gets a look at your POA, the document you have created will be paying you handsome dividends in the form of greater self-confidence, greater self-understanding, and a firmer sense of direction.

"The contents are important, obviously," Professor Fanning says. "But it's a great career diary as well. It forces you to look at everything you're doing and see how it would look to corporate America. It's a great job-hunting tool. It can get you a job."

The personnel or human resources department may not know what to do with your POA; the manager you want to work for will.

A word to the wise: Once you have compiled a POA and made up your mind to use it, do not send it to your prospective employer's personnel or human-resources department. Most will not know what to do with it. Share your POA only with the manager to whom you are going to report and with whom you are interviewing for the position.

But whatever you do, do not delay getting started on your POA. Memories fade. Details get lost. People who figured importantly in your career drift out of it, taking information with them. Without a diary—or at least a quickly jotted log of your comings and goings—you are likely to forget exactly what you did six months or a year ago that got you to where you are today. Try for a few moments to reconstruct what you did in your last job and to get it on a sheet or two of paper in correct POA style. You may have to review a stack of documents and interview a handful of colleagues before you can recollect accurately what you accomplished and how you accomplished it.

Fanning, who learned about the value of POAs from the authors, offers this note on the "care and upkeep" of POAs:

> I insist to my students, if you want to do your POA right, make an entry in it whenever you get a new assignment. And every time a new year rolls around, I make it a rule not to start celebrating until I have reviewed my accomplishments for the past year and entered them into the POA. It will always be—if nothing else—a great reminder of memories.

But the fact is, those notations will become a great deal more than entries in a personal scrapbook or journal once you have written them into your POA. They become the basis for *the most* important report you'll ever write!

PRACTICE

Writing Your Own POA

The best time to start working on your own portfolio of accomplishments is now. Write your own POA. When it's finished, get critiques from at least three different people: (1) a peer, (2) a friend from outside your business life, and (3) someone from your area of business who outranks you. Based on those three critiques, revise your POA. Then, at least once a year, you will need to revise it again.

Appendix A
Sources For
Business Research

GUIDES TO BUSINESS SOURCES AND RESEARCH

Guides are a quick way to learn about business-research techniques and the wide array of business reference sources available in libraries and information centers. Choose the one best suited to your particular research problem and read the pertinent chapter or pages. Remember to ask a librarian for additional suggestions if you do not find exactly what you need reasonably quickly.

DANIELLS, LORNA M. *Business Information Sources*. 3d ed. University of California Press, 1993. Long a classic in the field and well known to business librarians, this guide is intended for the librarian, the business student, and the business person. It includes not only descriptions of reference sources, but also of books and texts in several business subfields.

FULD, LEONARD M. *Competitor Intelligence: How to Get It; How to Use It*. Wiley, 1985. Describes the techniques of gathering and obtaining information about a competitor (or any company or industry) from library basics to creative backdoor approaches. An excellent manual for the seeker of corporate intelligence/market research information.

How to Find Information About Companies: The Corporate Intelligence Source Book. 8th ed. Washington Researchers Publishing, 1991. A do-it-yourself guide for company researchers, prepared by a professional information-gathering firm. Provides tips and suggestions for using printed materials and library resources, state and national government agencies, company and industry experts, and professional information and investigation services.

LAVIN, MICHAEL R. *Business Information: How to Find It, How to Use It*. 2d ed. Oryx Press, 1992. Intended for both experienced and novice researchers, each chapter begins with an explanation of the business concepts necessary to understand the materials introduced. Not a comprehensive guide, but one focusing on the most widely available and well respected business research materials.

STRAUSS, DIANE WHEELER. *Handbook of Business Information*. Libraries Unlimited, 1988. Intended for students and researchers as well as librarians, this guide identifies and describes business reference sources with illustrations of how they are used. It also explains many basic business concepts for the inexperienced user.

WOY, JAMES B. *Encyclopedia of Business Information Sources*. 9th ed. Gale Research, Inc., 1992. A suggested list of information sources (such as statistics, directories, associations, and periodicals) listed by industry or product. A good starting place for the researcher who wants to identify the specialized publications of an industry.

INDEXES AND DIRECTORIES OF PERIODICALS AND NEWSPAPERS

Periodicals and newspapers are a major source of current information about all aspects of business. Learn here about the activities of companies and industries, the state of the national economy, the latest in economic and financial statistics, new products and technologies, or the latest in management techniques. To guide yourself through the maze of available articles, choose an index and search for your subject. The index will direct you to articles with a citation including journal title, date, and page number. Sometimes an abstract or summary of the articles will be included. Several of the indexes below are available electronically as on-line databases or compact-disc products in addition to the traditional printed format.

General Business Indexes

Business Periodicals Index. H. W. Wilson. Monthly. *BPI* is a subject index to approximately 350 periodicals in all areas of business. Both popular and research journals as well as trade magazines are analyzed. In addition to subjects, company names and products are also indexed. A good index for periodical articles on any business topic.

Predicasts F & S Index United States. Predicasts. Weekly. An excellent index for current information on U.S. companies, products, and industries, *F & S* covers a wide selection of trade magazines, financial publications, business-oriented newspapers, and special reports. The *Index* is divided into two sections: part one contains industry and product information arranged by Standard Industrial Classification (SIC) number; part two has company information arranged alphabetically by company name.

Business Index. Information Access. Monthly. Available on either microfilm or a compact disc, this index covers several hundred periodicals, including many regional and trade journals plus the *Wall Street Journal* and the financial section of the *New York Times.* A good starting point for many business topics, but additional indexes should be used for complete coverage.

ABI/INFORM. UMI/Data Courier. Weekly or Monthly. Available as an on-line database or a compact disc, it provides indexing plus abstracts or summaries of articles from more than 800 business and economics periodicals.

Specialized Business Indexes

Accounting and Tax Index. UMI. Quarterly. Formerly published by the American Institute of Certified Public Accountants, this subject/author index to accounting periodicals covers accounting, auditing, data processing, financial reporting, financial management, investments and securities, management, and taxation. Some books and government periodicals also are included.

Journal of Economic Literature. American Economic Association. Quarterly. About half of each issue of *JEL* is devoted to a table-of-contents list of approximately 200 economic journals, followed by a classified subject index of the articles. Emphasis is on economic theory and method, but management, finance, labor, industry, and consumer economics are also covered.

Index of Economic Articles. American Economic Association. Annual. Annually cumulates the journal articles indexed in the *Journal of Economic Literature* and adds a selection of books containing essays, as well as conference proceedings and papers. The *JEL* subject-classification scheme is also used here, with a topical guide added to facilitate use. Publication of these annual volumes runs four to five years behind the *JEL*.

Work Related Abstracts. Harmonie Park Press. Monthly. Indexes and abstracts about 250 professional and academic journals for articles on the workplace, labor market, unions, compensation, occupational safety and health, and human-resources management.

Related Periodical Indexes

Applied Science and Technology Index. H. W. Wilson. Monthly. A subject index to English-language technology and engineering periodicals. Useful for the application of technology to a wide spectrum of business and industry.

Social Sciences Citation Index. Institute for Scientific Information. 3/year. Based on the relationship between an article and its footnoted sources, this index covers over 2,000 social science journals, including many in business, finance, economics, management, and personnel. Access is by title keyword, author, or cited author.

PAIS International in Print. Public Affairs Information Service. Monthly. Emphasizing public policy issues, this subject index covers research journals and a selection of books and government documents. Business topics are extensively covered, particularly economics, management, and political and social interactions.

Psychological Abstracts. American Psychological Association. Monthly. This abstract index of the world's psychological literature devotes one of its sections to applied psychology, which includes management, personnel, organizational behavior, and marketing and advertising.

Reader's Guide to Periodical Literature. H. W. Wilson. Semimonthly. This familiar author/subject index to general-interest popular periodicals is a good source for the most recent developments in a wide variety of fields and for articles on consumer interests.

Newspaper Indexes

Wall Street Journal Index. UMI. Monthly. Indexes the major U.S. business newspaper. The *Index* is divided into two parts: part one is devoted to corporate news listed by company name; part two has general news arranged by subject. Since 1982, an annual index to *Barron's* has been included.

New York Times Index. New York Times. Semimonthly. U.S. and international news from America's best-known newspaper has been indexed since 1851. Includes the extensive financial section. Subject entries give date, page, column, and approximate length of each article.

Directories of Periodicals and Newspapers

GRANT, MARY M. and RIVA BERLANT-SCHILLER, comps. *Directory of Business and Financial Services*. Special Libraries Association, 1984. Lists and describes the many looseleaf services used in the business world on subjects ranging from investment advice to business law to personnel management.

UHLAN, MIRIAM. *Guide to Special Issues and Indexes of Periodicals*. 3d ed. Special Libraries Association, 1985. Lists regularly appearing special issues of over 1000 periodicals, especially trade journals.

Ulrich's International Periodical Directory. R. R. Bowker. Annual. Contains information on more than 100,000 periodicals from around the world. Especially useful is the indication of where a title is indexed.

Gale Directory of Publications and Broadcast Media. Gale Research, Inc. Annual. Directory of newspapers, magazines, radio and television stations arranged geographically. Includes data on key personnel, rates, and other relevant material.

Editor & Publisher International Yearbook. Editor & Publisher. Annual. A directory of daily newspapers from around the world with data on circulation, editorial personnel, subscription rates, special issues, and more.

DIRECTORIES OF COMPANIES AND ORGANIZATIONS

Directories provide quick access to facts about companies and organizations. Location, telephone number, and the name of a contact person are commonly listed, but many other facts may also be included, depending on the purpose and scope of the directory. Several national business directories are available; all states have a directory of manufacturers located within their borders; and hundreds of additional specialized directories are published each year.

Company Directories

Million Dollar Directory. Dun & Bradstreet Information Services. Annual. Contains directory information for 160,000 U.S. businesses. Provides address, product or service, SIC code, approximate annual sales, number of employees, and chief officers and directors. Has geographic and SIC indexes.

Standard & Poor's Register of Corporations, Directors, and Executives. Standard & Poor's. Annual. Volume 1 is a directory of 45,000 corporations with addresses, SIC code, annual revenues, number of employees, officers and directors. Volume 2 has brief biographies of the executives; volume 3 has indexes by SIC codes, geographic location, and corporate family.

Thomas Register of American Manufacturers. Thomas Publishing Co. Annual. Over twenty-five volumes provide a comprehensive directory of American manufacturers. Several volumes list firms by specific product manufactured; two volumes are alphabetical, giving address, branch offices, and an asset classification for each manufacturer, plus a list of trade names. Additional volumes contain company product catalogs.

Ward's Directory of U.S. Private and Public Companies. Gale Research, Inc. Annual. A directory of over 100,000 large and small companies. Volumes 1–4 list companies alphabetically and geographically. Volume 5 ranks companies by sales within industry categories.

Directory of Leading Private Companies. National Register Publishing Co. Annual. Includes the following information about 7,000 companies with sales over $10 million: address, business lines, number of employees, state in which incorporated, number of plants and facilities, and outside service firms (accountant, bank, insuror). Brief financial data where available.

Directory of Corporate Affiliations. National Register Publishing Co. Annual. A guide to corporate links of over 5,000 major U.S. public and private companies and their 50,000 divisions, subsidiaries, and affiliates. Includes NYSE and Amex companies, Fortune 1000 as well as OTC and private companies.

Companies and Their Brands / Brands and Their Companies. Gale Research, Inc. Annual. The *Brands* volume lists nearly 230,000 trade names, trademarks, and brand names and identifies the company that manufactures or distributes each item. The *Companies* volume lists the same names alphabetically by company.

Principal International Businesses. Dun & Bradstreet International. Annual. With 50,000 companies in 140 countries, this directory covers most of the top companies of the world. Although the information provided is brief, it includes address, telephone, lines of business, top executive, number of employees, sales, and founding date.

Directories of Organizations

Encyclopedia of Associations. Gale Research, Inc. Annual. A guide to national and international organizations in the United States, including trade and professional associations. Each entry includes address, telephone, director, staff and membership numbers, purpose, publications, annual meeting date, and other information.

National Trade and Professional Associations of the United States. Columbia Books. Annual. A directory of over 6,000 trade and professional organizations and labor unions with directory information, key personnel, and budget size.

Business Organizations, Agencies, and Publications Directory. 6th ed. Gale Research, Inc. 1992. Useful in identifying experts in various fields, this directory covers U.S. and international organizations, government agencies, research and educational facilities, and information services and publications.

Consultants and Consulting Organizations Directory. 12th ed. Gale Research, Inc. 1992. Arranged by broad subject categories, this directory provides location, principals, description of services, geographic scope, special services and more for each consulting firm.

Directory of American Research and Technology. R. R. Bowker. Annual. Lists over 11,000 laboratories and R&D centers reporting to corporations and other nongovernment organizations. Included for each unit listed are the number of staff with advanced degrees and areas of research activity within the unit.

Research Centers Directory. Gale Research, Inc. Biennial. Reports on the programs and staffing of over 12,000 nonprofit research units in all fields. Also includes university research parks and technology transfer centers.

Directory of U.S. Labor Organizations. Bureau of National Affairs. Biennial. Contains information on 300 American labor organizations. Lists all AFL-CIO headquarters and central offices across the nation plus the national headquarters and their key personnel.

World Chamber of Commerce Directory. World Chamber of Commerce Directory. Annual. Provides contact information for Chambers of Commerce throughout the United States and Canada. Also includes addresses of local industrial development boards, state tourism offices, U.S. and foreign embassies.

Directories of Directories

Directories in Print. Gale Research, Inc. Annual. A guide to more than 14,000 directories in a variety of fields, many of them trade and industry. Provides description and purchase information.

BIOGRAPHICAL DIRECTORIES

Keeping up with the career moves of business executives is easier if you start with a biographical directory. Don't expect to find many middle managers or small business owners here, however, as most directories concentrate on top executives with major national firms or individuals with national reputations.

Who's Who in America. Marquis Who's Who. Annual. Biographical information on the best-known individuals in the United States, chosen on the basis of prominence and achievement or official position. Supplemented by regional editions.

Who's Who in Finance and Industry. Marquis Who's Who. Biennial. A well known business directory containing career sketches of over 20,000 top corporate executives in the United States and Canada. Each profile contains personal data, education, career history, political or civic affiliations, and special achievements.

Reference Book of Corporate Management. Dun & Bradstreet Information Services. Annual. This multivolume set is arranged by company name. Listed under each of the 12,000 companies included are brief biographies of their top executives and directors. Included are date of birth, education, employment history, and position currently held.

Biography and Genealogy Master Index. Gale Research, Inc. Annual. Provides an index to hundreds of published sources of collective biography, covering individuals in all fields of endeavor. The scope of the biographical sources analyzed is very broad, but most individuals included are of some national prominence.

DICTIONARIES, ENCYCLOPEDIAS, AND HANDBOOKS

Need a quick definition of a term or maybe a few examples of how a particular theory can be applied? Reach for a dictionary or handbook or turn to an encyclopedia or almanac. Many are published each year. Most fields of business have several volumes devoted to their particular area; those listed below are only a sample. Check the business guides listed on pages 205–206 or ask a librarian to suggest a volume for your field if these don't answer your questions.

The Business One-Irwin Business and Investment Almanac. Dow Jones-Irwin. Annual. A compendium of facts about business drawn from many sources. Helpful in identifying sources of more detailed or up-to-date information.

GREENWALD, DOUGLAS. *The McGraw-Hill Dictionary of Modern Economics.* 3d ed. McGraw-Hill, 1983. A well respected and widely available dictionary of business and economic terms.

ROSENBERG, JERRY M. *Dictionary of Business and Management.* 2d ed. Wiley, 1983. Another respected and widely available dictionary of business terms.

The New Palgrave: A Dictionary of Economics. Stockton Press, 1987. Updates an earlier encyclopedic dictionary first published in the 1890s. Presents a "comprehensive and critical" account of economic thought at the end of the twentieth century.

MUNN, GLENN G. *The St. James Encyclopedia of Banking and Finance.* 9th ed. St. James Press, 1991. A basic source of information on the field of banking, containing both brief definitions and longer articles on specific topics.

HEYL, CARL. *The Encyclopedia of Management.* 3d ed. Van Nostrand Reinhold, 1982. Provides a good general summary of many basic business concepts, with a core list of additional sources for most topics.

The Thorndike Encyclopedia of Banking and Financial Tables. 3d. ed. Warren, Gorham & Lamont, 1987. A compilation of tables in several categories including mortgage and depreciation, compound interest, and installment loans.

Exporter's Encyclopedia. Dun & Bradstreet Information Services. Annual. A world marketing guide with information for specific countries, including export-import regulations, customs, shipping services, and documentation requirements.

Dictionary of Occupational Titles. 4th ed. U.S. Employment Services, 1991. Provides a list of job titles with brief descriptions of the scope of responsibilities and duties required of each position.

ECONOMIC STATISTICS

The federal government is a major source of economic statistics. Although many departments and agencies provide data to the public, the Department of Commerce and its Census Bureau and Bureau of Economic Analysis are among the best known and most prolific producers of statistics. All federally published statistics are widely available in libraries and federal offices throughout the nation, both in printed and electronic formats. Start your search for statistical data in the library, but contact a federal office directly if you need assistance in interpreting data or access to possibly unpublished data.

In addition to the federal government, several commercial publishers, trade associations, economic-research institutes, university research centers, and state government agencies also provide economic data to the public. The indexes to statistics noted below will direct you to some of these sources; ask a librarian for other suggestions.

Federal Statistical Sources

The chief sources of comprehensive statistical data on the United States are the U.S. Census publications. The censuses of population and housing are taken every ten years and include extensive data on the entire United States as well as on individual states, counties, Metropolitan Statistical Areas (MSA's), and cities. In addition, a series of economic censuses measuring the nation's industrial and business activity are taken every five years. Publications are widely available in printed and electronic formats. Most census publications appear from one to three years following the surveys.

Statistical Abstract of the United States. U.S. Bureau of the Census. Annual. This is the first stop for many statistical questions because it serves both as a primary source for U.S. industrial, social, political, and economic statistics and as a guide to further sources of information. Most tables profile the United States as a whole, but some regional, state, and metropolitan data may be included.

County and City Data Book. U.S. Bureau of the Census. Irregular. Comparative statistics for U.S. counties and cities in a variety of demographic, social, and economic categories. Most data are drawn from the U.S. census surveys.

Survey of Current Business. U.S. Bureau of Economic Analysis. Monthly. An important source for current U.S. business statistics. It covers over 2000 statistical series, including general business indicators, prices, labor, employment and earnings, foreign trade, finance, and several industry categories.

Business Statistics. U.S. Bureau of Economic Analysis. Biennial. A supplement to *Survey of Current Business*, this publication contains an historical summary for the statistical series drawn from the monthly publication.

Economic Indicators. U.S. Council of Economic Advisors. Monthly. Presents current data on major economic indicators such as output, spending, income, employment, production, and prices.

Employment and Earnings. U.S. Bureau of Labor Statistics. Monthly. A statistical publication presenting employment data from the census surveys and state employment-office reports.

Occupational Compensation (formerly *Area Wage Surveys*). U.S. Bureau of Labor Statistics. Annual. A useful source of wage comparisons across the nation, although limited primarily to technical and clerical occupations.

CPI (Consumer Price Index) Detailed Report. U.S. Bureau of Labor Statistics. Monthly. Provides complete price-index tables of the items reviewed for the Consumer Price Index. CPI data for about twenty-five major cities are included.

Monthly Labor Review. U.S. Bureau of Labor Statistics. Monthly. Includes a statistical section with summary data on employment, wages, price indices, and productivity.

Federal Reserve Bulletin. U.S. Board of Governors of the Federal Reserve System. Monthly. Contains a summary statistical section with data on money supply, interest rates, foreign-exchange rates, and U.S. government finances.

Economic Report of the President. U.S. Council of Economic Advisors. Annual. A review of the nation's economic condition with summaries of current policy and projections for future directions.

Other Statistical Sources

Standard & Poor's Statistical Service. Standard & Poor's. Monthly. Provides monthly updates for statistics in banking and finance, production and labor, price indexes, income and trade, and various industries.

Predicasts Basebook. Predicasts. Annual. A publication measuring the cyclical sensitivity of various products, industries, and economic indicators over a period of ten to fifteen years. Indicates the source of the data and the annual percentage growth rate for each item.

Predicasts Forecasts. Predicasts. Quarterly. This publishing service has short- and long-range forecast statistics for basic economic indicators and for individual products. The source of each forecast series and an annual percentage growth rate are also given.

Cost of Living Index. American Chamber of Commerce Researchers Association. Quarterly. Provides useful measures of cost-of-living comparisons among a selected group of about 300 urban areas across the nation.

Guides and Indexes to Statistics

Standard Industrial Classification Manual. U.S. Office of Management and Budget. 1987. The Standard Industrial Classification (SIC) scheme, developed by the federal government, is a numeric classification of all industries. The system is used by the Census Bureau and other federal agencies and has also been adopted by many nongovernment publishers for use in indexes, directories, statistics, and guides. The *SIC Manual* is a guide to the appropriate SIC codes for a particular industry or product.

HOEL, ARLINE, et al. *Economics Sourcebook of Government Statistics.* Lexington Press, 1983. A guide to over fifty widely used government-produced economic indicators of business and financial conditions—what they are, what they are based on, their potential limitations, when they are released, where estimates can be obtained, and whom to contact with questions.

O'HARA, FREDERICK M. and ROBERT SICIGNANO. *Handbook of United States Economic and Financial Indicators.* Greenwood Press, 1985. A guide to over 200 indicators produced by government agencies, trade associations, financial publishers, and many others. Explains what they are, how they are derived and used, and where to find their current and historic values.

Statistics Sources. Gale Research, Inc. Annual. A guide to statistics, many of them economic, financial, and industrial, available in over 2,000 sources of all types.

American Statistics Index. Congressional Information Service. Monthly. A master guide and index to the statistical publications of the U.S. government, its agencies, and departments.

Statistical Reference Index. Congressional Information Service. Monthly. Provides access to a large body of business, financial, and social statistics produced by or available through U.S. associations and institutes, business organizations, commercial publishers, and state agencies.

Index to International Statistics. Congressional Information Service. Monthly. An index and description of the statistical publications of international agencies such as the United Nations, the European Union, and the Organization for Economic Cooperation and Development (OECD).

CORPORATE FINANCE AND INVESTMENT SERVICES

Knowledge of a corporation's financial position is essential for many aspects of business research. As a business scholar, you are well aware of the value of a corporation's annual report to stockholders in illuminating its fiscal standing. Along with the audited financial statement—the balance sheet and income statement—the annual report also provides insight into the firm's management strategies, current activities, and plans for the future. Annual reports are available for the asking from the corporation itself, and most libraries also maintain collections.

Proxy statements, which are the official notices sent to all stockholders before the firm's annual meeting, are increasingly important for corporate analysis, since they contain information on items to be voted on at the meeting. All proposals on items such as executive compensation, voting rights, financial policies, proposed mergers or acquisitions, and social issues such as animal testing will be outlined and accompanied by the management's position statement. Proxy statements are not widely available, but large libraries will have microfiche collections or electronic access to them.

Less well known are the financial disclosure statements that publicly owned corporations must file with the U.S. Securities and Exchange Commission. Principal among them is the 10-K report, an itemized list of questions the firm must answer annually regarding its current position. Much of the information corresponds to that found in the annual report, but without the traditional hype. The 10-K report also requires more detail in some areas than the annual report does. The 10-K report is updated by the quarterly 10-Q report.

If you are a student, you may be able to find either the SEC documents you need, or electronic access to them, at your university library. Many public and academic libraries (and most corporate libraries) also have access to this information. Unless you are working with a sizable budget, you may find it advisable to avoid corporate information brokers. The recent explosion of electronic access to information is making travel to distant sites or recourse to expensive professional services less necessary when it comes to finding this kind of information. In addition, the SEC now provides Internet access to its financial filings through its Electronic Data Gathering, Analysis, and Retrieval (EDGAR) system.

The SEC has regional offices in Atlanta, Boston, Chicago, Denver, Fort Worth, Los Angeles, New York, Philadelphia, and Seattle, but its documents are available for public inspection only at its headquarters in Washington, D.C. and at the Chicago and New York offices. The addresses for the SEC's headquarters and the Chicago and New York regional offices are:

Headquarters:	Securities and Exchange Commission
	450 Fifth Street, N.W.
	Washington, D.C. 20549
	Public reference room hours: 9:00 A.M.–5:00 P.M. (EST)
Chicago:	Securities and Exchange Commission
	Northwestern Atrium Center
	500 West Madison Street
	Chicago, Illinois 60661
	Public reference room hours: 9:00 A.M.–4:15 P.M. (CST)
New York:	Securities and Exchange Commission
	75 Park Place
	14th Floor
	New York, New York 10007
	Public reference room hours: 9:00 A.M.–5:00 P.M. (EST)

Filings made with the SEC in Washington or at any of its regional offices during roughly the past five years are available at any of the public reference rooms. The public reference room in Washington maintains filings for approximately the past four months in print; filings prior to that time are on microfiche. The Chicago and New York regional offices maintain filings only on microfiche. Filings older than five years are also available from the public reference rooms but may take from twenty-four hours to two weeks to obtain. The public reference rooms also have computer terminals with access to filings made via the SEC's Electronic Data Gathering Analysis and Retrieval (EDGAR) system.

Filings may be copied at the SEC's public reference rooms for a fee. Hard copy of filings made via EDGAR may also be obtained from the SEC's public reference rooms for a fee.

In addition to obtaining filings directly from the SEC's public reference rooms, filings may also be obtained for a fee from any number of information-retrieval-and-delivery companies. The listing below is only a partial one, and it is not to be construed as an endorsement of any of them. Disclosure, Inc., is the only one specifically authorized by the SEC.

Company	*Telephone No.*
Brokerage Securities Retrieval	(202) 347-3001
D.C. Documents	(202) 638-1357
Capital District Information, Inc.	(202) 265-1516
Disclosure, Inc.	1-800-638-8241
DocuPro, Inc.	(202) 628-4100
Docutronics Information Services	(212) 730-7140
Federal Filings, Inc.	(202) 393-7400
Global Securities Information, Inc.	1-800-669-1154
Lisa Gomez Associates	(202) 737-0829
Meredith Hurt & Associates	(202) 628-9628
In Depth Data, Inc.	(405) 232-0700
Pearson & Co.	(516) 921-7070
Prentice-Hall Legal & Financial Service	(202) 408-3120
Research Information Services	(202) 347-6666
Securities Document Service	(202) 737-4636
Securities Information Services	(202) 393-6017
SNL Document Retrieval	(202) 347-2724
Tymus and Company	(202) 628-6776
Vickers Stock Research Corp.	(202) 783-3400
Washington Document Service, Inc.	(202) 628-5200
Washington Service Bureau	(202) 508-0600

If you have the budget for it and cannot get the information any other way, it *may* be advantageous to engage one of these information services when you need material from the SEC, since dealing with government agencies can be time consuming. Though any of the companies listed on the previous page can obtain SEC documents for you, be aware that Disclosure, Inc. is the SEC's "official" commercial copier and makes all of the SEC's microfiche.

In addition to these primary documents available from the SEC, there are many other sources of financial data and investment analysis for publicly owned corporations. Listed below are the most widely accessible and best known of these.

Summary Financial Profiles

Moody's Manuals. Moody's Investors Service. Annual with updates. Cover corporations listed on U.S. stock exchanges in a variety of business areas. No investment analysis, but information for each company usually includes a brief corporate history, subsidiaries, plants and properties, business or products, officers and directors, comparative income statements, balance-sheet statistics, selected financial ratios, and outstanding securities. A center blue-page section in each manual provides useful industry statistics. Titles in the series include: *Bank and Finance Manual, Industrial Manual, Municipal and Government Manual, OTC Industrial Manual, OTC Unlisted Manual, Public Utility Manual,* and *Transportation Manual.*

Standard Corporation Records. Standard & Poor's. Daily updates. Similar in content and scope to *Moody's Manuals,* but all in one alphabetical sequence, this seven-volume set has both a financial and a narrative profile of publicly-owned U.S. companies, including balance sheet and income-statement data.

Standard and Poor's Industry Surveys. Standard and Poor's. Quarterly. A valuable source of basic data and outlook for approximately twenty-five major industry categories, including financial comparisons of the leading companies in each category. Each "Basic Analysis" is revised annually; each "Current Analysis" is updated quarterly.

U.S. Industrial Outlook. U.S. International Trade Administration. Annual. A survey of current trends and outlook for over 350 industries. Changes in supply and demand for each industry, developments in domestic and foreign markets, employment trends, and capital investments are covered.

Investment Analysis

Value Line Investment Survey. Value Line, Inc. Weekly. Analyzes and reports on the market status of approximately 2,000 corporations and 90 industries on a rotating quarterly basis. Data for each company is a one-page summary with a ten-year statistical history of key investment factors plus analysis and estimates of future stock performance over the next three to five years.

Moody's Handbook of Common Stocks. Moody's Investors Service. Quarterly. Price charts and concise annual financial statistics for about 1,000 common stocks of high investor interest are contained in this handbook.

Standard & Poor's Stock Reports. Standard & Poor's. Weekly. Brief reports for corporations listed on the New York Stock Exchange, American Stock Exchange, and Over the Counter market analyze a stock's current position and outline its prospects.

OTC ProFiles. Standard & Poor's. 3/year. Brief reports on about 750 smaller, less actively traded companies listed in the NASDAQ system or the U.S. regional stock exchanges.

The Outlook. Standard & Poor's. Weekly. Weekly analyses and forecasts for business and stock market trends. Discusses individual stocks and industries and makes recommendations for investment.

The Wall Street Transcript. The Wall Street Transcript. Weekly. A weekly financial newspaper with investment reports and recommendations from brokerage houses. Also contains speeches and interviews of company officials and investment managers.

Bonds, Mutual Funds, and Other Investments

Moody's Bond Survey. Moody's Investor Services. Weekly. Gives weekly commentary, analysis, and opinions on the bond and money markets and on individual issues.

Morningstar Mutual Funds. Morningstar. Biweekly. Surveys about 1,300 mutual funds, providing basic background and financial data about each fund plus analysis and a rating from a Morningstar analyst.

Weisenberger Investment Companies Services. Wiesenberger Financial Services. Annual. An important source of basic information on mutual funds and investment companies. Provides background, management policy, and annual financial records for leading U.S. and Canadian investment companies and funds.

Standard & Poor's/Lipper Mutual Fund ProFiles. Standard & Poor's. 3/year. Covers 750 mutual funds of prime investor interest. Brief data are provided on fund investment policy, performance evaluation, portfolio composition and financial-performance data. Lists of funds are grouped by objective and by complex.

Commodity Year Book. Commodity Research Bureau. Annual. Includes detailed statistical data on about one hundred commodities from apples to zinc. Contains a review of the past year's supply and demand plus ten to fifteen years of prices and production.

Best's Insurance Reports: Life-Health. A. M. Best. Annual. *Best's Insurance Reports: Property-Casualty*. A. M. Best. Annual. Information on U.S. and Canadian insurance firms with brief corporate history, management and organization, assets and liabilities, investment data and financial statistics. Most firms are rated by Best's for financial stability.

Investment Statistics

Daily Stock Price Record. Standard & Poor's. Quarterly. Contains daily and weekly stock price information for the New York, American, and OTC markets.

Security Owner's Stock Guide. Standard & Poor's Corp. Monthly. *Security Owner's Bond Guide*. Standard & Poor's Corp. Monthly. These pocket guides concisely present descriptive and statistical information on common and preferred stocks and on corporate bonds.

Analyst's Handbook. Standard & Poor's. Annual. This statistical handbook contains annual and quarterly per-share data for over eighty industries, together with selected income-account and balance-sheet items and related ratios for Standard & Poor's industry groups.

Security Price Index Record. Standard & Poor's. Annual. Offers monthly updates and annual stock and bond averages and indexes dating back forty to one hundred years.

Dividend Record. Standard & Poor's. Annual. *Moody's Dividend Record*. Moody's Investor Services. Annual. Both provide detailed data on the dividend disbursements of corporations.

Moody's Bond Record. Moody's Investor Services. Monthly. A monthly statistical summary of domestic and foreign corporate and government bonds.

Financial Ratios

Industry Norms and Key Business Ratios. Dun & Bradstreet Information Services. Annual. Covers 800 industries, both manufacturing and nonmanufacturing. Balance-sheet and income-statement figures are given for each industry group. The fourteen ratios presented are divided into median, upper, and lower quartiles.

RMA Annual Statement Studies. Robert Morris Associates. Annual. Contains product breakdowns for manufacturing, wholesaling, and retailing plus a selection of service industries and construction.

Each product line is presented in four asset-size groups and an aggregate. Balance-sheet and income data are also given for each product line. The time lag between the financial data used and the date of publication is generally no more than one year.

TROY, LEO, ed. *Almanac of Business and Industrial Financial Ratios.* Prentice-Hall. Annual. Provides a limited number of ratios for a variety of industries, including services and financial institutions. Ratios for up to twelve asset-size groups within each product group may be given, together with operating and financial data. The time lag between the financial data used and the date of publication is generally no more than three to four years.

Financial Studies of the Small Business. Financial Research Associates. Annual. Provides financial ratios and balance-sheet/income-statement data for firms having a total capitalization under $250,000. About fifty industries, primarily retail and service industries, but also a few manufacturers, wholesalers, and contractors are covered. Data for four asset-size groups and a total for all groups are given. The ratios are subdivided into median, upper, and lower quartiles.

Guides to Investment Data

Financial Stock Guide Service. *Directory of Obsolete Securities.* Financial Information. Annual. A list of companies whose identities have been lost through such events as name change, merger, acquisition, reorganization, or bankruptcy.

WOY, JAMES B. *Investment Information: A Guide to Information Sources.* Gale Research, Inc., 1970. Chapman, Karen J. *Investment Statistics Locator.* Oryx Press, 1988. Guides to locating specific investment statistics such as daily stock prices, industrial-stock averages, high-low bond prices, and treasury-bill prices.

MARKETING AND ADVERTISING RESOURCES

In the broadest sense, every item in this list of business reference sources is useful to a marketing or advertising researcher. In this section, however, are those items directly related to the field. Most of them should be widely available. Be aware that many highly specialized marketing materials such as product research reports, market-share data, television and radio audience data, lifestyle analysis, and market segmentation reports are often proprietary in nature, not widely known, or very expensive. Few, if any, libraries will have such materials in their collections, or even electronic access to them. These items will be much harder to obtain, but a determined researcher may find alternative ways to get the needed information from them.

Market Data

Editor and Publisher Market Guide. Editor and Publisher. Annual. Provides market data for U.S. and Canadian cities served by a daily newspaper, including location, population, number of households, major industries, banks, utilities, retail outlets, transportation, climate, and newspapers. Also included are statistics and rankings of income, population, and nine categories of retail sales.

Commercial Atlas and Marketing Guide. Rand McNally. Annual. In addition to detailed state maps, this atlas contains a variety of statistical data ranging from population and income to retail sales and auto registrations for counties and for cities with populations over 25,000 in size.

Demographics USA. (Formerly *Survey of Buying Power Data Service.*) Sales & Marketing Management Magazine. Annual. An annual survey of consumer buying power presenting detailed market, population, household, and retail-sales data by location, and also market-data projections, effective buying income, and buying-power index. Data are available for the United States as a whole, and for states, Metropolitan Statistical Areas, counties, and TV areas of dominant influence (ADI's).

Study of Media and Markets. Simmons Market Research Bureau. Annual. An extended annual survey of consumer buying habits and preferences coordinated with demographic characteristics and media preferences. Ten volumes analyze media audience and reach; thirty are devoted to products.

Advertising Expenditures and Rates

Ad $ Summary. Leading National Advertisers. Quarterly. The *Ad $ Summary* provides total advertising media expenditures by brand and parent company. Rankings of company expenditures by industry, media total, and media type also are included.

Standard Rate and Data Service. Standard Rate & Data Service. Monthly. Comprises several publications that provide current advertising rates and specifications as well as circulation data for trade publications, consumer magazines, direct-mail lists, newspapers, radio, and television. The sections dealing with newspapers, radio, and television include brief marketing statistics for states, counties, cities, and metropolitan areas.

Do's and Don'ts in Advertising Copy. Council of Better Business Bureaus. Continuous updates. Published for advertisers and advertising agencies, this service clarifies and explains the Advertising Code of American Business and various other definitions and standards that regulate the advertising industry.

Directories

Broadcasting/Cablecasting Yearbook. Broadcasting Publications. Annual. Surveys the broadcasting industry, including radio, television, and cable, with brief station profiles. Also includes data on programming, advertising, professional services, and satellites.

Television and Cable Factbook. Television Digest, Inc. Annual. Comprised of two volumes: Volume one has detailed profiles of all U.S. and Canadian TV stations with maps of station coverage, market data, ad rates, and technical data. Volume two covers cable systems and television-industry services.

Standard Directory of Advertisers. National Register Publishing Co. Annual. Lists about 20,000 companies, both public and private, that annually budget for national and regional advertising campaigns. The advertising agency used is noted and the amount spent and media used by each company may also be included.

Standard Directory of Advertising Agencies. National Register Publishing Co. 3/year. Lists over 4000 agencies with their top personnel and major accounts. Total approximate annual billing and a breakdown by media type are available. Also provides a geographic index and a Special Market Index for agencies specializing in certain target markets.

Green Book: International Directory of Marketing Research Houses and Services. American Marketing Association. Annual. Lists marketing research agencies in the United States, Canada, or abroad with a description of the services and facilities available from each.

GOVERNMENT INFORMATION

In addition to compiling the statistical data noted above, the federal government passes legislation and issues regulations that affect many aspects of business and industry. Remaining aware of these laws and regulations and developing the ability to track them as they pass through committee to Congress and the President and on to the regulatory agencies is a challenging research task. Most large libraries have the texts of these materials in their collections plus guides and indexes to get you started. You can also call your local congressman for assistance in obtaining copies of legislative documents, should your library not have them. Here are only a few of the reference materials that can help you track legislative and regulatory action.

Directories

U.S. Government Manual. U.S. Office of the Federal Register. Annual. A guide to the agencies of the federal government, especially the cabinet departments, independent agencies and quasi-governmental organizations. Includes organization charts, regional offices, and key personnel.

Congressional Directory. U.S. Joint Committee on Printing. Biennial. Guide to the members of Congress, their aides, and Capitol employees. Includes profiles of committees, their members, and key staff.

Federal Laws and Regulations

Federal Register. Office of the Federal Register. Daily. Contains the regulations and legal notices issued by federal agencies in order to carry out legislation passed by Congress and approved by the President. Starting in 1984, the *CIS Federal Register Index* provides a detailed subject index to this material.

Code of Federal Regulations. Office of the Federal Register. Annual. This is the annually revised codification of rules and regulations published in the *Federal Register* by the executive departments and agencies of the federal government.

United States Code. U.S. House of Representatives Judiciary Committee. Irregular. Contains the general and permanent laws of the United States currently in force. Indexed by subject, there is also an "Index of Acts Cited by Popular Name."

Summaries of Legislative Activity

CQ Weekly Report. Congressional Quarterly. Weekly. This timely and informative publication contains summaries of current legislative activity in a variety of subject areas. Provides information on both sides of controversial issues, on major activities in the executive and judicial branches of government as well as Congress, and roll-call votes.

Congressional Quarterly Almanac. Congressional Quarterly. Annual summary of the *CQ Weekly Reports*. Material is divided into broad subject areas (such as education, energy, and transportation) with summaries of Congressional action and major national political issues.

Aids in Tracing Legislation

Congressional Index. Commerce Clearing House. Weekly. One of the best sources for finding the current status of a bill. Legislation can be traced by subject, sponsor, or bill number.

CIS Index. Congressional Information Service. Monthly. Provides access to U.S. Congressional committee hearings and reports and public laws. Use the Index volume to find subjects, names, or document numbers. The Abstract volume summarizes the contents of the hearings and reports, including names of witnesses who testify. From 1984, legislative histories are contained in a third volume.

Monthly Catalog of U.S. Government Publications. U.S. Superintendent of Documents. Monthly. Lists and indexes publications of U.S. government departments and agencies, in addition to Congressional and judicial publications.

ELECTRONIC INFORMATION SOURCES

A growing body of information of all kinds is available in electronic format. Business information is no exception. Of the items noted in the preceding sections, many are available in an electronic format, whether computer tape, on-line database, or compact-disc product. In addition, many highly specialized or previously restricted materials are now available for more general use in an electronic format. The only restriction to access in many cases is cost. Users are generally charged a fee, and for business materials this can often be considerable.

Many business materials in electronic form are accessible in libraries. The best guide to availability is simply to ask a librarian what is accessible and what costs are associated with use. Many corporate offices provide electronic links to business information through their in-house computer systems, particularly if access to fast-changing financial or market data are essential to their daily operations. With your personal computer and a modem, you have access to additional information files and bulletin boards through national computer networks such as Bitnet and Internet.

You do not have to be a computer hacker to use these computer networks, but you may need some help getting started. Ask someone in your computer center for assistance with your initial connections as well as some simple navigation instructions. You will find a number of library catalogs around the United States and abroad available on the networks, plus the full text of books and reference manuals, statistical data, and other new items every day. Information in the public domain may also be downloaded from the network to your own computer. To provide a glimpse of the possibilities, here are a few guides to electronic information resources.

Information Industry Directory. 13th ed. Gale Research, Inc., 1992. Provides details about information producers and vendors, on-line services, library networks, and other providers of electronic information, especially information on how to find out about access and fees.

Directory of Online Databases. Gale Research, Inc. Semiannual. Lists and describes over 5,000 databases available through on-line services worldwide. Both textual and numeric databases are included.

STRANGELOVE, MICHAEL and DIANE KOVACS. *Directory of Electronic Journals, Newsletters, and Academic Discussion Lists.* 2d ed. Association of Research Libraries, 1992. Lists and describes electronic information sources available through national networks, with information on how to subscribe. New lists and bulletin boards are added frequently, so this directory is quickly dated.

Appendix B
Suggestions For
Further Reading

ANDREWS, DEBORAH C., and WILLIAM D. ANDREWS. *Business Communication*. 2d ed. New York: Macmillan, 1992.

BAKER, SHERIDAN. *The Practical Stylist*. 7th ed. New York: Harper and Row, 1990.

BATTEIGER, RICHARD P. *Business Writing: Process and Forms*. Belmont: Wadsworth, 1985.

BLAKE, GARY and ROBERT W. BLY. *The Elements of Business Writing*. New York: Macmillan, 1991.

JANIS, HAROLD J., and HOWARD R. DRESSNER. *Business Writing*. 2d ed. New York: HarperCollins, 1991.

LANHAM, RICHARD A. *Revising Business Prose*. 2d ed. New York: Macmillan, 1987.

LICHTY, TOM. *Design Principles for Desktop Publishers*. Glenview: Scott, Foresman, 1989.

LOCKER, KITTY O. *Business and Administrative Communication*. 2d ed. Homewood, IL: Irwin, 1992.

McKEOWN, TOM. *Powerful Business Writing: Say What You Mean, Get What You Want*. Toronto: McGraw-Hill, 1992.

MIELACH, DONA Z. *Dynamics of Presentation Graphics*. 2d ed. Homewood, IL: Dow Jones-Irwin, 1990.

MUNTER, MARY. *Guide to Managerial Communication*. 3d ed. Englewood Cliffs, NJ: Prentice-Hall, 1992.

OLIU, WALTER E, Et al. *Writing That Works: Effective Communication in Business*. 4th ed. New York: St. Martin's, 1992.

PAXON, WILLIAM C. *The Business Writing Handbook*. New York: Bantam, 1990.

SCHELL, JOHN, and JOHN STRATTON. *Writing on the Job: A Handbook for Business and Government*. New York: Penguin, 1984.

STRUNK, WILLIAM JR., and E. B. WHITE. *The Elements of Style*. 3d ed. New York: Macmillan, 1979.

WHITE, JAN V. *Great Pages: A Common-Sense Approach to Effective Desktop Design*. El Segundo: Serif Publishing, 1990.

WILLIAMS, JOSEPH M. *Style: Ten Lessons in Clarity and Grace*. 3d ed. Glenview, IL: Scott, Foresman, 1989.

Xerox Publishing Standards: A Manual of Style and Design. New York: Watson-Guptill Publications, 1988.

Index